DATE DUE

JAN 12 1971			
JAN 31 1972			
FEB 15 1972			
MAR 9 1972			
MAR 23 1972			
8-7-72			
DEC 2			
DEC 9			
OCT 22 1981			
OCT 27 1981			

Tracy
and
Hepburn

ALSO BY GARSON KANIN

PLAYS
Born Yesterday
The Smile of the World
The Rat Race
The Live Wire
Come On Strong

(*Musicals*)
Fledermaus
Do Re Mi

(*Adaptations*)
The Amazing Adele
The Good Soup
A Gift of Time

NOVELS
Blow Up a Storm
Do Re Mi
The Rat Race
Where It's At

SHORT FICTION
Cast of Characters
(twenty stories)

FILMS
The Rat Race

(*with Ruth Gordon*)
A Double Life
Adam's Rib
Pat and Mike
The Marrying Kind

(*in collaboration*)
From This Day Forward
The More the Merrier
The True Glory

(*Original stories*)
High Time
The Right Approach
The Girl Can't Help It

(*Original screenplays*)
It Should Happen to You
Where It's At
Some Kind of a Nut

NONFICTION
Remembering Mr. Maugham

Felix Frankfurter: A Tribute
(*Contributor*)

Tracy and Hepburn

Garson Kanin

An Intimate Memoir

THE VIKING PRESS NEW YORK

First published in 1971 by The Viking Press, Inc.
625 Madison Avenue, New York, N.Y. 10022
Published simultaneously in Canada by
The Macmillan Company of Canada Limited.
SBN 670-72293-6
Library of Congress catalog card number: 71-163875
Printed in U.S.A.

Third printing November 1971

TO KATE AND SPENCE

Preface

The past, recalled, is a flowing cornucopia of visions, sounds, aromas, emotions, gaieties, terrors, faces, and places.

We do not remember chronologically, but in disordered flashes. We are not, after all, programed memory machines. People are less efficient and orderly—but consider the compensations: freedom to associate; to roam and rummage in the attic of our yesterdays; to let one thing lead to another.

The ability to relive those parts of life that have been significant is a gift equal to life itself.

The following pages contain a record of friendship set down in the random way it was lived, with the conviction that it is worth not only remembering, but recounting.

There comes a time in life when the desire to pass on what one knows becomes intense.

I want to share my vision of Katharine Hepburn and Spencer Tracy, individually and as a team. She is a nonesuch. He was a master. Both valuable, useful human beings. Spencer had a great deal to give and he gave it. Kate is one of the pre-eminent women of her time.

Both pose many mysterious questions to which I have been unable to find answers. Like so many of the great ones, they always reserved an important part of themselves to themselves.

I have no doubt that each of them will one day be the subject of a comprehensive biography. This is not it. Far from it. I know her and knew him far too well to attempt such an undertaking, which requires, above all, objective detachment. In the matter of Tracy and Hepburn I am something less than unbiased.

Biography is a field that requires delicate expertise. How does one go about finding the needle of truth in the haystack of facts? Who, among informants, is telling the truth about a given incident? Or is it possible they are *all* telling the truth—their truth? Shades of *Rashomon* and the memory of my father saying, in fruity Yiddish, "Remember, *mein gold*. There are three sides to every story: yours and his and the truth."

I found Spencer consistently fascinating. The years went by but he did not grow old. He grew up. The same can be said of Kate.

They influenced each other more than they realized. They brought out the best in each other, in life and in work.

One

Katharine Hepburn is tall—not as tall as she thinks she is, but tall. For a long time, she owned several pairs of specially built platform shoes (has them still for all I know) that she wore whenever she felt the occasion warranted. To my eye they seemed ugly, suggesting deformity. She agreed, but was willing to go as far as to seem clubfooted, so long as she attained her impish aim: to put down—literally—the men with whom she came in professional contact.

It happened that during the time she was under contract to Metro-Goldwyn-Mayer, the upper-executive echelon was made up mainly of physically smallish men. Benny Thau, Eddie Mannix, Sidney Franklin, and the formidable L. B. Mayer himself were all under, say, five foot nine inches.

This meant that even with ordinary ladies' shoes and her extraordinary posture and her hair piled high, she was, from their point of view, imposing.

With the addition of the trick shoes, which added three or four inches to her height (and caused the men to shrink a cowering inch or two), she *towered* over them. At least she felt she did and what is more important, *they* felt she did.

Someone once called them her Seven-League Boots, and she invariably put them on whenever she started climbing the Beanstalk—up, up, up into the forbidding Front Office where the Giants lived. She did not make the trip often, but, when she did, she emerged with what she wanted.

Was it her wicked sense of fun that made her choose to wear them on the day she was to meet Spencer Tracy for the first time in order to discuss *Woman of the Year?* He was a big man—in every way—but not exceptionally tall: five foot ten and a half inches. Joe Mankiewicz, the producer, introduced them.

"Hello," she said.

"How are y'?"

She looked Spencer over, tip to toe, as though she were considering buying him. Then she smiled her friendliest smile and said, "You're rather *short,* aren't you?"

"Don't worry, honey," said Mankiewicz, trying desperately to extinguish Spencer's glare. "He'll cut you down to size."

With this as a beginning, it is not surprising that they went on to become one of the most celebrated teams in American film history. The leading man–leading lady Bad Beginning has been a staple of dramaturgy for as long as it has been turging. In American romantic movies, especially, we have come almost to *expect* the two leads to bite on each other in their first scene together. It may be that Tracy and Hepburn instinctively acted their opening scene the minute they met because they sensed they were meant to play together, that they were ordained to be a team.

Before long, the question of billing arose. It is a subject I have never fully understood—possibly because I have never been a star—but billing appears to be as important as breathing to some actors and actresses. Important films with ideal casts have fallen apart on the issue of billing.

In 1936, Maurice Chevalier left the United States and returned to France when he was so much as *asked* to take second billing to Grace Moore at M-G-M. (He says it signaled to him that his star was fading here, and it was his professional judgment to leave and wait to be urged to return. With first billing, of course.)

Co-stars have allowed a tossed coin to decide; have split the billing: half the posters and prints and so on, you—the other half me. Two names have been lettered in the shape of an X. Some settle for below the title, but in a *box!* What does it all mean? Status? Ego? It has always seemed to me that the audience determines the billing for itself after seeing the performance; but, as I have said, it is all a dead key on my personal piano.

I know of no man to whom the word "gentleman" applies more aptly than to Alfred Lunt. Yet for fifty years the billing has read: "Alfred Lunt and Lynn Fontanne in . . ." Even in conversation, no one has ever heard them referred to as Fontanne and Lunt.

I once asked him, "Has it ever occurred to you to switch billing once in a while?"

He thought for a moment and replied, "No. It never has."

So it was with the team of Tracy and Hepburn. The gentleman came first.

Tracy's position as a Metro superstar meant that there was nothing to discuss, and, in those days, Kate did not particularly care about billing.

It was always Tracy and Hepburn.

I chided him once about his insistence on first billing.

"Why not?" he asked, his face all innocence.

"Well, after all," I argued, "she's the lady. You're the man. Ladies first?"

"This is a movie, chowderhead," he said, "not a lifeboat."

Woman of the Year was followed in 1943 by an I.A.R. Wylie story, *Keeper of the Flame*. It was prepared for the screen by Donald Ogden Stewart and aimed high, telling the story of the unearthing of an American fascist. Although the film turned out to be an overintellectualized account, it served to solidify the team. Audiences clearly wanted to see Tracy and Hepburn together again. They did not do so until 1945, when Kate convinced Metro to film Philip Barry's *Without Love,* with which she had failed in the theater some three years earlier. It was directed by Harold S. Bucquet and fared not much better in its film version. Kate is inclined to be a die-hard about such things.

Two years later, Kate, having made in the interim *Undercurrent* with Robert Taylor and played Clara Schumann in *Song of Love,* was reunited with Spencer in Elia Kazan's film *The Sea of Grass,* adapted from Conrad Richter's beautiful novel. The film was a success in every way.

The following year, Spencer Tracy was teamed with Claudette Colbert to make *State of the Union* under Frank Capra's direction. At the last moment, a contractual dispute arose between Miss Colbert and the studio. She resigned from the picture and Kate, although unprepared, was asked to replace her immediately so that the film could start on schedule. The result was a disappointment, yet the team continued to flourish.

A year later came *Adam's Rib,* after which Kate did *As You Like It* on Broadway and *The African Queen* in Africa. In 1952, Spencer and Kate were again teamed in *Pat and Mike.* After a five-year hiatus, they made *Desk Set* for Twentieth Century–Fox; and finally, in 1967, *Guess Who's Coming to Dinner* at Columbia, under Stanley Kramer's direction. All told, there were nine Tracy-Hepburn films from 1942 to 1967. Twenty-five years. A small number considering the impact the team made.

The surprising aspect of their joint success was that they were so different. Kate's working method and approach was opposite to Spencer's. She is a careful, thorough, methodical, analytical, concentrated artist. She reads and studies and thinks. By the time she was ready to begin shooting *The Lion in Winter,* for example, she knew enough about Eleanor of Aquitaine to write a master's thesis on the subject. She loves to rehearse and practice and try things and make just one more take. Spencer, conversely, was an instinctive player, who trusted the moment of creation, believed it was possible to go stale by over-rehearsing, and usually did his best work on the first take. He was a firmly rooted subjective artist.

Imagine, then, his discomfiture on the night he was unavoidably trapped in a roomful of colleagues discussing Acting (with a capital A) as a profession, an art, a craft, a business, and even as a way of life. The Method was attacked and defended; views on Coquelin, Stanislavsky, Kean, Booth, Garrick, and Olivier were served up like after-dinner bonbons. Spencer sat quietly through it all, listening and, perhaps, trying not to listen. After some hours, Kate pressed him for *his* opinion.

"Well," he said, "it's taken me forty years of doing it for a living to learn the secret. I don't know that I want to give it away." Urged, he relented. "Okay," he said, "I'll tell you. The art of acting is—learn your lines!"

He left. It was not entirely a joke. That is about what it was to him.

They were different, yes; but the same as well—both dedicated to excellence and high standards, both consummate professionals, each admiring and respectful of the other.

On the conscious level, they jealously guarded individuality. As they worked together, however, there came to be a trading of energy, an adjustment of taste, an understanding of the other's world. They helped each other in many ways. Spencer kept his partner-friend down to earth. She can be flighty, whimsical, impractical, wildly overimaginative, and often unrealistic. Spencer kept his sharp eye on her and used the tender weapon of humor to reveal her to herself; to show her a better way.

A few of the more perceptive critics felt the vibrations of the pairing almost at once, noting, subliminally, the effect that these two players (people) had on each other.

About *Woman of the Year,* Donald Kirkley wrote, in the *Baltimore Sun,* "Her performance is a constant pleasure to watch. Mr. Tracy is an excellent foil for her in this particular instance. His quiet, masculine stubbornness and prosaic outlook on life is in striking contrast with her sparkle and brilliance. They make a fine team, and each complements the other."

The reviewer for *Time,* James Agee, wrote, "Actors Hepburn and Tracy have a fine old time in *Woman of the Year.* They take turns playing straight for each other, act one superbly directed love scene, succeed in turning several batches of cinematic corn into passable moonshine. As a lady columnist, she's just right. As a working reporter, he is practically perfect. For once strident Katharine Hepburn is properly subdued."

And the benign *Christian Science Monitor* commented, "Miss Hepburn and Mr. Tracy are admirably paired. Mr. Tracy's easy style with an undertone of firmness convinces one that his Sam is the man to cope with Miss Hepburn's combination of detachment and restlessness as Tess the career woman."

We have a way of associating film characters with the actors who play them. In this instance, the reviewers seemed to be writing about Tracy and Hepburn as much as they were about the characters in *Woman of the Year*. This time, they were beautifully right.

All careers in the arts resemble life on a roller coaster. First, the painstakingly slow and steady climb: next, reaching a peak; now a sickening plummet from grace. Up again, up, up—and *down!* Again and again. Observe, however, the interesting laws of physics in action as the downward thrust gives flowing momentum to the climb up to the next leg of the journey. Without the downs, there would be little self-generated energy for the ups.

There are some who are so shook up by the ride that they stop riding; others hang on grimly, without enjoyment; a number drop out or jump off and kill themselves; but a rare few—Kate among them—enjoy it all the way, the heady ups and the screaming downs. These are the born roller-coaster riders.

"I'm bad about lots of things," says Kate. "About taking criticism—that's one of the main ones. I can't take criticism. Oh, hardly anyone can, but I'm worse than most. My mother once told me that when I was very small, a relative, sitting out in the garden with us, happened to mention that I was too skinny and frail, and wondered out loud if I was really in good health and—

I don't remember this, but my mother said that just to show her up—the relative, I mean—I took off and ran head first into an enormous tree we had."

"No wonder you don't remember it," says Spencer.

"I used to shave my head almost every summer when I was a kid," Kate recalls.

"What do you mean, 'kid'?"

"Oh, eight, nine, ten—until I was about thirteen."

"Why?"

"I've often wondered—maybe it was to keep cool or maybe it had to do with the fact that boys used to pull girls' hair in those days, and I thought if I didn't *have* any hair, they wouldn't pull it. I'm not sure now exactly why I did it—I must have looked quite peculiar."

Spencer says, "Christ, if there's anything I hate, it's being interviewed. They always ask the same dumb things, and I never know what to say. 'How did you happen to become an actor?' for instance. There's one for you. How the hell do *I* know? Back there in Milwaukee, I don't remember ever *seeing* an actor and I certainly never thought about it when I was in the Navy. In fact, when I *was* in the Navy I thought I wanted to be a sailor. And maybe if the family hadn't been so dead set on me finishing high school, I would've stayed in the Navy, but when I got out, I did go back to high school and then—I don't know—automatically, I suppose, college."

"What college was that?"

"Ripon. I must have been a real pain in the ass—arguing all the time with everybody—because one of the professors there finally sucked me into being on the debating team. From there I suppose it was only a short hop to the drama club. Then, well, you know how it is. Everybody starts to tell you how good you are and you start to believe it. Even so, nothing would've happened probably if our debating team hadn't been invited to debate up at Bowdoin College in Maine, and on the way we had to stop off in New York for a day. And I went over to the American Academy of Dramatic Arts—I'd seen about it somewhere—and auditioned for Franklin Sargent. They must have been pretty short of men because he offered me a scholarship. When I got out of college, I went to New York and took him up on it. Pat was there, too. Pat O'Brien. We'd known each other as kids. We had a room together somewhere in the West Fifties. We were in the same class. Neither one of us very impressive. I don't know why. We sure tried."

In 1966, Spencer wrote a blurb for a magazine advertisement at the request of the American Academy of Dramatic Arts:

> I shall always be grateful to the American Academy for what I was taught there—the value of sincerity and simplicity, unembellished and unintellectualized.

The statement needs to be read and read again for its full import.

Spencer was a true intellectual, but he believed that acting should be a matter of instinct rather than design. He would study his parts secretly and thoroughly and think about them, but when it came to actual performance he would let go and follow his instinct.

"It's the only thing I have, really," he often said.

Spencer had an aversion to make-up. To most actors, beards and mustaches, putty noses and tooth work, wigs and contact lenses are not only tools, but toys. Spencer shuddered at the thought, believing that characters had to be created from within rather than with artifice.

Laurence Olivier once said to him, "I admire so much about

you, Spence, but nothing more than the fact that you can do it all *barefaced.*"

"I can't act with stuff all over me," said Spence morosely.

"But don't you feel as though they're looking at *you?* Don't you feel naked?"

"Only when I have to say a lousy line," said Spence.

This attitude once caused friction between us. When I directed him on Broadway in *The Rugged Path,* there was a scene in which the character he played reached an island in the Philippines, having survived a torpedoed battleship.

Eddie Senz, a brilliant make-up artist, devised an easily applied piece to simulate a beard growth. When he demonstrated it, Spencer turned and went to his dressing room. I joined him there a few minutes later.

"Has he gone?" asked Spence.

"May I ask you one question?"

"No."

"How could a man drift in the sea for eight days and turn up clean shaven?"

"Guess," he said.

"I know your feeling about all this, kiddo, but you're not going to tell me you can *act* unshaven!"

"Watch me," he said.

In performance, he did precisely that. I still find it difficult to believe.

Katharine Hepburn has created, with diligence and intention, a world of her own, and she lives in it happily ever after.

She is its Empress, its leading citizen, and the most common of its commoners. Her world has a Constitution (with the customary Amendments), laws, morals and manners, sports, customs, two religions: Friendship and Behavior, tradition, policies, aims and aspirations, a language, and—at the moment—even a population explosion.

When you enter her world you are expected to observe its

strictures and you do so without question. You eat a cooked fruit with every meat dish; you arrive on time and leave as early as possible (say, on her third yawn); you do not gossip; you agree with every one of her many opinions and approve each of her numerous plans; you do not get drunk no matter how much you drink; you love her dog, Lobo; you applaud the efforts or output or creations of all her friends (whether they or their works are known to you or not); you do not complain (you may, however, rail); you say nothing that may not be repeated; you refrain from lies, dissemblances, and exaggerations; you omit discussion of your physical state, symptoms, or ailments (unless preparatory to asking her advice); you take her advice; you do not use obscene, coarse, or lewd expressions.

Nonetheless, she is the very definition of friendship, meaning that she is more interested in her friends than she is in herself. The problems and concerns of those about her become her own.

Vivien Leigh, on the verge of nervous collapse, was saved by Kate's strong helping arms and medical supervision and innate wisdom. Donald Ogden Stewart, plagued by political blacklisting and driven from the United States by the virulence of McCarthyism, found her staunchly at his side. Tom Heaton, the son of her dentist's technician, was launched and sped on his acting career by the rocket fuel of Kate's enthusiasm.

New and old friends, employees, servants, and co-workers become part of her vast personal family and come to know the unfailing generosity of her hand and spirit.

She still maintains a neat relationship to Ogden Ludlow (Ludlow Ogden Smith) although they were divorced over thirty-seven years ago, after a six-year marriage. During this time their surname was changed from Smith to Ludlow. Some say it was Kate who insisted on the change because she did not want to be known as Kate Smith—or even as Mrs. Smith.

When one sees her with Luddy (as she calls him), it is clear that they share the compassionate interchange of two people who, once, long ago, were in a bad accident together but survived.

Kate has always lived in an expanding world; Spencer's, conversely, diminished as his years went on. Cronies died and were not replaced because they were irreplaceable. Friendships faded and few new ones were made. Travel became more and more of a burden and so, in time, was confined to that which was necessary for work or commitment.

Kate, all her life, has been a house person—even an apartment seems to her an artificial, temporary abode. Spence was perfectly content in a hotel room. For many years, his home was a pleasant suite on the third floor of The Beverly Hills Hotel.

Later on, Kate would introduce him to the pleasures of nest building and furnishing, helping him to set up a magically comfortable living machine; one of the three bungalows on George Cukor's West Hollywood estate.

Before Kate, Spencer's life was bounded on the north by his studio of the day: Fox, U.A., Warner's, Columbia, Metro; on the south by The Hill, the home of his wife and children; on the east by Romanoff's and Chasen's and Perino's; and on the west by short jaunts to Las Vegas, Catalina, Newport, or secret hideaways.

"I've always liked to live in small places," he said to me once, "because I live a small life."

He took a dim view of his colleagues who turned into tycoons.

"I notice it doesn't help their acting much," he said. "Me? All I know is it takes all I've got to give a fair day's work on the set. I never even see Ross except on an off day."

He was referring to his business manager, Ross Evans, with whom he held regular and comprehensive sessions. His disclaimers notwithstanding, Spencer's business acumen was keen and he patiently built a fortune by careful and judicious steps.

His social life was meager and selective; his interests, few. Theater, literature, Catholicism, politics, and the opposite sex.

His genius and his myriad life problems had a single wellspring—loneliness. Out of his solitude and his contemplative life came his rich-flowing work. It also triggered his sometimes excessive drinking (a bottle can be a comforting friend), his moods, his outbursts, and his increasing inability to compromise.

Yet, his merry eye saw the fun in everything. To Spence, it was all—save his religion—a surpassing joke.

In the classic syndrome of an acting life, Kate paid dearly for her early success.

Much has been said and written about her return to the stage as the star of *The Lake* in 1933. Too much. It should have been —*was,* in fact—no more than another part in another play in the course of a career. But the demanding theater world would not have it so. Kate had gone to Hollywood and in her first picture, *A Bill of Divorcement,* had exploded in the manner of a nova.

She says, "I was lucky—*A Bill of Divorcement* came up at just the right time—I'd made quite a splash in *The Warrior's Husband* and I knew, well, *everyone* knew, that they were looking for someone to play the girl in *A Bill of Divorcement.* It's one of those sure-fire parts—made a star of Meggie Albenesi in London and certainly didn't do Kit Cornell any harm when she played it in New York—everyone seemed to be testing for it and not making it. When I got a chance to test, I looked at the scene, and I thought, Well, hell, no wonder—the *scene's* no good—so I made some excuse and said I couldn't do that scene for the test, but would they let me do a scene of my own? They didn't care one way or the other—in those days they used to make about two hundred tests a day in New York for the different studios—everyone was always testing away—so I used a scene from *Holiday*. I'd been Hopie Williams' understudy for a year and had got the scene down absolutely perfectly. Naturally, it worked. I'd gotten Alan Campbell—he hadn't married Dorothy Parker as yet—to do the scene with me. He'd been in

The Warrior's Husband with me, too. I asked him to sit back-to. I didn't want that nonsense about the one helping with the test getting the job—they used to do that quite a lot—gave them a sense of discovery—Alan was fine. I could imagine what it was like sitting in a projection room watching one girl after another play the same scene—over and over again. Finally, they get so immune to the scene, it doesn't have any meaning—so when I came on, looking sort of strange and mysterious—and may I say, photogenic?—they heard a new scene—and a damn good one too, by the way—and it worked. I'm not going to deny that luck has a lot to do with everything good that happens to us, but there's a little brain-work mixed up in it, too—don't forget that."

She returned to California, solidified her position with *Christopher Strong,* and topped herself with *Morning Glory,* for which she won the first of her Academy Awards. This was followed by the classic *Little Women.* All these in a single year.

She was now an undisputed star, but felt that staying in films was not the final answer. She did not confuse being a star with being an actress. She was still stage-struck, and wanted to do a play.

Jed Harris, one of the outstanding theater talents of his time, had seen a play in London, called *The Lake,* by Dorothy Massingham and Murray MacDonald. Although a tragedy, it was a huge success and Jed had bought the American rights. There were several good parts, and he wanted Kate for one of them, Stella Surrege.

He was planning, simultaneously, an American production of another London success: the notorious, highly controversial drama of homosexual life, *The Green Bay Tree,* by Mordaunt Shairp, for which he had already engaged the spectacular young Laurence Olivier.

He had a scheme, and went to Hollywood in order to outline it to Kate.

He pointed out to her that nothing is more dangerous than a flashing young new star who has made it big in pictures suddenly turning up on Broadway in a lead.

"They'll be laying for you," he said. "They'll make it tough. You know how suspicious they are."

"But for God's sake, Jed," she said, "I'm not a starlet. I've been on Broadway. I've been in *several* plays on Broadway, and I *starred* in the last one."

"It was nothing," said Jed. "They've forgotten it."

"Well, what do you want me to do?"

"Let's outsmart them," said Jed craftily. "Here's the idea. I'm going to do a play, tremendous. *The Green Bay Tree.* I've got James Dale and this fantastic new English actor named Laurence Olivier. It's about homosexuality. I'm so God-damned sick of seeing English kings played by English queens! This is different. Two real men playing classy fairies. A superb play, and there's a part in it for you. You'd be perfect. It's not the lead, you understand. It's not even the second lead. I'd call it the third part, but it's the only woman in the play. You play it. It'll be a tremendous gesture. It'll show respect for the theater and for your craft. You're sure to hit. Then, after you've scored in this supporting part, we star you in *The Lake*."

Kate looked impassive.

"I know what you're thinking," said Jed, quickly. "You're thinking, 'This son-of-a-bitch is trying to promote me. He's got a play with nobody in it and he'd like to shore it up. So he's trying to con me into doing it with these crazy arguments.' Isn't that what you're thinking? Also you're thinking 'Why the hell should I? He'll do *The Lake* with me whether I do this other play or not.' That's what you're thinking. Am I right?"

"You're a mind reader," said Kate.

"All right. It's true. I *will* do *The Lake* anyway, but you'll see. It would be better my way. Think it over."

Leland Hayward, Kate's agent, was outraged when he heard of Jed's proposal. A row took place.

In the end, Kate did *The Lake.*

It is recorded as a famous disaster, and one cannot help but reflect on the possible wisdom of Jed's proposed strategy, since *The Green Bay Tree* proved to be a stunning success for all concerned.

It was in the lobby of the Martin Beck Theatre, during the first intermission of a performance of *The Lake,* that Dorothy Parker made one of her most celebrated remarks.

Someone said to Mrs. Parker, "Kate's wonderful, isn't she?"

"Oh, yes," agreed Mrs. Parker. "She runs the gamut of emotion all the way from A to *B!*"

The crack is remembered better than the play.

It should be noted that by this time Mrs. Parker had married Alan Campbell, who had been one of Kate's many beaux.

Some years later, I was working on a film with Dorothy Parker. In the course of a casting discussion, she began to sell Katharine Hepburn. I was astonished.

"I thought you didn't like her," I said.

Those great brown eyes became greater and browner.

"Me?" said Dottie. "I don't think there's a finer actress anywhere."

"But what about 'all the way from A to B'?" I reminded her. "Or didn't you say it? Or do you think she's improved?"

Dottie sighed. "Oh, I said it all right. You know how it is. A joke." She looked distressed. She shrugged and swallowed. "When people expect you to say things, you say things. Isn't that the way it is?"

I did not see *The Lake* on the first night, but I had read it. It seemed to me then, and seems to me now, a meretricious piece, but when finally I did get to see it, in the sixth week of its run, I recognized it as one of those plays that works. Moreover, Katharine Hepburn was giving a most interesting performance.

Shortly after we met for the first time, we talked about *The Lake.* I mentioned this discrepancy to her.

"Well," she said, immediately warming to the subject, "it was fascinating. What happened was this. We rehearsed. I was scared. I knew almost right away I was wrong for that damned part. It wasn't only that I was too young, which I was by about twenty years, but the whole temperament of the woman, her whole outlook and make-up was completely foreign to me—I couldn't get under her skin—and when you don't have the cloak of a character to put around you, you walk out on that damned stage and you feel absolutely stripped stark naked—that's what I felt like, all the time we were rehearsing. And Jed wasn't much help—a great director, all right, but *he* must have seen, too, that he'd made a mistake—made him irritable and cantankerous and unreasonable—and he took to bullying. The whole thing was a shambles. Then on opening night—well, opening nights are bad enough at best, and during this one, I was simply petrified. My voice went all loony, and I must have been stiff as a board. Anyway, I'm sure I gave a foul performance—*chaotic*. One night, someone came back with Frances Robinson-Duff—I'd worked with her—and I asked her, quite frankly, 'What do you think?' And she said, 'Well, you're not very good. You could be, but you're not. There's no center to your performance.' So I said, 'Do you think you can help me?' And she said, 'I'm willing to try.' So we set to work—I worked with her every day—I'd asked Jed to close the damned thing but he wouldn't. Perverse as hell, so I knew I had to keep playing it, and I thought, what the hell?—as long as I have to keep playing it, I may as well use the time to learn something. I'd work every day with Duff, and then I'd go on at night and try stuff—and as the weeks went by I got better and better. I think eventually I got pretty good in it, but by then it was too late. Nobody much was coming to see it."

"Me," I said.

"That's what I said. Nobody."

This is the essence of Kate's approach to work. It is never a chore to her, always a challenge.

Many years later, although she had succeeded brilliantly in *Coco,* she said to my wife and me, months after it had been running, "Come and see it again sometime—Don't tell me when—I can't bear it. I never like to know who's out front, but come and see it again—it's much better and so am I."

We did so. She had indeed embellished her performance, found fresh values, new climaxes, and was firmly in charge of the stage.

On the 10th of June, 1970, we phoned her from Edgartown. It was the third anniversary of Spencer's death and we wanted to talk about him with her for a while. We did so, remembered some jokes, laughed, and missed him.

Suddenly she said, "You know I'm finishing at the end of July—definite this time—And listen—would you please come again before I close?"

"We've seen it quite a lot," I reminded her.

"You haven't seen it as good as this," she said. "I'm really quite marvelous—don't tell me when."

Kate never says, "That will do." She does not settle for less. She goes on deepening, refining, improving each role she plays, including the role she plays in daily life: Katharine Hepburn.

That is why she has been able to produce and perfect the finest Katharine Hepburn in the world.

There are those who make strong efforts and take considerable pains in order to appear eccentric or singular or unique. There is a fretted child inside them still clamoring: "Lookit *me!* Look *at ME!!"* To this end, they dress outlandishly (remember Petruchio's wedding getup, designed to obliterate the hapless Katharina?); they voice outrageous opinions; they behave shockingly; they devote themselves to any and every sort of jumping-up-and-down attention-getting.

The result they achieve is irritating and tedious since we recognize easily the phonyboloneyness of it all.

Then there are your true peculiars, the natural born eccentrics, the honestly different. These, we instinctively revere. We know, atavistically, that they are the ones who dictate styles, cause progress, revise standards, create the new, and move the earth. ("The unique must be fulfilled."—Martha Graham.)

Of the latter group, my friend Katharine Hepburn is Chairman of the Board.

The unusual comes naturally to her. Observe her, in the opening scene of *Adam's Rib,* pouring a cup of coffee for her husband. Her hand comes down over the creamer. Does she pick it up by its handle? No. Her long, graceful fingers reach out and envelop it firmly. She lifts it and pours the cream into the coffee in what is all at once a clearly better, more practical way. Further, it has infinite elegance.

A small point, I grant, but works of art are composed of thousands of small points.

Did the director, George Cukor, stage it, I wondered? I asked him.

"No," he replied, "it's just another one of Kate's own-way things."

He goes on. "It reminds me of the test she made for her first picture, *A Bill of Divorcement*. I'd watched dozens. But on she came and there was a glass on the floor—I don't know why—and she bent down and picked it up in a way that was so sensitive and meaningful. Moving. I was infinitely impressed. That one moment struck me so hard that it made her stand out. And, of course, she got the job."

Here is another own-way thing. Jules Dassin submits a play to Kate. It is an English adaptation of a French success, *Days in the Trees,* by Marguerite Duras. Dassin hopes to interest Kate in a Broadway production. She reads it at once, goes to her desk, sits down, begins to write. "My dear Mr. Dassin: Thank you so much for sending me this *fascinating* play. I found it most interesting, but unfortunately . . ."

She stops. Her false tone offends her. She picks up a new sheet of paper and begins again. "Dear Jules Dassin: Try as I will I cannot make head or tail of this *confusing* manuscript, and therefore . . ."

She stops again. Once more, "Mr. Dassin: This is surely the most idiotic and *depressing* piece of claptrap I have ever in all my life . . ."

No. She has gone too far, she thinks.

Finally, "Dear Mr. Dassin: I am grateful to you for thinking of me in connection with your play. I am returning it to you unread, as, alas, I am not available at this time, and have no idea as to when I might . . ."

No, again. Why lie?

Later, she tells us of her struggle to find the proper response, and quotes these four beginnings.

"And what did you decide in the end?" asks Ruth.

"Oh, I just put *all four* of them into an envelope and sent it off to him!"

These days actresses (and actors too!) strip to the buff at the drop of a direction and think nothing of it, but how many of them would be willing to remove the protective façade of their minds or spirits or opinions?

It has been said that we owe the greater part of our social and scientific progress to the eccentrics. Those who firmly follow the rules of the game, the status quo, the that's-how-things-are-done we've-always-done-it-this-way school of thinking, are not likely to break out and contribute much that is new. It is the original, the nonconformist, the iconoclast, the I-don't-give-a-damn type who audaciously leads us to take a new step, or an old one in a new direction.

The danger is that unconventional people are likely to be ridiculed, and sometimes ostracized. The strong among them persist. The young today understand this principle well as they rally around their trenchantly coined dictum of "doing your own thing." Unfortunately, there is a trap here, too, since it is possible to conform with nonconformity. Look about you.

But the true line of American originals: Thoreau, Jane Addams, Edison, George Washington Carver, Gertrude Stein, Margaret Sanger, Carrie Nation, Robert G. Ingersoll, Charles Ives, Dashiell Hammett, Eugene V. Debs, Samuel Gompers, Jackson Pollock, and Ralph Nader remain true to their personal vision of self and what is yet to come. Kate is part of this continuing substream.

We are all related—by ink, if not blood—to Walter Mitty. We all have dreams of glory, aspirations, plans, schemes, and designs. Why then are so few of them executed and why do only a small number come to fruition? It is because too many lack the nerve it takes to step out of line, and it is this brand of courage in Kate and her eccentric compatriots to which we respond.

Laurence Olivier once observed that the dramatization of human courage, if done even reasonably well, scarcely ever fails as a literary or theatrical or film subject. The courage may take various forms: physical, as in *High Noon;* moral, as in *A Man for All Seasons;* military, as in *The Way Ahead;* Freudian, as in *Hamlet;* youthful, as in *Easy Rider.*

Kate has her own sort of courage. That is why those who observe her life and work in action respond with admiration.

Like most originals, Kate had a difficult time getting started. We are so accustomed to hearing about "a young Jimmy Stewart," "a new Shirley MacLaine," "a sort of Audrey Hepburn." Too many producers and directors are comfortable only with what they have seen before, or with a reasonable facsimile. When faced with a new style or a fresh presence they tend to become confused. Martinet directors are often in the habit of attempting to turn actors and actresses into *other* actors and actresses.

This was Kate's major problem from the start. Rehearsing her first good professional role, in *The Big Pond,* she seemed promising enough as long as she stayed within the bounds of accepted, conventional ingenue practice. On the first night, when in contact with the audience her own personality made a brave if awkward attempt to prevail, she was summarily discharged. She had the same experience later in *Death Takes a Holiday* and in *The Animal Kingdom.*

Once they got on to her and left her alone—as soon as they were willing to take a chance on a new style—she began to come through and to communicate with her audience.

In 1930, she had a small success as Judy Bottle in *Art and Mrs. Bottle* by Benn Levy, but not before she had been fired and rehired. At last she won the part of the Amazon, Antiope, in *The Warrior's Husband,* opposite Romney Brent in Julian Thompson's play. She was probably cast more for her physical attributes than for her talents. Romney Brent, who is short, played her husband, and beside him Kate seemed tall indeed. It was a superior play and Kate gave a rousing performance.

She had made a hit at last, even though the play was no more than a mild success.

Yet she did not totally conquer the theater until after she had become a film star.

Even as late as 1937, after a rare run of film successes, when she did *Jane Eyre* for the Theatre Guild it toured but never came in to New York.

It was not until *The Philadelphia Story,* in 1939, that she made an authentic Broadway success.

She acted professionally for over ten years before achieving New York stardom.

A large part of Kate's inner strength derives from the crucible of early experience. Not many adolescent girls are called upon to deal with mysterious death. Here are the bare bones of the story:

Kate is twelve. Her brother Tom is fifteen. They are in New York for an Easter weekend. There is a party on Saturday night. On the morning of Easter Sunday, Tom seems to have disappeared. Kate looks everywhere for him, all through the house. She reaches the attic and finds him there, hanging. She cuts him down and runs for help, although she is quite sure it is too late.

She bangs on the door of a doctor's house in the neighborhood. A maid appears.

"Please, can the doctor come?" she asks desperately. "I think my brother is dead."

"Well, if he's dead," says the maid, "the doctor can't help him."

She slams the door shut.

The mystery of Tom's death has never been fully explained. It would appear to have been a suicide, but suicide generally has a motive. It might have been a prank. The family wants to think it was, or a boyish experiment of some kind, but the coroner's report said he had been dead for at least five hours when he was found. This meant that the hanging had occurred at three o'clock in the morning. Kate's father had often told a story about a phenomenal Southern black who could perform a startling trick: tightening his neck muscles, he would hang by his neck for half an hour at a time. With his help, a group of collegiate pranksters at Randolph-Macon once stupefied a visitor from the North pretending to have carried out a lynching.

Also, not long before the tragedy, Tom and Kate had gone to see a musical production of Mark Twain's *A Connecticut Yankee in King Arthur's Court,* in which a similar stunt was enacted.

Tom was a great favorite of hers, a part of her life, and it can easily be imagined what a traumatic effect the event had on her.

Carroll (Spencer's only brother) and I are spending an evening together. Toward the end of it, he says, "Spence was always different—I'm talking about right from the beginning. So nothing he ever did or does surprises me. Good or bad." He looks off into memory and continues. "Except one time. He did surprise me. And the old man. And Mother. And Aunt Moom. Everybody. It was when he all of a sudden said he'd decided to go for *priest!* Jesus. We could hardly *believe* it. Any of us. Our mother was pleased, of course. Dad said, 'Fine, fine.' But I could see he wasn't too sure. What I mean is, Spence had been—up to that time—a full-scale hell-raiser. The idea stuck with him for a while, though. Then, I don't know—one thing and another—it just petered out, I guess."

Not long afterward I ask Spencer to verify Carroll's report. He smiles gently, remembering, and says, "Yuh. True. I can't explain it, even now. I was seventeen, maybe sixteen, and I was going to a Jesuit school—Marquette Academy. And you know how it is in a place like that—the influence is strong, very strong, intoxicating. The priests are all such superior men—heroes. You want to be like them—we all did. Every guy in the school probably thought some—more or less—about trying for the cloth. You lie in the dark and see yourself as Monsignor Tracy, Cardinal Tracy, Bishop Tracy, Archbishop—I'm getting gooseflesh!"

I hate jokes, avoid listening to them, and refrain from telling them but he has cued me powerfully into a vaudeville wheeze and I find myself repeating it. It is a rabbi-priest-on-a-train story: The rabbi inquiring, "And *then* what could you get to be? . . . And *then* what? . . . The Pope, yes . . . And *then?*"

"And then, nothing," says the priest. "I can't get to be Jesus Christ, can I?"

"Well, one of *our* boys made it," says the rabbi.

Spencer frowns.

"What I meant was," he says, "it's the idea, the aim. Like in Washington. Didn't you once tell me that every single man in public office there—congressman or senator or cabinet or whatever—somehow, sometimes pictures himself as President of the United States?"

"That's what I've observed."

"It's the same in a school like that."

"What do you suppose happened," I asked, "to turn you off?"

"Well," he replies, "it was wartime. Nineteen-seventeen. And the uniform seemed more appropriate than the habit. Or more glamorous. Everybody was joining up. So we did, too. Carroll and Pat and I into the Navy. And I guess that's where Cardinal Tracy started turning into Admiral Tracy."

"So we have the Navy to thank for Tracy the actor, eh?"

"No," he says. "The *Church* has the Navy to thank."

"You'd've made one helluva priest," I suggest.

"Don't you believe it. Anyhow, you don't know anything about it!" His flare-up is only momentary and dies away. He goes on. "I'll tell you something. . . . No, I'd better not."

"Come on, Spence. Don't do that."

He thinks it over, decides to acquiesce. "Well," he says, "it's only this. Every time I *play* a priest—and I've done my share, Father Flanagan in those two *Boys Town* ones and Father Mullin in *San Francisco* and Father Doonan in *The Devil at*

Four O'Clock—every time I put on the clothes and the collar I feel right, right away. Like they were mine, like I belonged in them, and that feeling of being—what's the word?—an intermediary is always very appealing. Those were always my most comfortable parts, and if you ever tell anyone I told you this, you son-of-a-bitch, I'll break you in half."

I never have. Until now.

Dinner at Kate's with Edwin O'Connor, the author of *The Last Hurrah*.

We are asked because it was I who originally sent the book to Spencer, at the request of O'Connor's editor, Edward Weeks, of Little, Brown.

It is the beginning of a fine, long friendship. O'Connor turns out to be a sainted man with extraordinary charm, and impressive acting ability.

Toward the end of the evening, Spencer asks, "And what are you writing now, Ed?"

"Well," he replies, "I never like to talk about work in progress, but I'll say this much—it's the story of a priest."

Spencer nods, interested.

"A middle-aged, American priest."

Spencer looks up.

"And the story—well, I won't go into that. But the character—the priest—happens to be an alcoholic."

Spencer thinks for a time, and says, "I see. Well, yes—I think I could handle that."

There is little understanding of the creative process and of the labor that goes into supporting an ability. Ruth Gordon, my wife, has said, "It isn't enough to have talent. You also have to have a talent for *having* talent."

Someone else: "The use of talent is far more important than the possession of talent."

We all know of artists who have misused their talent, or sold it cheaply, or prostituted it, or evaded it, or expanded it into turgidity, or drowned it in alcohol, or dulled it with drugs.

Kate is one of the few who has made the most of her gifts, but it is often forgotten that her career had a sticky beginning, a discouraging first few years. And even after she had made her considerable mark, there came a series of leans and fats which might easily have destroyed someone less resilient.

At the very outset, her father objected to her choice of a career. He himself was a distinguished but private person who believed that publicity was vulgar and demeaning. He could not understand the desire of his coltish eldest daughter to go off and display herself in public. He offered her little or no support in the beginning and allowed her to take her first job in the Baltimore, Maryland, stock company only because he was certain she would fail, or would come to her senses. Some time later, when he realized she was determined to go on with it, he began to send token support, always in a euphemistic guise.

"This twenty-five dollars," he once wrote her, "was won playing golf. I do not believe in gambling and so don't wish to keep it. Do what you like with it."

On another occasion, when she asked him for the financial support she needed to acquire training from Frances Robinson-Duff, he came through generously and swiftly.

"If you're determined to do it," he said, "you may as well learn your busincss."

In the years to come, he became resigned to her activities and took great pride in her achievements.

Her mother, a born rebel, was on Kate's side from the beginning but, for all Mrs. Hepburn's work in the fields of women's suffrage, birth control, and related causes, the Hepburn household was a classic patriarchy. Dad was the undisputed boss.

Certainly Mrs. Hepburn did much to interpret Katharine to

her father and her husband to her daughter, but it still made for a difficult beginning.

Kate is frequently thought of as being one of the loved and envied. Didn't it all come easily to her? A rich girl. A great beauty. Innate talent, along with energy and the controlling factor—luck.

It is worth remembering that although she did indeed win her first Academy Award only five years after her first professional appearance (as a lady-in-waiting in *The Czarina* in Baltimore stock in 1928) she was not to win another Academy Award for thirty-four years: in 1967 for *Guess Who's Coming to Dinner*.

It was a surprise win, even to her. She was in France, making *The Madwoman of Chaillot* when the news came through by telephone. Her housekeepers, Willie and Ida, phoned her from Hollywood, awakening her just before 7 A.M., French time.

"You won, Miss Hepburn!" they shouted. "You won the *Oscar!*"

"Did Mr. Tracy win it, too?" she asked.

There was a pause before Willie replied, "No, Madam."

"Well, that's okay," she said. "I'm sure mine is for the two of us."

The following day, Gregory Peck received a cable:

> IT WAS DELIGHTFUL A TOTAL SURPRISE I AM ENORMOUSLY TOUCHED BECAUSE I FEEL I HAVE RECEIVED A GREAT AFFECTIONATE HUG FROM MY FELLOW WORKERS AND FOR A VARIETY OF REASONS NOT THE LEAST OF WHICH BEING SPENCER STANLEY SIDNEY KATHY AND BILL ROSE. ROSE WROTE ABOUT A NORMAL MIDDLE AGED UNSPECTACULAR UNGLAMOROUS CREATURE WITH A GOOD BRAIN AND A WARM HEART WHO'S DOING THE BEST SHE CAN TO DO THE DECENT THING IN A DIFFICULT SITUATION. IN OTHER WORDS SHE WAS A GOOD WIFE. OUR MOST UNSUNG AND IMPORTANT HEROINE. I'M GLAD SHE'S COMING BACK IN STYLE. I MODELED HER AFTER MY MOTHER. THANKS AGAIN. THEY DON'T USUALLY GIVE THESE THINGS TO THE OLD GIRLS YOU KNOW.

The following year, 1968, she won it again for *The Lion in Winter,* sharing the honor with Barbra Streisand of *Funny Girl.*

This time, she could have appeared, was urged to do so, as a presenter. Gregory Peck, then president of the Academy of Motion Picture Arts and Sciences, made a special, personal appeal, pointing out that as a two-time winner, her appearance would be infinitely appropriate.

"I'd love to do it, Greg," was her response. "I'd do it for you if I could, but I can't. I'd faint on camera, and spoil the whole damned show."

Between the first two awards, there were many nominations, but the final accolade was withheld. (Some thought it had to do with the fact that Kate would not play the Hollywood game, would not campaign, would not enter into the social scene. In short, she would not become a member of the club. This may or may not be so, but the final result would seem to vindicate her position.)

In 1935, she was nominated for her performance in the title role of *Alice Adams,* but the award went to Bette Davis, for *Dangerous.* In 1940, for her performance as Tracy Lord in *The Philadelphia Story,* she won the New York Film Critics' Award, was nominated for the Academy Award, seemed a shoo-in, but lost to Ginger Rogers, who had made *Kitty Foyle.* In 1942, she was nominated for her performance as Tess Harding in *Woman of the Year,* and the award went to Greer Garson as the patriotic *Mrs. Miniver. The African Queen* and her performance as Rose Sayer in 1951 brought still another nomination, but Vivien Leigh won for *A Streetcar Named Desire.* In 1955, Kate was nominated for *Summertime* and her beautiful performance as Jane Hudson, under David Lean's direction. The award went to Anna Magnani for *The Rose Tattoo.* The following year, 1956, Ingrid Bergman in *Anastasia* won over her Lizzie Curry in *The Rainmaker.* In 1959, Kate played Mrs. Venable in *Suddenly, Last Summer,* and the award went to Simone Signoret for *Room at the Top.* In 1962, she gave what many believed to be her greatest screen performance as Mary Tyrone in *Long Day's Journey into Night.* This time she lost to Anne Bancroft in *The Miracle Worker*.

The obvious injustice of some of these outcomes irritates her friends, not her. Kate considers neither life nor work to be a matter of prizes or awards. She has spoken passionately and vehemently against them. She understands, as do most creative people, that artists do not, in the strictest sense, compete with one another as do race horses. Rather, they complement one another, each providing a color and size and shape to the great creative mosaic of the time. To put them in a position of vying with one another is degrading and anti-art.

The argument on the other side is that the public at large does not understand such esoteric maunderings, does understand a baseball game, knows a winner from a loser, and takes great pleasure in watching a contest. We are a nation of sports lovers. Even our jury system is based on a numerical score, as is a decision of the Supreme Court of the United States. Seven to two, five to four, four to three, means a great deal. Sometimes life or death.

Not only does she break many of the rules of life and of professional practice, but she establishes rules of her own. For a long time, she refused to give autographs. Of late, she has softened, and will occasionally scribble her signature for someone, saying, "Do give up this autograph nonsense. It's idiotic, wasting your time and mine. Here."

Kate, the only actress ever to win three Academy Awards, has never attended a single Academy Awards presentation. She appreciates the honors but cannot find it within herself to be part of the hoopla.

"It would give me dyspepsia," she claims.

Spencer's first Academy Award was for his performance as Manuel in *Captains Courageous* in 1937. The competition that year was formidable: Robert Montgomery for *Night Must Fall,*

Paul Muni for *The Life of Emile Zola,* Fredric March for *A Star Is Born,* and Charles Boyer for his portrayal of Napoleon opposite Greta Garbo's Countess Walewska in *Conquest.*

"I knew I was going to lose," Spencer says. "Three of the five were Metro—Bob and Boyer and me. So the studio couldn't very well campaign for *one* of us or pass the word without getting a million-dollar beef from *somebody.* They were boxed in. Warner's was pushing Muni hard; and, of course, Selznick was all out for Freddie. And remember that not only was Selznick the greatest operator in the history of Hollywood, but in this case he had what most people—including me—thought was the best performance to plunk for. God damn, that Freddie was good. Anyway, I don't have to tell you, Jasper, I may be a lunk about *some* things but not about acting. I know I'm pretty good, and in *Captains* I was a little better, maybe *very.* I mean, I'm a good actor, but I'm a son-of-a-bitch if I thought I had an expression in my box to put on my face when they announced the winner, Fredric March—and sitting there in soup and fish, to top it off. And I sure didn't want to reach for the kind of liquid help I was going to need to get through an evening like *that*—not in that particular group. So . . . it was a situation. The studio was insisting I show—there was going to be hell to pay if I didn't. Finally, I got an idea. Dr. Dennis—you know, Howard—was not only my doctor, he was my friend. And I went to him and laid it on the line. I told him I couldn't go through with it. So he said, 'Well, what do you want *me* to do? Pick it up *for* you and make a speech?' And I said, 'No, Dennie, but you know my hernia.' 'You haven't got a hernia,' he said. 'You told me I did have.' 'No, no. I said "incipient hernia" and that at some point, elective surgery might be preferable to emergency.' 'That's it!' I said. 'Elective. How about electing next week? Say February 8?' And he said, 'Oh.' 'But *you* have to elect,' I said, 'because if *I* do, trouble.' Well, what can I tell you? Dennie was a friend, and he shot me into the hospital and I didn't have to go to the Academy goddam banquet. Of course, I *did* have to have the operation. And can you imagine what I felt like—lying there, in all those itchy bandages around my middle, and plenty of pain—when the word came through, I'd won it?"

The following year, 1938, Spencer made motion picture history by winning the Award again. This time, for *Boys Town.*

Spence says, "When I got the one for *Boys Town,* I got up and made my speech and I don't remember the words exactly but something to the effect that I didn't deserve it, that it belonged to Father Flanagan and that all I'd done was let his light shine through me and so I wanted to thank him for the privilege of impersonating him and accepting the Award for him. Something like that. And I sat down. In those days you used to go back to your seat after getting it. I guess I must've overdone it a little, because ol' Frank Morgan was sitting right behind me, and he leaned forward and whispered, 'I didn't see you in the picture, Spence, but you sure deserve that statue for the performance you just gave up *there!*' "

He was nominated several times after that; in 1958 for *The Old Man and the Sea,* in 1960 for *Inherit the Wind,* in 1961 for *Judgment at Nuremberg,* and in 1967 for *Guess Who's Coming to Dinner.*

Some of us thought he should have won some of those times but Spencer insisted on putting down the Academy and its awards at every public opportunity, offending many of the members.

It should be remembered that the voting membership of the Academy has, across the years, totaled no more than thirty-seven hundred. Of this number, about eighty per cent vote. It can be seen, therefore, what a small number of members are needed to cause a victory or defeat.

"I hate it," said Spencer. "The whole thing. Whenever I'm up for it—and mind you, who asked them?—I always feel like a horse at Santa Anita."

Yet if personal popularity had been all that was ever at stake, and if everyone in the motion-picture world, everywhere, had a vote—Spencer Tracy would have won annually. Despite his often erratic behavior, his sometimes curt manner, and his general nonavailability, he was ever, in his lifetime, our Most Popular Boy in the Class.

Nineteen thirty-eight. RKO. I am directing my first film, *A Man to Remember.* It is full of brilliant old character actors whom I have admired on the New York stage: Edward Ellis, John Wray, Granville Bates, Frank Thomas, Charles Halton, and Harlan Briggs.

I am standing outside of Stage Four with Harlan, discussing an approach to the scene we are about to shoot. Kate dashes by. She stops for a moment. We exchange hellos and she greets Harlan cordially.

"Don't tell him our secret," she says to him as she moves away.

Harlan glances to me and says, "I guess she wants me to tell you our secret." He looks after her admiringly and says, "A girl like that—well, I don't know why I say a girl like that. There *is* no other girl like that. What I mean to say is, *that* girl is my idea of an inspiration. What she was talking about was eight or nine years ago when we were in a play together."

"Which one was that? I never saw you in anything with her."

"Well, she wasn't in it finally."

"Why not?"

"It was *The Big Pond,* for Eddie Knopf. He'd tried it out in his stock company in Baltimore and decided to do it in New York. We went into rehearsal. Kenneth McKenna was in it—playing a Frenchman, for God's sake! And this skinny kid everyone said was a society girl was in it playing a little part, a secretary or something, and they were having trouble with the leading girl and about a week or so before the out-of-town opening—Great Neck, I think it was—they got rid of her and shifted Hepburn from the bit to the lead. Well, that was interesting and I must say she was pretty damned good, too. I played her father. Of course, she was inexperienced and—have you ever noticed *that* in the theater? Somebody amateurish or a beginner will go on and be simply fine. Then the longer they play it or the more they rehearse, the worse they get. I guess that's the difference between a professional and an amateur, huh? The professional gets better, the amateur gets worse. Well, nobody noticed it much, but I could see—playing as much with her as I was—she was getting more and more tense as it got closer to the opening date. A funny thing used to happen to her voice. Whenever she got nervous, it would start to get high and sort of unpleasant—*grating,* don't y'know—and naturally she was nervous a lot of the time. All of us were.

"Everybody remembers opening nights—every suffering one of them—but I remember that one especially because when they called half hour, Miss Hepburn wasn't there. I think the first notion was that she'd just taken off in fright, but finally she got there and the play started. Right at the opening she had a little thing to do where she had to do something with a French accent, imitating McKenna, y'see. She did it fine and got a hand, what's more. Well that threw her, I think. Because instead of acting she started acting *up* and got steadily worse all night. Overconfidence, I guess you'd call it.

"By the end, nobody knew what to say. I remember we drove into New York together that night. I'd already heard they were going to replace her, but I couldn't tell *her* that. . . . And, damn it, isn't it a wonderful thing when you look at this marvelous girl today, this great actress, and realize it all didn't just happen for her, that she's worked and struggled and been knocked down, and gotten up again. That's what I mean by inspiration."

The following Sunday at Larry Olivier's, Kate comes to lunch. I ask her for *her* memories of *The Big Pond.*

"Oh, my God!" she says. "Did Harlan tell you? It was sheer terror—I recall it but as though it never happened—I remember it in the way one remembers a bad dream—I simply wasn't prepared and they threw this damned huge part at me and I got increasingly nervous—I could have played it if I'd had some handling, but it wasn't a terribly professional group—true, that, about my coming late to the opening night—I'd gone out trying to calm down and had a picnic supper all by myself in a field." She looks off. "I remember the dress I wore—a humdinger—Also that they'd given me someone's underpants and I was standing in the wings getting ready to make my entrance and the damn things started to tickle—I'd never worn lace pants before—knew they were going to throw me—so just before I went on I reached under and pulled them off and handed them to the assistant stage manager and went on—I still can't imagine what he must have made of *that.*" She laughs that all-out, full-bodied laugh of hers which is so infectious that people across the pool begin to laugh, too, although they have not heard a word of the story. A sudden frown cuts Kate's laugh in two.

"I wasn't much good that night—could have been if they'd stuck to me but Lee Shubert—one of the producers, was pig-headed and stubborn and wouldn't give me a chance, so I was out. They couldn't even tell me themselves, the mutts! They got Frances Robinson-Duff to do it when I went in to see her the day after opening night. It certainly stunned me and I said, 'Well, I'll go out and say good-by to everybody.'—and she said that wasn't the professional thing to do and I said I was going to do it anyway—I wasn't going to slink around—so I went down and played the part of a good sport—I got to thinking later if I'd been able to act on opening night as well as I acted then, maybe I wouldn't have got fired.

"But it was an important occasion for me—that one ghastly night—because Arthur Hopkins happened to be in the audience and he sent for me and gave me a little part in *These Days*—ran about three days—but then Arthur gave me the job of understudying Hope Williams in *Holiday*—so actually it did get me going—nice man, Harlan Briggs."

One mellow after-dinner time at George Cukor's, we talked of beginnings.

"I'd have quit the stage completely," said Spencer, "if it hadn't been for George M. Cohan. I was sort of chunky and funny-looking. I knew I was good, but I couldn't seem to get anywhere. The parts just weren't coming up. Then I got this bit in a show by Cohan. My hero. Selena Royle got it for me. Chester Morris was in it, and Hale Hamilton. Selena . . ."

He stopped and returned to the present.

"Tell them the rest of it, Spence," said Kate.

"No."

"Tell them what he said to you that time."

"No."

"The thing that made the whole difference. The turning point."

"No."

"Why not?" she said, exasperated.

"Because, you cluck," he shouted, "it's not the kind of thing you can tell people about *yourself!*"

"We're not people," said Ruth.

"Go on," I urged.

"Tell it, for Chrissake," said George. "Don't be coy."

Spencer, cornered, took a long swig of his coffee and said, "Well, the play was *Yellow* and he'd cast me in this part. Cohan had. Not the lead, but damn good. And Cohan kept watching me—more than anybody—all through rehearsals. At least, that's what I felt. I could tell he thought I was awful; so of course I got more discouraged by the hour—and worse—but he never said a word. He just kept watching me. I started to think maybe the smart move would be to quit before I got fired. I hated getting fired."

"You'd have gotten used to it," Kate interrupted. *"I* did."

Spencer looked up at her.

"Don't hector him, Kate," said George. "He's liable to stop right in the middle. You know how he is."

A long pause, after which Spencer continued.

"Well, one day—it might have been that fifth day when you could get let out without getting paid anything. . . . They were torture, those days. The whole cast, practically, being sick inside. Well, I got through my first scene somehow and at the end of it, George M. came down the aisle toward me. I knew what was coming, but what could I do? I just sat there. He put his hands on the footlights and looked up at me and said, 'Kid, you're the best actor I've ever seen,' and went back to his seat. That was the day I decided to stay on the stage."

Kate and I have been close for thirty years, but she seems to have been a vital part of my life always, in one way or another. She was there even before we met, when she was that skinny stunner floating around on the periphery of Broadway. Her career in those days appeared to consist of understudying and getting fired. Yet we all knew (all us hopefuls sitting around in Sardi's or the Penn-Astor Drug Store, standing in Shubert Alley or in the hallway outside Chamberlain Brown's office) that this high-class broad "A" broad was going to make it. What is more, *she* knew it, too.

There are actors and actresses who go through life and career perfecting their faults. Kate has made her life and her work a single pursuit, and has very nearly perfected her dazzling style.

Evidences of it were apparent even in the old days; the cut-through voice, the proud posture, the self-possession, the suffragette's determination to remold this man's world, the melting smile with its perfect teeth, the beguiling femininity, the pants.

We met, finally, in Hollywood, in 1938, when we were both under contract to RKO, and I was trying to get to make Shaw's *Saint Joan*. I was also trying to get to make Miss Hepburn. Both projects were doomed to failure.

Kate was a movie queen at the time, but there soon followed several years of ups and downs, mainly downs.

Tyrone Guthrie once said, in another connection: "Ah, yes. 'Uneasy lies the head that wears a crown'—especially if it's a *prop* crown!"

To some, failure is a debilitating experience, eroding confidence and obstructing further action. Kate uses failure as a basis for success.

A fat-headed exhibitor once ran full-page trade-paper advertisements to label her—along with Greta Garbo, Marlene Dietrich, Mae West, Joan Crawford, and Fred Astaire—"Box-Office Poison."

(I have often wondered what he thought as he observed Kate continuing to work and triumph, to hold on to her audience, to build a new one and remain as important a star as exists. Her most recent theater appearance was the occasion for the largest advance sale in the history of the American theater.)

The famous infamous campaign was effective and set off a mindless, panicked chain reaction involving distributors, exhibitors, and craven studio heads who instinctively believed whatever they saw in print. She found herself, almost overnight, embarrassingly *persona non grata* at her own studio. The accepted technique in those master-slave movie days was to assign an unwanted contract player to inferior parts in cheap pictures. This would result in making the unimportant pictures seem slightly more important; or else causing the player to balk, thereby breaking the contract.

Kate refused to play this ignominious game, went to the front office, bought her way out of her contract, and returned to New York. There she scored decisively in Philip Barry's *The Philadelphia Story,* produced by The Theatre Guild. The play ran for a year in New York and could have gone two, but Kate was restless and wanted to tour the country. She did so for a year, thus demonstrating that the lady called "Box-Office Poison" at box offices that sold tickets for fifty-five cents, was able to cause a run on box offices demanding three dollars and thirty cents.

Before long, every film company in Hollywood was bidding for the rights to *The Philadelphia Story.* They discovered, to their consternation, that Kate had already shrewdly acquired the rights from Barry and the Guild. Thus, she was in an enviable position to deal. She insisted on playing her own part. Metro-Goldwyn-Mayer bought the rights, but still troubled and to protect itself gave her two leading men—Cary Grant and James Stewart—as well as George Cukor to direct. The result was one of the studio's outstanding successes.

Kate then took the play on tour again, and tells this about the closing night in Philadelphia:

"I told the stage manager to watch me. I didn't tell anyone what I was going to do but I told him to keep his eye on me—I'd give him the instructions. After the performance—it had gone very well—friends out front—I signaled him to leave the curtain up—I came forward and made a little speech—don't remember the words exactly, but what I said to them in substance was that we'd just given the last performance of *The Philadelphia Story* that we were going to give ever, anywhere; that it was terribly sad for me because the play had meant something special in my life—I hadn't been doing well—was considered sort of a flop in pictures—came to New York and played the play and it had gone so well that I was able to go out and make the movie and then tour the play again. And I said all plays were sad to close but some more so than others—that this one was the saddest of all because it had been such a friend and had meant so much to me and now I was leaving it—but I had decided that the curtain would *never* fall finally on *The Philadelphia Story;* and I signaled to the stage manager to leave it up, and we all just walked off the stage, and the audience left the theater and the curtain was still up, and that was it—I liked that—Doing that."

On a balmy summer night in 1953 in St. Jean-Cap Ferrat, I am sitting up with Spencer, who is not feeling well.

Knowing that he always enjoys theater talk, I try to distract him with some.

"I remember just perfectly, absolutely plain, the first time I ever saw you, Spence. Nineteen-thirty. February. I went to see *The Last Mile.* I got one of those last-minute, cut-rate, fifty-five-cent tickets at Gray's Drugstore on Forty-third Street, and ran like a thief over to where you were playing: The Sam H. Harris Theatre on Forty-second Street. Right?"

"Right," he replies. "You sure keep your head full of trivia, don't you? It's a damn wonder there's room for anything else in it."

"That's not trivia," I argue. "That's one of the most important theater decals on my memory pan."

Spencer blushes, of all things. I go on.

"I remember whamming up those second-balcony steps, two and three at a time, because I didn't want to miss the opening which one usually did on those tickets. That night I made it. I don't care if you believe this or not, Flannel, but I thought you were great right off. Sure, Jimmy Bell had that first act showy part—and Joe Calleia—but I went for you, boy. All out."

"I think I'm feeling a lot better," says Spence. "Want to go into Nice and look for some girls and take 'em dancing?"

"Of course by the end of the play I was knocked out. A total wreck. And something happened to me that had never happened before."

"You fell out of the second balcony."

"No. Edith Evans once said that when you leave a theater, if you don't walk several blocks in the wrong direction, the performance has been a failure. Well, that night, I left the theater and started walking, and the next thing I knew I was standing in front of Macy's where I'd worked the year before, for a year. That was some performance, boyo."

"And some part," he says. "Clark Gable didn't do badly in it. On the Coast. Got him into pictures. Have you ever noticed how few people can tell the difference between a good part and a good performance?"

"That's the way it should be," I suggest. "The actor and the role have to become one in the mind of the audience. Otherwise there's no illusion. I learned that lesson once at the Capitol Theatre, watching Robert Montgomery in a Metro comedy called *Forsaking All Others*."

"I remember it. Damn good."

"And Montgomery delivered one of the solid punch lines—I don't know whose it was, the original author's or Joe Mankiewicz's or whose, but no matter. It got a terrific laugh. And a popcorny girl, sitting in front of me, turned to her girl friend and said, 'I *love* that Bob Montgomery. He's always got a comeback.' And thinking about it, I realized that—sure that's the way it is—the one who says it is the one who gets the credit on a then-and-there basis. And should. I mean, it would be awful if when some actor playing a character says something, and you think, 'By God, that George S. Kaufman is witty.' "

Spencer fixes me with a searching look and asks, "How come you'd never seen me before *The Last Mile?"*

"Never *seen* you? I'd never even *heard* of you."

That famous mock-hurt, outraged expression comes over his craggy face and he begins. His voice, a tone or two higher than normal. "You mean you didn't see me as the Ninth Robot in *R.U.R.?* Or as Holt, the Second Detective in *A Royal Fandango?* How come you didn't come to Stamford to catch me in *The Sheepman?* And *Yellow?* I was a hit in that. Where were you? You missed *The Baby Cyclone?* And *Whispering Friends?* And those were all Broadway, buddy—big time—aside from the sensation I was in stock, in Baltimore and Trenton, and Grand Rapids and White Plains, and Providence and Cincinnati, and Lima for God's sake Ohio. And on the road, in Chicago. And what were you doing in 1929—the year of the crash? I stayed right in style that year and did three big flops in a row; *Nigger Rich, Dread,* and *Veneer*. What do you *mean,* you'd never heard of me, you bastard. You just weren't trying!"

"Sorry," I tell him. *"The Last Mile* was the first time."

He stands up and walks over to the window. Looking out, he thinks back. "I ran into Ring Lardner one night, and he asked me what I was doing. I told him I was going to Brooklyn with *Dread* and he said, 'Is there any other way? . . .' Then *Veneer,* that last turkey I went into after it had opened—around The Lambs, it was always referred to as 'Venereal.' But then, God be praised, came *The Last Mile* . . . at last. . . . Funny, isn't it," he muses, "how we never know? What is it? Cockeyed perspective? Self-delusion? What? All through rehearsals of *The Last Mile* I was *sure* it was another bust. Maybe after three in a row, I'd just gotten into the habit. I couldn't *imagine* a hit. I think Shumlin liked me all right, but I had the feeling, all through, that Chet Erskine—he was directing, you remember—was on the verge of firing me every day. But the play got over finally, not just me—the whole show—everybody. Chet certainly had a hot bat going at the time—four big hits in a row. *Subway Express, Harlem,* and another one I forget, and then us. And he was twenty-three years old! What days. . . . Beat it, will you? I want to go to sleep."

The next time I saw Chester Erskine, I asked him if it was true he had lacked confidence in Tracy during rehearsals.

Chet shakes his head. "You know our Spence. Anything to create drama. Of course, he's wrong. I was bowled over by him at the first reading, and he got better every day. He was the best actor I'd worked with up to then—or since, I may say. There'd been a lot of guys up for the part of Killer Mears, but when we decided on Tracy it was unanimous—Herman, Wexley, and I. . . . About his worry during rehearsals? I don't know. He never showed it, thank God. It was a tough show. Revisions every hour. But all of us—out front at least, even after a rocky out-of-town opening—were confident. It was a fine play. Very strong. We all succeeded. Everyone connected with it. But there's no question that the triumph was Tracy."

For years the Hepburns had a summer cottage at Fenwick, near Saybrook, Connecticut, on Long Island Sound. The kids all grew up there, and became proficient at sports. In 1938, during the violent hurricane that hit the New England coast, the cottage was demolished.

Kate relishes the memory of that adventure. "I was there with Mother—knew Dad would be worried—so off I went right through the blow—my God, it was something—*devastating*—and unreal—like the beginning of the world—or the end of it—and I slogged and sloshed, crawled through ditches and hung on and kept going somehow—got drenched and bruised and scratched—*completely* bedraggled—finally got to where there was a working phone and called Dad. The minute he heard my voice he said, 'How's your mother?'—and I said—I mean shouted—the storm was screaming so—'She's all right. All *right,* Dad! But listen, the house—it's gone—blown away into the sea!' And he said, 'I don't suppose you had brains enough to throw a match into it before it went, did you? It's insured against fire, but not against blowing away!—And how are *you?'* "

Characteristically, the Hepburns decided to build another house on the same site. Kate went, one afternoon, to the F.A.O. Schwarz toy store on Fifth Avenue and Fifty-eighth Street in New York, and bought an elaborate box filled with toy house-building blocks. She took it to Hartford, where the whole family sat around, playing with the blocks and constructing a collectively conceived ideal house. After many changes and arguments (and a few broken blocks), a plan was agreed upon, and the house was built. It still stands, occupied permanently by her brother Dick, and from time to time by various members of the ever-growing family.

Jeff Selznick has a memory of adventure at the place:

"Kate. I guess she was the first girl I was ever in love with. It didn't seem strange to me because she never treated me as though I were young and she were older. There wasn't any of that adult-child nonsense. I was a boy and she was a girl and even though I don't think anybody could say I'd lived a sheltered life, I sure had never run into anything like her. Once when I was about—I don't know—fourteen or fifteen, I was visiting Fenwick and we went out in a twenty-two-foot boat. There was Kathy Grant and one of the other nieces and we were going along fine, and don't ask me how it happened, but all of a sudden we lost the motor. I mean it just fell overboard. So I sat there looking down and the next thing you know, Kate dove right in. We were scared to death and kept yelling at her that we were in the marshes and that it was dangerous and please cut it out, but she kept diving over and over, getting madder and madder. She couldn't find it, so she got a fix on exactly where we were and the next day she got us all to go back there. Well, no. Not the girls. She got her brother, Richard, and me, and we went back to the spot and she supervised the whole operation and got Dick and me to dive down, looking for the motor. I was terrified but since she'd done it the day before it would've seemed sissy not to. After a while Dick found it, but he couldn't raise it. About this time, I was exhausted—breathing hard and gasping. She pulled me back into the boat. Dick was saying, 'The hell with it.' You know what she did? She pulled up the anchor and started fishing for that motor with the anchor. Next thing you know, she'd hooked it. She started to pull on it and yelled for help, and we all pulled on it and pulled. All of a sudden, we had the goddam motor back in the boat!

"It means a lot to a kid growing up, hanging around with a dame like that."

In the spring of 1939, I was at RKO directing John Barrymore in *The Great Man Votes.*

Between shots, one morning, we sat and chatted.

He looked at me quizzically, those legendary eyebrows awry, and said, "I'm told you go around with the Hepburn woman. Is that true?"

"I don't know what you mean by 'go around with,' " I said, rather stiffly.

"I don't know," he said. "What do *you* mean?"

"She's a friend of mine."

"Impossible!" The word was spat.

"Why do you say that, Mr. Barrymore?"

(It was one of the rules I had laid down on the production. Everyone was to call him "Mr. Barrymore." The great American actor had, by this time in his floundering career, degenerated into something of a sloppy clown. I reasoned that if we all treated him with respect he might begin again to respect himself. It worked.)

"I say that," he replied sonorously, "because I *know* her. A creature *most* strange. A nut. She must come from Brazil. 'Where the *nuts* come from.' *Charley's Aunt.* Glorious farce. Brandon Thomas. Do you know it?"

"I find Kate extremely intelligent. And awesomely talented."

"I didn't *say* she wasn't *talented,*" he snapped. *"Most* talented people are nuts." He snorted the famous Barrymore snort. "I made a picture with her around here, you know—Is this RKO? Yes. —about a year ago." (Actually, it had been *A Bill of Divorcement, seven* years earlier.) "And let me tell you. We'd been shooting for a few days, and getting along famously. She was playing my daughter, so it was difficult to get the customary licks in, if you take my meaning."

"Yes."

"I gave her the eye a few times, then I stopped till *she* gave *me* the eye. After a few more days, we gave each *other* the eye. So I knew the time was ready. I'm *never* wrong about such things. I never *have* been. I said to her, 'How about lunch?' She said, 'Fine.' We went over to my dressing room. I locked the door and took my clothes off. She just stood there looking at me, and finally I said, 'Well, come on. What're you *waiting* for? We don't have all day. Cukor's one of those finickers who goes into a *spin* if you're five minutes late.' She didn't move, so I did and started to grab her, but she backed away and practically plastered herself against the wall, by God. I said, 'What's the *matter?*' And she said, 'I *cahn't!*' I said, 'Never mind, I'll show you how.' She started babbling, 'No, no. Please. It's impossible. I *cahn't!*' I've never *been* so damned *flabbergasted*. I said to her, 'Why *not?*' And what do you think *she* said?"

"I've no idea."

He saved his uncanny imitation of Kate for his punch line.

"She said, 'My father doesn't want me to have any babies!' "

I changed the subject as swiftly as I could. When I asked Kate about this account, she said, "Well, I won't say he lied, but I do think his memory betrayed him a bit. He did *not* ask me to lunch in his dressing room—I'd have understood that —I'd been around by then. Actually, he suggested we run over the scene we were going to shoot after lunch—imagine how I leaped at *that* chance—to be coached by John Barrymore—I was absolutely fascinated by him. What an actor! I went over to his dressing room, not with him—he was already there. We ran the scene—and he did help me—enormously—then, as I was getting ready to go, he suddenly took off his dressing gown—

one of those ridiculous, flannel ones, the kind we used to wear when we were children—his was absolutely repulsive—filthy, food-stained, and caked with make-up on the collar—simply *revolting.* Anyway, he whipped it off and stood there—stark naked. My first thought was to get out, but I simply couldn't move—I was petrified—couldn't speak—eventually I did, I suppose, but don't ask me to remember what I said—I'm willing to take his word for that part of it—God knows, what he reported *sounds* like me back in those days. I do remember, though, even now, how terrified I was—and I recall that he was furious—hardly spoke to me for the rest of the picture."

"What you must understand," I explained, "is that this was routine with him. He was, after all, John Barrymore, stunningly beautiful, considered by some to be the greatest American actor ever, sexually magnetic. So who'd say no to him—except a nut like you?"

John Barrymore's leading lady in *The Great Man Votes* was Katherine Alexander, and I was delighted to have her. The part was small but she played it, I suppose, because it was opposite Barrymore.

He behaved in something less than a gentlemanly way with her and it surprised me. One day, during a scene, he was so beastly to her, that I saw her literally shrinking. All at once, I recognized the problem. She was taller than he, that was all.

There was nothing I could do with him, but I took her to lunch to let her know I was aware of the difficulty. She was more than understanding and said, "Would you mind if I took my shoes off when we continue?"

"Not at all."

"Do you think *he'd* mind?"

"God only knows. It's worth a try, though. Wear slippers or something."

"All right. I've always had a scratchy time with leading men," she said, chewing on a piece of her sandwich and reminiscing. "Spencer Tracy, the best, I suppose, was one of the worst."

"Tracy?" I said. "But you never worked with him."

"Oh, yes. It was almost ten years ago, when the talkie thing hit with such an impact. There hadn't yet been any such thing as an all-talking picture, but out in Brooklyn, at Warner's, they'd begun to make shorts. Musicals, mostly. With Martinelli, the opera singer, and others. And then they decided to go into shorts. It's a surprise, looking back, how few legitimate players were willing to go into them. For one thing, they worried about how they'd be photographed and recorded. They didn't want to spoil their chances at a real movie fling that they thought might come later on. And for another, there wasn't much money in it, and it was a sort of giveaway that you were hard up. Well, I was and I didn't see why there should be any secret about it. The first one was called *Taxi Talks,* if you can believe it—a two-reel melodrama. Mayo Methot—she was married to Humphrey Bogart then—was in it with us. I remember riding out there with her on the subway. Spencer played a gangster of some kind. The whole thing was shot in about three days. I never saw it, not because I didn't want to—I just never could find out where it played. Still they must have thought it was pretty good and they must have liked us because Spencer and I were hired for a second one. *One* reel this time. I think we worked *two* days. It was called *The Hard Guy.* He played the title role. It was all strange and new and uncomfortable and rather embarrassing, but honestly, playing even the shortest scene with him there was simply no question that he was a brilliant actor.

"I've read just about everything about him that's been published, but I've noticed he never mentions those shorts. So perhaps I shouldn't have, either. Oh well, in the end, what does it matter?"

In the RKO hairdressing department, during the same period, I eavesdropped, over a half-wall, on a 6 A.M., over-coffee conversation, involving Lucille Ball, Barbara Stanwyck, Ginger Rogers, and several unidentifiable voices. Lucille and Ginger were making *Stage Door* with Kate at the time. Barbara Stanwyck was on *The Mad Miss Manton.*

There was general studio agreement that Katharine Hepburn was a dazzling actress and a star, but there was some question as to whether she was going to become box office.

The voices said:

"She's so *gorgeous*. How can she miss?"

"Takes more than gorgeous, sugar."

"Yeah? Like what?"

"Talent."

"Luck."

"Hits."

"That's it. Hits. Listen to *her*."

"So? She's had hits."

"Not lately."

"What do you call 'lately'?"

"What about *Alice Adams?*"

"Two years ago."

"All right."

"All right if she'd done nothing since, but she's had strike-outs in the two years. *Sylvia Scarlett*."

"Help!"

"Break of Hearts."

"I liked it."

"But Kokomo didn't."

"Mary of Scotland. Wasn't that a hit?"

"No."

"Yes."

"No!"

"No."

"A Woman Rebels."

"She should've, before she said yes to *that* turkey."

"Quality Street?"

"They say she picked that one herself. Well, whoever. The people didn't want it."

"She's gonna score in this one, though. Boy, is she ever great."

"Yeah, but we're talking about star. The ones people come to see, no matter what. Gable, Tracy, Harlow, Bette. Like that."

"Maybe Hepburn's too special."

"What does that mean?"

"Too, like—well, like high-toned. Not like us."

"I'm high-toned, you *pisspot!"*

The unmistakable cut-through voice of Lucille Ball took over. "Listen, biddies, don't worry your pretty little heads—and I do mean little—about Miss Katie. She'll make it just fine. She knows the combination of the safe. To everybody's safe. Have you ever noticed something? How every time she gets into a new scene, no matter where, or on what stage, and she's wearing a new outfit, every son-of-a-bitch on this lot, from every department, finds his way over there—or her way—to stand around and gawk? Why *is* that? Don't ask me, but they sure all want to look at her, and watch her, and see what she does. I do it myself. And the grips from the other sets and cutters and messengers and readers. They all find their way and stand around taking her in like out-of-town visitors. I notice they don't do it for any of the rest of us. Only for her. So why is that? Don't ask me. But I claim anybody who can get a routine like that going for them, without trying even, has got to become a big star, and, what's more, *stay* a big star. She's news, that's all. Hot news. All the time."

The instinctively sagacious Lucille, who wound up owning that very studio, had recognized it. Call it news, hot news, call it "it," as Eleanor Glyn did for Clara Bow, or call it, as we do these days, charisma. Katharine Hepburn had it and has it.

Humphrey Bogart, not a man to fawn or curry favor or flatter, once said, "As far as actors go—living ones—I'd say Spence is the best by far. He and I have our ups and downs personally—he's a moody son-of-a-bitch—but professionally I rate him tops. The thing about his acting is there's no bullshit in it. He doesn't go in for those hammy disguises some clowns think is acting. Disguises! Jesus, they're for detectives or for Owen McGiveney. Spencer *does* it, that's all. Feels it. Says it. Talks. Listens. He means what he says when he says it, and if you think that's easy, try it."

Clark Gable, long called The King (a name bestowed upon him by Spencer), said, "The only thing I mind about him is that humble act he does once in a while. Don't you believe it. He knows how good he is. And that's as good as anyone has gotten up to here and now in this business. Any actor or actress who's ever played a scene with Spence will tell you—there's nothing like it. He mesmerizes you. Those eyes of his—and what goes on behind them. Nobody's better than when they act with him. It's like playing tennis with someone better than you—*you* get better."

"He's more than an actor," says Jean Simmons. "He's a sort of sorcerer. When I was with him in *The Actress*—playing his daughter—well, I confess I'd never known anything like it. When we met, he was pleasant and professional; later, a bit flirtatious, but that was to be expected—it was his habit, I gather. Then we began to shoot. All at once, he looked at me and he wasn't the star—he was the father. *My* father. And I wasn't me—I was his daughter. I fairly broke out. And it would happen again and again—startling, really. One never quite got used to it. To him."

Spencer made a director's complicated work uncomplicated. Aside from his considerable imaginative contributions, he created an atmosphere on the set that made for pleasant hours.

Edward Dmytryk says, "You believe him. Audiences believe him, and *in* him. They never feel the strain of acting in him, so they can relax and enjoy it. Of course, it's all illusion. Actually, he works as hard as anyone I know—but it's all inside. Hidden. You never see the strings."

John Ford says, *"He* directed *me* twice. Once at the beginning of his career and once toward the end. In between, we talked a lot. He was a great actor—the greatest, I guess, in my time."

George Cukor directed more Tracy films than any other man. "An astonishing actor," is Cukor's comment. "I have—with the help of several expensive pho-sycians, and these lenses—excellent eyesight, and as a rule, I'm concentrated on the set, too concentrated sometimes. I'd watch him act—print up what I thought best. Then I'd go to the dailies and *always* there would be something he'd done that I hadn't seen. Some look or subtlety or meaning. Communication. It was as though he and the camera were in private cahoots. It went on happening right through the five pictures we made together. From *The Keeper of the Flame* through *The Actress*. And what's even more important than the fact he was a marvelous actor, was the fact that he was equally good as my tenant. Paid his rent on time, no complaints, quiet, respectable, and did all his own repairs."

"Tracy movies are murder to edit," says Henry Ephron. "You're tempted every minute to stay with him. You feel it's a shame to cut away. That great face never gets monotonous. Not even in long extended close-ups—the way you see them often in the rushes. And of course that voice—it's compelling. You *can't* not listen."

Spencer, who loved praise and appreciation as much as anyone, nevertheless did not feel the necessity to repay in kind. His public utterances were as rare as they were taciturn, but in private he was frequently withering, often witty.

Talking to me of Kate, he said, "You see, the trouble with Kath is—she understands me."

One night, we were watching an old movie of mine on television. Charles Laughton and Carole Lombard in *They Knew What They Wanted*. Somewhere in the middle of it, Kate asked aimlessly, "What did Laughton die of?"

"Acting," said Spence.

The inflated status of movie stars troubled him.

"Why do actors think they're so goddam important? They're not. Acting is not an *important* job in the scheme of things. Plumbing is."

One night, by careful prearrangement, we all watched a television program: Laurence Olivier in Somerset Maugham's *The Moon and Sixpence*.

Not a word was said as it played, not even during the commercials.

When it ended, Spencer stood up and said, "Ladies and gentlemen, you have just seen a professional actor doing his job."

One of Kate's shortcomings is that she does not wear clothes well and never has. This may be due to an over-all lack of interest in frippery.

Wearing clothes, as any expert knows, is a matter of instinct and experience, involving many nuances.

There is an account of Florenz Ziegfeld being sued by his backers for being wasteful, even profligate, with their money.

Under cross-examination, Ziegfeld was asked, "Is it true, Mr. Ziegfeld, that you imported petticoats made of rare Irish lace for your showgirls?"

"Yes, sir. That is true."

"Is it also true that at no time in the course of the production could any part of these expensive petticoats be seen by the audience?"

"That is absolutely true."

"How then, Mr. Ziegfeld, can you justify this great expenditure? This enormous amount spent on petticoats that the audience never saw, and could not possibly have seen."

"My dear man," explained Ziegfeld, with the patience of a master. "I specialize in presenting the most beautiful girls in the world. When these girls walk onto the stage and know they are wearing these unsurpassable, expensive petticoats, it makes them move differently, and stand differently; it changes the looks on their faces, it's one of the things that makes my beautiful girls beautiful. It's one of my secrets. I'm not going to tell you any of the others."

Ziegfeld was right. We have all observed how women in new and costly finery change in spirit and appearance before our eyes.

Not Kate. It has never mattered to her whether she was wearing an original Balenciaga or her traditional fatigues and T-shirt.

By the same token, she has always used a minimum of make-up, on and off, and usually does her own hair.

A bright, bitter young actress once said, "Well, of course she doesn't have to try to look like Katharine Hepburn. She *is* Katharine Hepburn!"

In the motion-picture world, the word "photogenic" is part of the professional lingo. What does it mean?

Webster's Third New International Dictionary, gives it as:

pho•to•genic \[1]fōd·ə[1]jenik, -ōta-, -jēn-, nēk\ *adj* [*phot-* + *-genic*] **1 a :** produced or precipitated by light <~ epilepsy> <~ dermatitis> **b :** marked by a tendency to darken on exposure to sunlight <the ~ property of a pigment> **2 :** PHOTOGRAPHIC **3 :** producing or generating light **:** PHOSPHORESCENT <~ bacteria> <~ organs of a firefly> **4 :** eminently suitable for being photographed esp. from the aesthetic point of view <~ hands> — **pho•to•geni•cal•ly** \-nek (ə) lē, -nēk-, -li\ *adv* *

This leads us to "photogene," where we find:

pho•to•gene\ʹfōd•ə,jen*n -s* [ISV *phot-* + *-gene;* prob. orig. formed in F]: an afterimage or retinal impression

Afterimage? Something which, for some reason, has a special glow?

What is finally meant is that because of some unexplained and magic combination of shades, planes, shapes, eye color, inner fire, and the mystery of personality, there are some players who are unquestionably more effective as shadows than they are as flesh and blood.

The camera does more than simply record, it also reveals. In many ways, it is more powerful than the naked eye. The moon to the eye is not the telescope's moon. A face in filmed close-up tells you more than it does in life.

Gary Cooper was one of the most photogenic players ever and Greta Garbo perhaps *the* most. The retinal impression she made on me is permanent.

I once said to Ernst Lubitsch, "Why is it that every time I see Cooper on the screen, he reminds me of Garbo; and every time I see Garbo, she puts me in mind of Cooper?"

"Naturally," said Ernst. "They are the same person."

* © 1966 by G. & C. Merriam Co., publishers of the Merriam-Webster Dictionaries. By permission of the publishers.

"What are you talking about?"

"I'm telling you. They are not two. They are one. Garbo and Cooper. The same."

I laughed at the wild Lubitsch slant.

"Yes, laugh," said Ernst. He narrowed his humorous eyes craftily, and added, "But have you ever noticed how you've never seen them in the same picture?"

He went on, seriously, to explain the nature of this phenomenon.

He told me he had worked with both Cooper and Garbo and had found them in real life to be bland, colorless people.

"Then," he said, "you photograph them in a scene, you go to the rushes and there is something up there which you never saw on the set. It's the great legerdemain of our métier."

Kate and Spencer, unlike Cooper and Garbo, were equally effective on the screen and off.

In the early days, cameramen liked Kate's face because it was easy to photograph, simple to light. Those high cheek bones, those luminous eyes, the long neck, took the light well and easily.

Spencer's face, too, could hardly ever be photographed uninterestingly.

Thus, they were both what we call "photogenic"—but in the largest, the most arcane, and inexplicable sense.

There is something of the schoolmistress in Katharine Hepburn. How you respond to this quality in her depends largely on your response to schoolmistresses in general.

She knows a lot about a lot and is only too eager, at any time, to pass it on.

Where to live and how. Which side of the street is great, which side is hopeless. Exactly where in the bedroom the bed should be placed. How to refrigerate food. What to put on a chigger bite. What to feed a dog. Dentistry. The common cold. Air travel. Skin care. The uses of the sea. How to get a cinder out of your eye, and what to do if you can't. Flowers and flower arrangement. Make-up, hair. Food. Marriage, sexual behavior, separation, and divorce. The right exercise and the wrong. Antiques, real and phony. Golf, tennis. How to keep water out of your ears when swimming. Literature. Weather. The tides. How to drive a car in the city, the country, on the road. Birth. Death. Morality. These are a few of the subjects on which she considers herself expert. Her desire to disseminate information has nothing whatever to do with showing off or dominating. It merely represents a way to do something to help her fellow members of the human race, most of whom, in her opinion, stand sorely in need of help.

I did not fully comprehend this side of Kate until I met her mother. Suddenly it all came clear.

Her mother, Katharine Martha Houghton, was born in Boston, Massachusetts; later moved with her family to Corning, New York, where the Houghtons still dominate the community. Her guardian was Amory Houghton, whose namesake-grandson was United States Ambassador to France from 1957 to 1961. She was graduated from both Bryn Mawr and Radcliffe, and went to teach school in Baltimore. There she met and married Thomas Norval Hepburn, a handsome and brilliant young medical student at Johns Hopkins. She gave up teaching—professionally. She was able to continue to exercise her instinct for this form of self-expression by rearing six children, each one remarkable in a separate way. Tom, deeply serious during his brief lifetime; Kate, independent, talented, and ambitious; Peg, unusually practical for a great beauty; Bob, becoming a doctor and a princely extension of his father; Marion, living a life cycle in which she went from political action to happy maternalism; and Dick, the youngest, mercurial, original, brilliantly gifted, and absolutely uncompromising.

Kate greatly admired her mother, an uncommon relationship in any generation. A result of admiration is often emulation and Kate has gone through life emulating, or attempting to emulate, her mother and her father.

When she undertook the practice of her profession, she began to add idols—some overt, others hidden.

One of these came to light on a long, snowy Saturday night in

New York, when she and Spencer and Ruth and I decided to stay in rather than risk the roads to the country.

I looked at Spencer and said, "Who do you think you are, really?"

"Are you well?" he asked.

I explained. "It's part of a game we invented accidentally, years ago, at the American Academy. I guess I must have been pretty hard to cast and so all through my senior year, the best I got to do was a few beards and a few bits, and as the term was ending, it began to seem clear that I wasn't going to get any good parts. I went upstairs to the office and complained to Mr. Diestel. You remember him. And I said that in view of the fact they hadn't given me any decent parts to play in my senior year, they ought to let me direct a play. He seemed rocked by the suggestion, said they'd never done such a thing, but that he'd take it under advisement. A few days later, to my surprise, he said it had been decided to let me direct a one-act play, to be done as a curtain raiser. I remember it well. *Eyes,* by Maxine Block, and a fine piece of heavy going it was, too. There was an excellent actor in our class named Bob Thomsen—you probably know him. He's a writer now at Metro—a tall, rangy, handsome redhead, a lot like Douglass Montgomery, who was going great guns in those days. In fact, I thought it might turn out to be one of the things that held Bob back. He was almost *too much* like Douglass Montgomery. So when I started to direct him in this play, I tried to get him to be different, which meant being different from himself. And he was having a hard time, not only with this problem, but with the fact that he was taking direction from a classmate. Well, along about the second week, things began to move badly—there was nothing but discord—and one day we had one of those shattering rehearsal blowups. And at the peak of it, when he had flatly refused to do something I wanted him to do, I yelled at him, 'Who the hell do you think you are?' And he said, automatically, 'Douglass Montgomery.' This stopped the argument cold till he said to me, 'Who do you think *you* are?' And I said, 'Jed Harris.' Well, as you can imagine, this broke the tension and we got to laughing, and asking everyone else around who they thought *they* were, and when they wouldn't tell, we'd guess. And it got to be a game around there for quite a while.

"The point was—is—that we all see ourselves in the shape of someone else. Someone we know about. Someone we'd like to be like, or who inspires us. It isn't necessarily a matter of imitation; more of standard. Sometimes people identify with strange others, or with characters in fiction. I remember once pinning down Burgess Meredith on the subject. It turned out *he* thought he was William Butler Yeats. Dick Rodgers and Larry Hart cheerfully confessed to Gilbert and Sullivan. Once I asked my boss, George Abbott, who he thought *he* was, and he said without any hesitation, 'Winchell Smith.' *His* old boss. Laurence Olivier doesn't mind admitting *he* identifies with Edmund Kean. So, come on, Spence. Who do you think *you* are?"

Spencer looked off into space, smiled, and said, "George M. Cohan."

"What about you, Kate?"

"Maude Adams," said Kate.

"Ruth?" I enquired.

"Ruth Gordon," said my wife.

We began to talk about Spencer as George M. Cohan.

The surprise was that although Cohan was an outstanding figure in the American theater, no one ever thought of him as a great actor. Still, it was his influence on Spencer's style that helped Spencer to evolve that remarkable relaxation, that seeming ease.

This was, of course, an illusion. In order to achieve the effect of relaxed spontaneity, Spencer would frequently tear himself apart inside.

We went together to see Laurette Taylor in *The Glass Menagerie*. Spencer admired Laurette more than any other American actress. He marveled at how easily she played. There was no sense of strain, no apparent attempt at projection, yet it was clear that with her most breathless whisper, she was holding the ear and the attention of the entire audience.

After the performance, we went back to see her. The great lady of the theater sat sprawled in a coming-apart easy chair in her untidy dressing room, her legs carelessly spread wide apart, her shoes and stockings off, a pair of old bedroom slippers on her feet, her make-up streaked.

Spencer was about to go into rehearsal in *The Rugged Path* and, having been off the stage for some fifteen years, was concerned about projection.

"Help me, Laurette," he said. "How do you do it?"

She snorted, "How do I do it? Like *this!*"

She reached down, picked up one of her feet and lifted it so that we could see its blistered and bleeding sole. She dropped it and showed us her other sole. The same.

"That's how," she said. "I grab that goddam stage with my two feet and send it right up from there through the rest of me and out to *them.*"

Even Spencer was astounded.

Kate's revelation of her affinity for Maude Adams was more difficult to understand because by the time Kate came on the scene, Miss Adams had long been retired from acting, and was involved in a project in Schenectady, having to do with the mechanics of stage lighting. Long afterward, she became a teacher of drama at Stevens College in Missouri. Thus, Kate had never seen her on the stage, and it is unlikely that they ever met. From what she had read and heard, however, something of the strong, independent spirit of Maude Adams attracted her. Miss Adams never married. Might this have reinforced Kate's indifference to the subject? Could her feeling about Miss Adams have influenced her to make films of Maude Adams' successes, *The Little Minister* and *Quality Street?*

There was a time when one used to hear Kate discussed as an ideal Peter Pan, one of Miss Adams' greatest roles. Alas, this never came about.

"Lord, you never know what influences you," says Kate. "How does anybody know at what precise moment they decided on this career, or that?—We're all just chunks of putty, molded by the people we meet, the experiences we have, the books we read, and the things that happen before our eyes—I remember, in Hartford, when we lived in the house on Hawthorne Street—

lots of land around it, and a brook, and all sorts of bushes, and trees—and over the mantelpiece in one of the rooms—Dad's study, I think it was—there was a sort of carved sign, and it read, 'Listen to the Song of Life.' I used to stare at it, and at first, I had no idea what it meant—so I asked Dad to explain it to me—he did and I still didn't understand—I asked mother, Tom—It got to be a joke—then, one day, I understood it all by myself, and I knew it was good advice and I've been listening ever since.

"Among other things, it means you've got to learn to live in the active tense—too many people seem to think life is a spectator sport—it isn't—not at its best, anyway—They sit around night after night watching other people converse on television—isn't it better to converse with someone yourself?—Be part of it?—That's all there is to life—being part of it."

She goes on. "Dad was an intellectual. I mean a real intellectual—a thinker—not just a memorizer. He was mad about Bernard Shaw—most people in Hartford hadn't even *heard* of Shaw—must have been because Dad was such a fan of Shaw's that he got to read that play by Brieux, *Damaged Goods*—you know, the one about syphilis that caused such a scandal—and because Dad was a urologist, the play had a special appeal for him—and he wrote to the Shaws—Mrs. Shaw had translated the play, I think, and GBS had done the introduction—Dad thought it superb—a great way to get this notion of what to do about it into the open—he made an arrangement of some sort with the Shaws and got the Connecticut Social Hygiene Association that he was connected with to disseminate copies of the play—but there began to be some trouble—he knew he needed some big names to support him. Well, one of the biggest in those parts was the president of Harvard, Dr. Eliot—Dad went and talked to him—he must have been impressed, because they say he could have had the job of Ambassador to the Court of St. James—instead he decided to stay in America and work on this thing of Dad's—So the Connecticut Social Hygiene Association went national and became the American Social Hygiene Association—Dr. Charles Eliot became the president—Dad was offered a big job in the thing, too—turned it down—I haven't any idea why. So you see he was more than *just* an intellectual—a firebrand, too—There are men of action, and men of thought, and if you ever get a combination of the two—well, that's the top—you've got someone like Dad.

"Mother always believed that a girl has as much right to go out and find the right man as the other way about—Lord knows, that's how she got Dad—Her sister, Edith, was studying medicine at Johns Hopkins and she went down there to join her in Baltimore—Edith introduced her to loads of fellows but she took a fancy to young Mr. Hepburn.

"Thomas Norval Hepburn, a great big red-haired athlete from Maryland—medical man. As soon as they were married, he got a job at the Hartford Hospital in Connecticut—they rented half a small house across the street from the doctors' entrance—thirty-two dollars a month—Tom, Junior, was born there and three years later—me—named for my mother.

"All this Women's Liberation noise, I'm for it, of course—what I'm against is their idea that they invented it—that they're on to something new—Good Lord, one of my earliest recollections is my mother making speeches, and raising hell—a real suffragette, and in those days, that wasn't an easy thing to be—about ninety per cent of the people in America—men *and* women—were against you if you were a suffragette—made fun of you—she didn't give a damn—it was something she believed in. Now with Dad trying to make a living as a doctor, of course it could've got in his way professionally—but they talked it over—decided people have to do what they feel—it wasn't only the vote that was the issue. She was in the birth-control thing with Margaret Sanger—got to know Emmeline Pankhurst—got all het up about prostitution—a hell of a lot of it in Hartford in those days—Imagine!—The newspapers used to go after her sometimes and I suppose, around Hartford, she must have been known as an oddball, the way I am now, around here.

"Dad believed in cold baths for everyone—didn't have showers in those days. He liked the idea of cold baths, the colder the better, and we all had to get used to them—I suppose that's why

I still do it—if I start with a hot shower, I always finish with a cold—trouble is, in California, the cold water doesn't run cold enough, ever."

Baths are one of Kate's many peculiarities. She takes endless showers, she says. Sometimes as many as seven or eight in the course of a day. Aside from her belief that cleanliness is next to Godliness, she uses cold baths as a hairshirt sort of self-discipline, to strengthen character and intention and drive.

In 1938, Mrs. Ogden Whitelaw Reid invited Kate to address the Herald-Tribune Forum. After a week of agonizing, she accepted. She wrote and delivered the following speech. Consider as you read that it represents the expression of a twenty-eight-year-old film star, three years prior to Pearl Harbor.

> I've never given a speech before and I don't think that any one but Mrs. Reid has ever asked me to give a speech before. As Beth so aptly put it in *Little Women,* "I have an infirmity, I'm shy." But I'll try to do my best because there are several things that I am very anxious to say to you about that much-maligned industry of motion pictures.
>
> I think that all of you will agree that moving pictures could be one of our greatest mediums of education today. Children don't have to be forced to go to the "movies," even as you and I. They like to go to them. We go to be entertained, to laugh, to weep, to think, and to be inspired. There are a great number of brilliant and talented producers, writers, and directors in Hollywood whose sole occupation is to provide us with an opportunity for just this, to say nothing of the bankers. They work day and night in a mad effort to give the public what it wants.
>
> Now in the field of the classics they have a comparatively free hand, and they have done a fine job. For some reason or other we do not seem to be so touchy about the political, economic, and moral problems of our grandfather's day, with the possible exception of the Constitution. We can face those problems simply and courageously without fear of the conse-

quences. In other words, we can face the past with a clear conscience and we can allow our children to do the same. But allow a "movie" to present situations in which we are all involved now; allow a "movie" to show people their plight and suggest a way out; allow a "movie" to present a political, moral, or economic topic of the day, honestly and simply, and they are told to do nothing, say nothing, and hear nothing.

They are sent scurrying back to the shelves to redraft that poor old story of boy-meets-girl. Then the producers are blamed for not having any originality. We are all creatures of habit. If we are fed on innocuous platitudes we cannot develop either mentally or morally. Are you going to allow this medium of public enlightenment to be stifled? The producers apparently do not dare fight this battle alone, and I don't blame them, because their risk is too great—they must have the public back of them.

Now, if you want intelligent censorship, that is, censorship which will give you "movies" which will not only entertain you but contain an idea or two, the women's clubs of America can certainly help. You can make this matter one for discussions at your meetings. You can all write your state censorship boards, insisting on a more liberal attitude, and you can write to the producers, encouraging them to produce better "movies," better modern "movies," and guaranteeing your support.

You who are responsible for the growth and development of the men and women of tomorrow must be very careful that in an effort to protect your children's morality, you are not crippling their minds.

As George Bernard Shaw says on the subject, rather wickedly perhaps, "A nation's morals are like its teeth, the more decayed they are, the more it hurts to touch them." Prevent dentists and dramatists from giving pain and not only will our morals become as carious as our teeth, but toothaches and plagues which follow neglected morality will presently cause more pain than all the dentists and dramatists have at their worst, since the world began.

It is saddening that her remarks are equally apt today, thirty-three years later; but it is hopeful that many of the new movies appear to be, at last, realizing Kate's long-ago vision.

Kate considers flying a perfectly natural act. Most people, even those who fly a great deal, are constantly aware that they are dealing with an abnormal situation. To Kate, flying is merely something one does. Apparently, it comes as a surprise to her that to do it one needs a complicated machine.

It has been said that the reason we are so often psyched by birds is that birds give us an inferiority complex; they can fly and we cannot.

Here, then, was still another of the contradictions she shared with Spencer, who always loathed it, was terrified of it, and grew more apprehensive every time he did it.

I comforted him once by telling him that George S. Kaufman lived a long life and never, in the course of it, stepped into a plane.

"I like terra firma," George once said, adding, "and the more *firma* the less *terra!*"

During the Presidential campaign of 1940, President Roosevelt invited a group of artists to lunch at Hyde Park. Kate, instead of joining the others in the travel arrangements that had been made, chartered the tiny, single-engine seaplane she frequently used for hops around the East, and flew up. There was some difficulty in finding a place to land close to Hyde Park. It was getting late. Kate instructed the pilot to come down as close to the shore as he could. He did so. She hopped out of the plane, waded through mud, and reached the river's bank. She hitchhiked to the gate of the Roosevelts' Hyde Park home, cleaned up her slacks as best she could, and proceeded to the luncheon. Her explanation of her bedraggled appearance delighted everyone, especially the President.

"Kate," he said, "you cannot imagine how flattered I am that someone would go through all that just to see *me*."

Spencer's admiration for President Roosevelt was boundless. In 1945, Spencer agreed to go abroad and tour a number of Army, Navy, Marine, and Air Force bases.

After being briefed in Washington, D.C., he was astonished to receive an invitation to call on the President. They chatted for a pleasant hour, whereupon the President told Spencer that he had a mission he wished him to perform. A message to deliver to someone, somewhere. It was important, top secret. There were reasons why it could not be conveyed even in code or by telephone. Having served in the OSS for three years, I recognized it as one of those off-the-record tidbits that sometimes came up. Spencer never revealed who, what, or where.

"The thing I couldn't understand," said Spencer, "was why me of all people. But of course I said nothing and agreed to do as I was told, that's all."

He recalled that as he left the White House, he felt that he was carrying a four-hundred-pound sack on his head. He went to New York and prepared to leave for Europe. The President died, suddenly. The tour was postponed. Waiting at the River Club, Spencer fell ill.

The whole abortive affair was one of the major frustrations of Spencer's life.

Two years later, in Washington, D.C., he and Bob Sherwood and I were having dinner at the Carlton. Bob was telling us something of his work as one of the President's speech writers.

". . . So he looked at the copy we'd brought in and had no more than glanced at the standard opening, 'My Friends . . .' when his pencil came out and he started to rewrite, furiously. We wondered what the hell. When he stopped, he said, 'I think this would be a better opening, don't you?' And he read, 'My Friends: soldiers, sailors, airmen, marines, men of the merchant marine, workers in industry, wives, mothers, parents, farmers, professionals, laborers, students, civil servants, railroad men, and all of you, my fellow Americans, tonight I wish to discuss . . .' He stopped and looked up and said, 'What do you think, Bob?' And I decided to tell the truth and I said, 'Well, Mr. President, it seems to me a little long getting to the matter.' And the President said—rather sharply for him—'Yes, well, that may be. But if I've learned one thing in this job, it's that what people mind most is being left out!' "

Spencer slammed down his fork as Bob finished the anecdote. "There it is!" he cried.

"What is?"

"The reason he gave me that message to deliver that time. It was probably nothing, but he wanted me to feel I was part of the act."

Spencer enjoyed a close personal relationship with Justice William O. Douglas, with Ambassador Lewis Douglas, and with the Kennedy family—but he made a point of not discussing them with anyone, ever.

"All the Kennedys," he once said, "remind me of my father."

Katharine is talking of her mother. "I'm not sure Mother always admired what I did on the stage or on the screen—not sure she *ever* did—I'd like to *think* she did. She'd come, of course, to everything, and sit through it and come back and say all the right things. But I couldn't help noticing a difference in her reaction to *other* theater things she'd go to—odd things, downtown, avant-garde, agitprop theater—When she talked about those, it was in another tone—she'd stay on the subject longer. What you said the other day, Ruth, is so true—that you can always tell how much they really liked it by how long they stay on the subject—I've had them come back and say, 'That was the greatest performance you've ever given in your life. In fact, it was probably the greatest performance *anyone* has ever given *anywhere*. Now are you sure you wouldn't like to come out to Twenty-One with us? Or how about coming up to the apartment for a bite? Have you heard anything from Irene?' And so on and so on. Well, hell, you just know you were a bust as far as they were concerned.

"I don't mean that Mother was like that—she simply didn't have it in her to be hypocritical, but I think she thought of most of the things I did as being sort of la-di-da commercial—She was one who believed you had to plunge your arms into life right up to the elbows, but she didn't think the things I did, the Phil Barry things, *The Philadelphia Story* or *Little Women* or things of that sort, had enough to do with what really mattered in the world."

Her face reveals unutterable sadness as she adds, "Of course, she died before I tackled Shakespeare—she'd have approved of that—I suppose that's why I did it, really—For her."

Because I knew this remarkable lady and understood Kate's attachment to her, I was once greatly staggered by a small event.

Cary Grant had made a new picture, *Memory of Love,* with Carole Lombard. It had not as yet been released. For reasons of her own (had she turned it down? I did not ask), Kate was eager to see it. Since the picture had been made at RKO, where I was employed, it was easy to arrange a confidential private screening, ostensibly for myself, in the home of a company executive who had a projection room.

Kate, wearing sunglasses and scarf, entered the house through a side door. We ran the picture.

As it was ending, she left in the same way.

I thanked the projectionist and left.

Later, Kate and I met and talked it over. I had liked it. Lombard was a great favorite of mine. Kate's reaction was negative. Sentimental, she thought it.

"God! It's given me the *melancholia,*" she said, employing one of her personal words. "I hate sappy women, sleeping around and then whining when they get bruised—there's not a game in the world you can play without the risk of getting hurt some—That's what makes it fun—worth doing—playing—what was the *matter* with that damn woman? Dumb. *Dumb!* What's the matter with her?"

"I'll call her up and ask her."

"I'm worried about you," she said, "going for rubbish like that. Dumb!"

"I hated it," I said.

Two nights later, at a dinner party at the Goldwyns', we encountered Cary.

He saw us, standing in a corner of the sitting room, waved, and started toward us.

"Careful," Kate warned through her nose.

I was unconcerned. I really *had* liked the picture and was prepared to say so. As for Kate—well—she would have to fend for herself.

I need not have been concerned. Cary was not in the least interested in my opinion. He moved in close to Kate and winked at her. She smiled at him, her face becoming the morning sun. They did not actually kiss—people did not kiss as much in 1940 as they do now—but their exchange was tantamount to a kiss. They had made four films together, *Sylvia Scarlett, Bringing Up Baby, Holiday, The Philadelphia Story,* and shared an affectionate regard.

"Well," said Cary, puffed up with confidence. "How'd you like it?"

"Like what?" asked Kate, using one of her melting looks from *Little Women.*

"My picture," said Cary, impatient for praise. "My picture!"

"Your picture?" she asked with that tiny, bewildered headshake that had laid me low when I first saw her do it in *Alice Adams.*

"Memory of Love," said Cary. "My new picture you saw last night."

As she played utter confusion, getting her body into it now, I thought: Holy Smoke! She's not going to try to beat *this* one, is she?

"I didn't see your new picture last night," Kate said calmly.

She *is,* by God!

Cary's jaw tightened.

"Yes you did, Kate. You saw it last night with *him,"* he said, pointing across the room, although I was standing right beside him. Excited, I suppose. He went on, correctly naming the time and place we had seen it and finished by shouting, *"Memory of Love!"* in the way one yells, *"Eureka!"*

What would she do now? I wondered, as I watched the Olympic Lying Finals. Turn it into a joke and pretend she had been teasing him? Say she loved it? Take a chance on the truth? What? Whatever, she had to face the fact that he knew she had seen it.

Not at all.

She made herself taller, looked down at him with her *Stage Door* hauteur and said, "You are mistaken, Cary, and you *must* stop insisting. It's *enervating.*"

"You're lying," said Cary, "and I can prove it."

I hoped he would not turn to me, nor did he.

At the word "lying" Kate gasped as though he had uttered some graphic, unspeakable obscenity.

Her incandescent eyes began sending danger signals. For a fleeting instant she suggested—tall and straight and flashing—a lighthouse; and Cary—a foundering ship. Their contretemps had attracted some, although not full, attention. My concern was considerable and growing—because although people did not kiss as much in those days, they did bat each other around even more.

Kate drew *Mary of Scotland* from her repertoire and became the Tragic Queen.

"Cary," she said softly in her solemn, royal voice, "I swear to you that I have not seen your picture, *In Loving Memory.*"

"Memory of Love," said Cary.

"Yes." She raised her right hand to the ceiling and possibly to God. I looked for crossed fingers. None. "I swear to you that I have not seen it. *Memory of Love.*"

Cary was wavering, but I could see he was unconvinced. Apparently, she could see it, too, because she went on, her hand still pledged, in fact, moving even higher as she proclaimed, "I swear it to you—*on my mother's life!*"

Cary blanched. Never mind Cary. I thought *I* was going to faint, especially when she looked from him to me.

Cary took her hand, which had returned from its mission up there.

"I'm *sorry,* Kate," he said. "Some stupid bastard thought he . . . Well, never mind. I *do* apologize. Forgive me."

She was graciousness itself and *Mary of Scotland* was held over as she touched his shoulder (Sir Cary?) and said, "Of course. No matter, dear."

Cary slunk away, but before I could say a word, Mr. Goldwyn had Kate's arm and was leading her in to dinner.

After dinner, we were separated; Kate surrounded, as always, by idolators.

At ten-thirty she signaled an exit. It was well past her bedtime. We said our good nights and left. I waited until we were well away from Laurel Lane and had started up Tower Grove Road before I spoke.

"Kate . . ." I said, and added a couple of meaningless sounds.

"Is something the matter?"

"That oath . . ."

"What?"

"With Cary. That oath you took with Cary. About seeing his picture. I mean *not* seeing his picture."

"What picture?" she asked. Her shoes were off and her feet were up over the dashboard. She seemed to be sitting on the back of her neck.

I realized she had forgotten the incident. How could she forget such a thing? I took several deep breaths.

"Kate," I said. "You swore on your *mother's life!"*

"Oh, *that?"* she said.

"Yes," I said. *"That."*

She waved her cigarette at me. "Nothing. It's an arrangement I have with my mother. She swears on *my* life, too. All the time."

"Life is habit," Kate says. "A good life is a collection of good habits and the other way about—you have to make a set of rules for yourself and then learn to obey them—what makes it complicated is that you're the only one who can set up the rules for yourself—what suits one might not suit another."

I agree and say, "Damn right. If I played tennis as much as you do, I'd be dead."

"You don't play at all."

"I know. That's why I'm not dead."

"That's one of your troubles, I think," she says, scrutinizing me. "You live too much with your head and not enough with your body."

"There's nothing wrong with my body."

"There *will* be," she says. "Haven't you noticed how people who let themselves get physically sluggish end up slow in the mind? And most people I know simply don't sleep enough."

"You sleep *too* much," I argue.

"I suppose so, but it's better than not enough. And who knows? Maybe I *need* as much as I get."

"Ruth says Charlie MacArthur thought sleep was one of the most dangerous things a person could do. And Gus Eckstein says there's a far-out body of physiological thought that holds sleep to be the normal state and claims it's only outside stimuli, such as light and noise and heat and cold and hunger that wakes us up."

"Ridiculous," says Kate, dismissing this part of the discussion. "It's entirely an individual matter."

"And different for different times and circumstances, wouldn't you say?" I ask.

"Of course. I don't seem to need as much sleep when I'm working, which is lucky, because I'm so charged up all the time."

"Gertrude Stein once said that we all take in and give out, that everybody's balance is slightly different, and that we fall ill when we disturb the proper balance of take in and give out."

Kate frowns, digesting this, and says, "Yah."

She does not often break a rule, but when she does, she does it dramatically.

In 1939, Vivien Leigh, Laurence Olivier, and I rented a Beverly Hills property together. I occupied the guest house. It was too expensive for us as individuals, but we reasoned that if we pooled our resources, we could handle it.

They were superlative days and nights. Vivien was making *Gone With the Wind,* and had much to report every evening. Larry was working on *Rebecca* with Alfred Hitchcock. I was shooting *Bachelor Mother* at RKO with Ginger Rogers and David Niven.

Although we were properly concentrated on our various projects, there was talk, from time to time, about future plans. For one of mine I was hoping to involve Kate.

"I'm out for dinner tonight," I announced, early one evening.

"But it's *goose,"* Vivien protested.

"Even so."

"Where are you going?" asked Larry.

"Up to Kate's. Business."

They looked at each other.

"Why don't you put it off?" said Larry. "Until tomorrow."

"Because I don't want to," I said, and left.

Shortly after dinner at Kate's I began to see that I had seriously captured her imagination. My idea was to make a picture called *Mrs. Grant* about the life of Julia Dent Grant, the wife of Ulysses S. Grant. General Grant was not to appear at all. The camera would stay with Mrs. Grant and reveal the part she played in shaping his life.

"I don't think it's any good for him *never* to appear," said Kate. "It turns it into a stunt. We should see him from time to time, but he should have a small part. He weaves in and out of the story, sort of shadowy, but *hers* is what you're telling."

"You may be right," I said.

"I *know* I'm right."

"But think of it, Kate. What a story. After all that early whirlwind romantic stuff and the tough time in the Army, we finally get to the point where they're living in Galena. He's been kicked out of the Army for drinking. He's tried the tannery business and gone bankrupt. So he has no career, no job, no money, and a bad reputation. And get this—he's forty years old, which, in those days, was a hell of a lot older than it is now. Then, starting from this base, Julia takes him in hand. He goes back to the Army, re-establishes his position, becomes Commander in Chief of the Union Army, wins the war, and is elected President of the United States for two terms. And I think it's fair to say that it was mainly Julia."

"I'm not surprised," said Kate.

"Who do you think to write it?" I asked.

"I don't know." She began to pace the room. "It's a hard one, God knows."

"What about Sherwood?" I asked.

She stopped pacing and said, "Perfect."

"And if, for any reason, we can't get him. . . ."

The phone rang. She answered it and said, "For you."

"Me?" I went to the phone. Kate left the room. "Hello."

It was Larry. "Sorry to trouble you, Cocky," he said, "but we'd like you to come right down here."

"What is it? Something happen?"

"No. Nothing. Everything's fine, but do come right down, will you?"

"I'm in the middle of something," I said. "I can't."

"Of course you can," he said. "It's imperative."

"Can't you tell me what it is?"

"Not on the blower."

"But what is it?"

The voice that replied to my question was Vivien's, startling me. *"Please!"* she said. "Will you *please* stop being mulish and come down here? We *need* you."

"All right," I said. "I'll be right down."

"Hurry," she said.

Kate returned. "What is it?" she asked. "You look troubled."

"I don't know *what* it is," I said, "but there's some situation. I have to leave."

"Oh," she said. "Do you?"

"I'm afraid so."

"All right," she said. "We'll talk about what's-her-name another time."

I could sense I had diminished considerably in her view in

the preceding minute. My behavior was certainly unprofessional. What—saving emergency—could possibly be more important than the conception of a new film? Interrupting a story conference at this point was frivolous. My position was especially weak since I could not say *why* I was leaving.

We said good night and I left, miserable. My depression turned into anger as I descended the hill and drove up Coldwater Canyon. By the time I reached the shared house, I was in a state of uncontrollable vexation. Not only had these so-called friends ruined my evening, but they had probably scotched one of the greatest pictures of all time, the beginning of a professional relationship with my favorite film actress, and who knows? Who knows what *that* might possibly have led to?

I stormed in, ready for a row, and found them both dressed in their best and wreathed in smiles.

"I suppose you've guessed it by now," said Larry.

"Guessed what?"

"Where we're going," said Vivien.

"What we're going to do," Larry added.

"I'm sorry," I said, shaking my head.

"Don't be dull, darling," said Vivien, impatiently. "We're getting married."

I looked about, in confusion, for the rest of the wedding party.

"Not here," said Larry. "In Santa Barbara, at Ronnie Colman's place. It has to be right after midnight, so if we leave about now . . ."

"You couldn't have *told* me?" I asked. "Before? Before I went up there?"

"I tried to get you to postpone it, didn't I?"

"But if you'd said why."

"Couldn't," said Vivien. "It has to be absolutely secret until it's done."

"Why does it?" I challenged.

Instead of replying, Vivien said coolly, "Well, I'm terribly sorry, I'm sure, to have ruined your evening."

"Ruined my *evening?*" I complained. "You may have ruined my whole *life!*"

"He's overwrought," she said to Larry.

"Nobody's ruined your life," said Larry. "Besides, you're going to be best man. Rather a good part."

"Great," I said. "Thank you very much. I'm honored. And who's my partner? You know, maid of honor. Dame May Whitty?"

"My God," said Vivien. "No one."

"Oh, come off it, puss," said Larry. "We don't need a maid of honor. It's not that sort of do. It's just a justice of the peace. In fact, if you want the truth, we don't even need a best man."

"Of course you do," I said, "and what's more, I'm going to get you a snappy maid of honor."

"Who?" asked Vivien.

"Kate," I said. "We'll stop and pick her up on the way."

"Lovely," said Vivien.

I was less interested in providing them with a maid of honor than I was in salvaging my own evening.

Twenty minutes later, I rang Kate's doorbell.

When the door opened, I saw Kate in pajamas, looking tousled and sleepy and furious.

I lost my nerve and said, "Larry wants to talk to you. He has a favor to ask. Vivien, too." I turned and called down to the car. "Larry! C'mere. Viv!"

We stood at the door, all three, explaining the situation.

"Good God!" said Kate. "Sure. It'll take me a few minutes. I'll have to take a shower and get dressed."

Larry glanced at his watch, nervously.

"Couldn't you skip the shower?" I suggested. "You probably just had one."

"Yes," said Kate, "but I've been to sleep and now I'm up."

"I see," I said. "Well, quick as you can, huh?"

Attempting short cuts, we lost our way. The most romantic and beautiful couple in the world, minutes from marriage, began to bicker. We arrived at the Colman ranch an hour and a half late. The justice of the peace, from whom the identity of the couple had been kept a secret, had wanted to leave after waiting fifteen minutes. He had been offered a drink every ten minutes from then on to hold him there.

By the time we arrived, he was smashed, and the ceremony itself turned out to be a forerunner of the Theatre of the Absurd.

Vivien wanted it done out of doors. We stepped out onto the rose-covered terrace.

I began to sneeze. Hay fever.

Vivien ordered me to stop as though she believed I was doing it purposely. The justice of the peace referred to Larry as "Oliver" and to Vivien as "Lay." Larry was asked if he took this woman to be his lawful-wedded wife, but the justice of the peace forgot to ask Vivien for her vow, and me for the ring, although I kept waving it under his nose.

Finally, there was a long pause and a silence, broken only by a few chirping crickets and my continuing sneezes.

The justice of the peace, weaving slightly, looked up and shouted, "Bingo!"

Vivien Leigh and Laurence Olivier were thus united in holy matrimony.

After a few bottles of champagne and a bit of food, we continued to follow the plan. Kate and I dropped the newlyweds at a crossroads where a car, which had been waiting for three and a half hours, took them to Ronald Colman's yacht for a short honeymoon cruise. I drove Kate home.

She had not been up past 10 P.M. for years, yet seemed totally unaffected by being called upon to stay up all night.

"Why all the secrecy, do you suppose?" I asked.

"Probably nothing," she said. "People do it sometimes because it's fun—Howard Hughes and I used to do it all the time—it's enjoyable, getting everybody into a tizzy—all this hush-hush—they're probably listening to the radio news right now, furious that no one has found out."

She was brilliantly correct. Larry later reported that they had, indeed, spent the whole day listening to the radio with increasing annoyance at having their great event ignored.

And Mrs. Grant? That dear lady, I fear, got lost in the shuffle

Spencer took the rough times in his career better than anyone I have ever known. There was no bitterness, no recrimination, no blame-shifting or faultfinding. He handled it all gracefully, philosophically, and kept hoping for a change in the weather.

Following the underrated *Broken Lance* (1954) and the extraordinary *Bad Day at Black Rock* (1955), there followed six years of more or less unsuccessful pictures, *The Mountain, The Desk Set, The Old Man and the Sea, The Last Hurrah, Inherit the Wind,* and *The Devil at Four O'Clock.*

Then came *Judgment at Nuremberg,* the narration for *How the West Was Won, It's a Mad, Mad, Mad, Mad World,* and *Guess Who's Coming to Dinner*—to end his career and his life in a triumphant blaze.

During the bad time, he and Kate were constantly reading and planning and scheming. Dozens of projects came and went. One never had a sense of retirement or retreat or defeat in the atmosphere. Still, the humiliations were many. Spencer made light of them.

"You remember that picture you worked on during the war, *The More the Merrier?*" he asked me on the phone one night.

"Certainly. Why wouldn't I? I wrote it with Bob Russell; and later, Frank Ross, Jean Arthur's husband, came in on it. What about it?"

"Columbia's going to remake it," he said. "Lay it in Tokyo during the Olympics. They own all this Olympic footage they don't know what to do with. What do you think?"

"I don't know. Offhand, it sounds nutty. Sort of manufactured. It was a pretty topical piece as I recall."

"But Sol Siegel, he's the producer, wants me to do it; the Charlie Coburn part that he says is going to be the lead in this new version."

"Well, Jesus," I said, "that's different! Sure. Could be. Why not?"

"Would *you* be interested?"

"In what?"

"Writing, directing, both?"

"Wait a minute, Spence. Whose idea is this? Yours or theirs?"

"What's the difference?"

"Plenty. Remember *Separate Tables?"*

I was reminding him of a family joke. When he was offered one of the four leading roles in that film, he accepted on condition that Laurence Olivier played the other male role as had been hinted. Subsequently he was told, no Olivier. Spencer stood by his guns. He would not do it unless Olivier did. So the picture was made with Burt Lancaster and David Niven.

I said, "Why don't you get the job for yourself first, and *then* worry about your friends?"

A few days later, Siegel called to invite me and my wife, along with Kate and Spencer, to screen *The More the Merrier* at his house.

The four of us had a bubbling, anticipatory dinner beforehand at Spencer's house, talking of the problems of film making in Japan.

Then to Siegel's house. The film is screened and seems even better than I had remembered it.

The talk afterward is blunt.

"How about it, Spencer?" Siegel urges. "Will you do it? Come on. I need you. Didn't I do all right by you on *Broken Lance?* What do you say?"

"Do it, Spence," I blurt out.

"Wait a minute," says Spencer.

Siegel looks at me and begins cautiously. "Does it interest you at all, Gar? I guess you want to think about it, huh? After all, I know you had something to do with it—even though you're not credited."

"Yes. I was in the Army at the time, you see. And under contract to RKO. Anyhow the whole thing was a lark—a favor for Jean Arthur."

"Well," he said. "Give it some thought and we can talk next week." He put his concentrated attention back on Spencer. "How about it, ol' buddy? You'd be great. Trust me."

In Basic Hollywoodese, Spencer was being made a firm offer, subject to terms and conditions being worked out. I, on the other hand, was being used as a pawn of some sort. The offer to me was made of pure quicksilver. Try to pick it up.

By the time the evening ended, Spencer had made a tacit agreement to do the picture.

In the ensuing weeks, he continued to talk to Siegel daily; tentative negotiations began; there were unofficial items in the trade papers about the project; and I heard no more about my own possible connection.

One evening I phoned Spencer and asked, "What's doing?"

"Hold on to something," he said.

"Now what?"

"I have got the parfor of the year for you! That's what."

In our lingo, the word was short for "par for the course" and applied to examples of the daily ironies and insanities that abounded in our life.

"Go ahead," I said.

"The Columbia picture? Siegel?"

"Yes?"

"I'm out."

"Jesus Christ, Spence," I shouted. "Not on account of *me?*"

"No, no," he said. "On account of Cary Grant."

"What?"

"He's in and I'm out. How about that? Do you think he's better-looking than I am? I don't."

"Can I come over?" I asked. "I can't handle stuff like this on the phone."

"Sure," he replied, "but come *after* dinner. We can't be feeding all you people around here all the time. Nobody's working."

So, we all put a good face on it, but it was no secret to anyone that these were painful days.

Spencer summed it up. "I don't mind losing a part—I'd hate to lose my talent."

In early 1941, Tess Harding (played by Katharine Hepburn) was named Woman of the Year in the Metro-Goldwyn-Mayer film of the same name. The award, which was the penultimate scene of the movie, was, of course, no more than a fiction, a part of the make-believe.

Some thirty years later, the editorial board of a popular magazine for women, sifting through dozens of candidates for a similar honor, finally and unanimously selected Katharine Hepburn. This time the recognition was real. In making the citation, the editors wrote:

> It has not been easy to choose *McCall's* first WOMAN OF THE YEAR. The Sportswoman, or Churchwoman, or even Mother of the Year would have been less difficult. Women today do so many things and play such varied roles that it is hard to name One. "But why, of all things, an *actress?*" highminded people may inquire. The answer is that we honor Katharine Hepburn as a woman, not actress though surely she is much of both. Beauty, grace, talent, devotion—Miss Hepburn has the traditional feminine virtues in untraditional ways. She is a raving individual. We should have more like her. Her beauty is in her reality; it ages but does not grow less. She is a creature without creams or formulas, a woman unmade-up. Her grace is in her gallantry, her sure sense of self. Always a public property—you can buy a ticket to see her weep or get drunk—she is doggedly a private person. Her capacity for devotion may be better sensed than seen. It remains the most private property of this wholly private woman. In sum, Katharine Hepburn is *McCall's* WOMAN OF THE YEAR because she has always been so much of her own.
>
> —THE EDITORS.

Kate once said, about another prize: "It's one thing to win one of these goddam things—it's another to deserve it—sometimes the two happen at the same time—then it's fine—I mean fine."

With the success of *The Philadelphia Story,* she had reached a crucial point in her career. Was this victory to be temporary, a new flash in the old pan? Or was it to be the foundation of a soaring comeback? All of us who loved her talked and thought and searched and read, hoping to find the vehicle to carry her forward.

I believed, at that time, that I had discovered the formula for a Hepburn success: A high-class, or stuck-up, or hoity-toity girl is brought down to earth by an earthy type or a lowbrow or a diamond in the rough, or a cataclysmic situation. It seems to have worked time and again. Consider these: *The Warrior's Husband, A Bill of Divorcement, Morning Glory, Little Women, Alice Adams, Mary of Scotland, Stage Door, Holiday, The Philadelphia Story*. Later, *Woman of the Year, Adam's Rib, State of the Union, The African Queen, Pat and Mike, The Millionairess, The Taming of the Shrew, Guess Who's Coming to Dinner,* and *Coco.*

I omit *Long Day's Journey into Night* as not strictly "a Hepburn picture." In this instance it was the rare circumstance of a great actress at work in an overwhelming play.

The Hepburn formula works, possibly because the audience is drawn to her, yet wants reassurance that she is real—that she is not entirely unlike itself. Nothing more endears a Queen to her subjects than a hiccup in public, a slip on the ice, a fall from a horse, or, best of all, a marriage to a commoner.

Once, after I had spent an evening with Dorothy Thompson, and had received a letter in the following morning's mail from Jimmy Cannon, an idea for a movie struck me: lady political pundit and hardheaded sportswriter work on same newspaper; clash in print about something; meet; clash in person; both wrong, both right—not bad!

Since I had just been greeted by the Selective Service System, I turned the germ over to two of the brightest screenwriters I knew: my brother Michael, and Ring Lardner, Jr. It infected them neatly and the result, *Woman of the Year,* won them an Academy Award for Best Original Screenplay of 1942.

A frantic, last-minute, all-night, final screenplay session comes to mind. The place: a bungalow at The Garden of Allah. The time: spring 1941. The participants: Kate, Mike, Ring, and I—and two clattering typists. The script is due to be delivered by Kate (who is masterminding it all) first thing tomorrow morning. She reads and responds, scans and frowns, suggests cuts and word changes, reads aloud—always with enthusiasm and optimism. She sends for food—gourmet stuff from Chasen's (to inspire confidence). The script is finished in time, delivered, accepted.

From the beginning, there was no question in anyone's mind, except Kate's, that Spencer Tracy was the man for the man. When at last the team was formed it became the longest-running acting partnership the movie business has ever known: twenty-five years.

The success of their relationship was founded on many things: a mutual respect and high regard for each other's talent; an exchanged generosity; a total lack of possessiveness; and, perhaps more than anything else, a gloriously shared sense of humor.

Their friendship and their life was less complicated than one might think, given the circumstances.

When they met, Spencer had been living away from home for some time, although he continued to think of himself as a family man, a responsible husband, and a doting father.

His first-born child, John, had suffered the serious handicap of deafness at birth.

Spencer's wife, Louise Treadwell, had long been a popular leading lady in stock. She retired from the stage in order to devote herself to the rearing of their son. She found that facilities and methods for dealing with deaf children were inadequate, and threw herself into the work of reform. She has continued this activity for almost fifty years. She is the founder, and still head, of the John Tracy Clinic, where not only deaf children but parents of such children are taught. She has become an outstanding, world-famous expert in the field, serves on Presidential Commissions, travels throughout the world, teaching and still studying, and two years ago, was named Man of the Year [*sic*] by the B'nai B'rith.

"Deaf and dumb" was a phrase that invariably infuriated Spencer.

"There's no such goddam thing!" he would insist. "People learn to talk by hearing. And if they can't hear, how the hell are they going to learn to talk? Johnny did, and got through college, and is as good and bright a guy as I know. Of course, he couldn't have done it without Louise."

Their daughter Louise (known as Susie) was born three years after John and grew up to be a fine broth of an Irish lass, resembling Spencer in many ways. He adored her, and, for a time, employed her as his efficient secretary.

Throughout the many years of Kate and Spencer, he continued to visit what he called "The Hill." One of the Beverly ones. High up.

During these times there was always something for Kate to do. A neglected friend, a postponed chore, or a long think by herself up around the reservoir. She never felt bereft or sidetracked. She understood the necessity for Spencer to stay close to his family, since she lived with like instincts.

She would take off to see her mother and father and brothers and sisters and nieces and nephews whenever she felt the time had come.

Family people.

The situation was clearly exemplified at the time when Kate's father fell ill in the East, while Spencer was still unrecovered in the West. She undertook the arduous routine of shuttling back and forth between the coasts, spending a week in Hartford and a week in Beverly Hills—in both places: tending, conferring, supervising, consulting, advising, caring.

She remembers her father saying to her during this time, "I have the feeling I must be getting ready to go someplace. I suppose I ought to get interested in it but I'm damned if I can."

Two

It is odd that Kate, for so many years a public figure, should be a private person. Privacy to her is more than a desired condition. It is a passion, a cause, an emotional necessity in the shape of a religion. Her life, she maintains, is none of your business.

This attitude has caused awkward complications in her professional life across the years. Stars are expected to give interviews, talk on the radio, appear on television, sign autographs; in short, do anything and everything to keep themselves and their product in the public eye. Kate considers this activity intrusive on the part of the interviewer and vulgar on the part of the subject.

She has often been awarded the Sour Apple. This is the strike-back of the Hollywood Women's Press Club bestowed upon "The Most Uncooperative Actress of the Year."

Kate has won it time and again.

As a matter of equilibrium, it should be noted that the actress who received the Golden Apple (for being the Most Cooperative) more than any other was Rochelle Hudson.

Katharine Hepburn has never been a darling of the critics in the way of, say, Helen Hayes, Julie Harris, Kim Stanley, Ethel

Merman, and others. Over-all the reviews of her work have been preponderantly unfavorable except in a few instances: *The Philadelphia Story, Long Day's Journey into Night, Morning Glory, The African Queen,* and *Coco*—for which her personal reviews were superlative.

The usually soggy notices, coupled with her traditional lack of cooperation with the press, makes one stop and think about the importance of these elements in her career. Kate is now in her fifth decade as a professional actress, shows no signs of waning, has conquered films and the legitimate theater in many parts of the world with equal ease, has remained a great, in-demand star in all the media—with television yet to come—and has done it *without* being consistently praised and encouraged.

Perhaps it is precisely *because* she has been constantly challenged or put down that she has developed the extraordinary resilience to which she owes her professional longevity. She has outlasted most of her critics.

Much of the personal criticism was distinctly unfair. Here is a typical example.

Kate and I had been driving around Beverly Hills one afternoon, talking about *My Sister Eileen,* in which I was attempting to interest her. At about five o'clock she said something about being thirsty. Drive-ins and soda fountains were out, but we happened to be passing Romanoff's and I suggested that if it were open, they would certainly give us some iced tea and that, at this hour, it was probably deserted. We went in. No one there but the staff preparing for dinner. The headwaiter showed us to a corner table. Kate asked for iced tea. I ordered a Coke. We continued our discussion. It went on longer than we had planned, and by the time we were approaching the end, we looked about and discovered, for the first time, that the restaurant was filling up. Kate reddened and felt trapped.

"Let's go," she said. "Quick."

"Wait a second. Check!"

As frequently happens in these instances, the check was slow in coming, but the instant it did come and I had paid it, Kate jumped up and strode out of the restaurant. I followed, not even waiting for the change. As I passed a table, someone said, "Who's your friend?"

I turned and saw Alan Campbell and Dorothy Parker in a booth with John O'Hara and, I suppose, O'Hara's wife.

I waved, said "Hello," and went on.

That was all there was to it. A few days later, John O'Hara wrote a piece for his then-current, widely syndicated column, in which he blew up this small incident. Kate was characterized as a show-off, a snob, a rude aristocrat *manqué,* whose principal aim in life was to shock the public with her perversity, and to attract attention.

I came off as a parasitic sycophant who ran after her, following her every mad whim. It was not only inaccurate reporting but betrayed built-in prejudice.

Kate may have done some reprehensible things in her life, but, as a witness, I can testify that she did not do one of them in Romanoff's restaurant on that particular afternoon.

My birthday. We celebrate it together, all four. There are embarrassingly splendid gifts. Dorothy, Spencer's sister-in-law, has baked one of her famous cakes. There are party favors on the table, a bottle of champagne. Kate is dressed up, which means she has a scarf around her neck. Spencer is wearing the St. Patrick's Day tie I gave him in March. It is a fine party, one of the best I have ever known.

After dinner, there is talk and since this is a birthday night, it centers on the subject of age and maturity; the curious compulsion in many of our friends to cling to their youth, not only cosmetically but physically; the obsession with games and sports and other activities of childhood.

I tell of a conversation I had the other day with David Niven.

"Well, David," I had said, "now that you and I are getting to be middle-aged men . . ."

"Hold it right there, cully," he interrupted. "Just what do you mean by 'middle-aged men'?"

"Well, I'm going to be fifty-five in a few weeks," I said.

"And how many men do you know," asked David, "who are a hundred and ten?"

Spencer was all at once testy and spoke to me sharply.

"What the hell *is* all this? Why don't you shut up? Jesus Christ, you're the youngest one in the room, so what're *you* popping off for?"

(With Spencer it was virtually impossible to know when he was pretending and when on the level. He had only real emotion; none of the stage or fake variety. Whether acting or not, he tapped the genuine source. In this instance not one of us could tell if he was truly angry and was about to leave us or ask us to leave him, or if this was one of his elaborate put-ons. Thankfully, it turned out to be the latter.)

When I suspected this, I picked up the argument.

"The hell you say," I said. "The way I see it, Ruth here is the youngest, then Kate, then you, and I'm the oldest."

"You sure *look* the oldest," he said. *"That's* a fact."

"I do?"

"What's more, you *think* the oldest. You wouldn't even go to the ball game when I asked you last week. And what about Las Vegas? Didn't you say we were going to drive to Las Vegas? Just you and me?"

"Okay, let's go."

"Bullshit. You're too old for me."

"Well," I reminded him, "Picasso says it takes a long time to become young, so maybe you're right. Maybe I *am* the youngest, after all."

"Oh, hell," said Kate. "Everyone knows that young isn't a question of numbers any more—Dad used to say, 'Health is youth.'—Of course, he's right—you're young while you have your health—when that breaks down, you're old—even in that week when you're suffering from a common cold—You're *old* that week—And when you get better, you get younger."

"I've always been young," said Spencer. "I was very young when I was born and I've stayed that way."

Ruth remembers a story about Alfred North Whitehead and

tells it: How Whitehead was retired by Oxford at the age of sixty-five; how he decided he was not yet through, and rather than stay in England where he would be considered venerable, solicited a post elsewhere; came to Harvard where he lived and accomplished his best, most significant, productive, and important work.

"That's what it's all about," says Kate. "Work and action. That's what worries me about the beatnik world. They don't seem to work much. They don't produce enough. We used to call people like that 'lie-abouts.' When they do work, it's just enough to get enough to pay the rent on a pad or a few ounces of marijuana. Now, *they're* what *I* call old."

I am reminded of something Ruth left out, and add it. When Felix Frankfurter, who'd been a professor of law at Harvard for about twenty-five years, was appointed to the Supreme Court, he went to say good-by to Whitehead with whom he'd developed a great friendship. Whitehead was, at this time, an ancient, and sat by the window looking out at his garden. He and Felix talked for an hour. Felix rose to go. They shook hands and Whitehead said, rather vaguely, "Washington. Yes. And what is it you're going to do there?"

"I thought you knew," said Felix. "I've been appointed and confirmed to a seat on the Supreme Court of the United States."

"Ah, yes," said Whitehead. "Good. Very good. I'm glad you're going, then. It's important work." His voice grew strong as he said, "We must have order."

Touched, Felix nodded and started out of the room. Behind him he heard a voice, "But Felix . . ." He turned. There was Whitehead, holding up an admonishing finger. ". . . not too *much* order."

Kate leaps out of her chair. "My God!" she shouts. "That's great. That is simply *great*. Thanks for telling that." She lights a cigarette and paces about the room, stiffly. (I note that her pacing is no better in real life than when she does it on the stage or on the screen.) "I've been working on that order thing so long I'm finally beginning to get it, and I swear I think now I have too *much* order. A few weeks ago—did I tell you?—One

Sunday, I ate three lunches—I mean I had to, because I'd accepted these three engagements and went to three lunches one after the other, and ate them all. Then last Sunday I didn't eat any lunch at all—I forgot about it."

"You call that too much order?" asked Spencer, his eyebrows arched.

"No, of course not. But the fact that I did those things worried me—kept me awake—that's what I mean—I'm sure if it happens that way let it happen—Hell with it—I've noticed something about artists' studios—they're always cluttered—maybe that's a good thing—maybe that's important—out of that clutter and chaos, they bring a kind of order and organization—and that's what art is, isn't it?"

"I don't know what it is," said Spencer. "I know it isn't what you and I do."

"I'm going to stop belting at myself about it," said Kate. "I think there's an awful lot to being a slob."

I tell of a poster I saw recently in a hippie shop on Fairfax. It said: "Buddha says—'Don't just *do* something, *stand* there!' "

Ruth recalls that Thornton Wilder once told Woollcott he was thinking seriously of giving up his academic and artistic life and going off somewhere to become a slob. And Alec said, "Well, ol' boy, you wouldn't exactly be starting from scratch, would you?"

"Ho, ho," says Kate, "and does that mean me?"

"Certainly not," Ruth assures her. "Just something to add to the gaiety of nations."

There is a pause, rare, because with the four of us always ready to pop off, pauses do not come often. In this one, Kate lights a cigarette, Spence sips coffee, Ruth reaches for the candy dish. I swallow water.

All at once, Kate says, "They're asinine."

"Who?"

"The insurance companies."

We wait for her to continue because so far it makes no sense.

She looks at us, all three, as though we were backward pupils, and continues.

"The insurance companies—they're the ones, or those asinine

actuaries who work for them—they've figured out that when a person reaches the age of sixty-five, he or she is no longer useful. Well, maybe not if you're a professional golfer, though I've known some damned fine ones over sixty-five, but good God, in law or in medicine or in literature, acting, directing, engineering, composing, painting, conducting—what's more important than a long life?—and a rich experience? Any doctor under fifty is not for me—he's a beginner and I'm no guinea pig—unless he's a genius—then it's okay."

"Coffee," says Spencer.

"It's right there," says Kate, moving to pour it.

"Cold," he says.

She touches the pot and withdraws her hand suddenly, burned.

As she sucks her fingers, Spencer repeats, "Cold."

Kate goes out to make fresh coffee.

Spencer was a nut on the subject of coffee. He could make it himself better than anyone, and often did, but never when Kate was around, not wishing to usurp her function.

We talk of other things for a time, but when Kate returns, I pick up the conversation where it had been when she left, to convey the notion that she had missed nothing.

"To be or not to be a slob," I say, "is a question that sure in hell has occupied a lot of my thinking lately. The first separation of humanity I can remember was between young and old. Us kids against the grownups. Later on, I saw it in another way. The whole world divided, not into young and old, but into Jews and Gentiles. Fortunately that passed, when my father consistently made fun of it and considered anti-Semitism in America a sort of joke. You may live on this street but not on that one. Belong to this club, not that one. So many of you may enroll in this school and no more. 'What's the difference?' said my father. 'It's a big country. That's why we came here.' Then, in a political period, the world began to be made up of the exploiters and the exploited. The rich and the poor. Still later, in work, I began to divide people into professional and nonprofessional, or talented and untalented. This led to the sensitive against the insensitive, the selfish against the unselfish. Wait. I think I left out the time when it was almost entirely men against women."

"And what is it now?" asks Spencer.

"Well," I reply, "I've finally come to believe that it's divided into slobs and nonslobs. It doesn't matter whether we're in England or France or Germany. It's the slobs who ruin life. They're the ones who don't give a damn about others. They don't really give a damn about themselves. Mind you, slobs often dress beautifully; take two baths a day; put in their time at the hairdresser's and beauty parlor—but they never answer a letter, or send a thank-you note. They don't return telephone calls. They're always late for appointments or skip them or cancel at the last minute. They reserve at a restaurant and don't show up. They're always coming into the theater late. They break laws, rules, regulations. They're thoughtless, cheat at games, interrupt, don't laugh at jokes, laugh at nothing, are too loud or too soft. Disagreeable for no reason. Rude to waiters and clerks. Slobs. So, Kate, don't give up that order thing entirely. Anyway, you couldn't. It takes slob talent."

"You mean, 'Don't become a slob,' " she says.

"You can generalize about this age thing too much," says Spencer. "Sure, in *that* guy's business—what was his name? Whitehead?—maybe being older was being better. He had time to study and acquire more and more wisdom and experience, but it doesn't help Mickey Mantle because every year after twenty-three or twenty-four, he's got to stand off those younger guys coming up who're just a little faster, a little stronger, whose reflexes are better. In sports, nobody much makes it past forty."

"Satchel Paige," says Ruth.

Spence is astonished. "How do you know about Satchel Paige?"

"Lloyd Lewis," says Ruth, and the talk goes on about old Satchel to Kate's delight. She has never heard of him and now wants to know all about him.

Spencer says, "Somebody once asked him how he kept his health and his condition so fine, and he said, 'Well, I take three awful hot baths every single day, and I eat *nothin'* but *fried foods!'* "

And Ruth repeats Lloyd's account of the time it was decided, on Satchel Paige's twenty-fifth anniversary or his fiftieth birthday or whatever, to give him a banquet in Chicago. All the outstanding sportswriters and sports figures in the country were invited. They assembled for the black-tie affair. Everything went perfectly except that Satchel Paige, the guest of honor, failed to appear. The dinner went on without him. All the speeches were made, but it was a hollow event. Meanwhile, runners were searching the city for him, but he could not be found.

The next afternoon, Lloyd phoned him, reached him and asked, "Where were you, Satch? Did you forget about it?"

"No, no, Mr. Lewis, I remembered."

"Well," asked Lloyd. "Why didn't you come?"

"Mr. Lewis," said Satchel, "I have found out . . . that the social ramble . . . just ain't *restful!*"

"That's me," laughs Spencer.

"And me," says Kate. "Wears you out, partying around—all right for people who need to get entertainment—but I always leave social events absolutely exhausted. I put *out* so much—never seem to gain anything—always putting out—and of course it always ruins the morning, doesn't it?—I like to get up at sunrise—just *before* sunrise—so I can see the sun rise—I always feel as though I'm being born again with the day."

Our long friendship was not without its bad times; occasions when it faded for a moment or longer.

There was the night in May 1941, when I went to Wilmington, Delaware, to see a tryout performance of *Without Love* by Philip Barry, in which the charming, mild-mannered Elliott Nugent played a powerful tycoon; and Kate, a soft, sensitive, dominated girl with whom he enters into a marriage of convenience.

I went backstage, directly following the performance, perfectly prepared to commit what Thornton Wilder has labeled "green-room perjury," but was told that Miss Hepburn was in conference with The Theatre Guild and would phone me later.

Later turned out to be 2 A.M., by which time I was not only querulous but crocked.

"I'm sorry," she began.

"Yah," I said, attempting an imitation.

"You're not irritated, are you?"

"Me? Why should I be irritation?"

"Are you all right?"

"Damn right, all right. But the play's not. You've got problems, baby."

"I know it. We all know it. We're working on it. Can you come over and talk a while?"

I worried about walking. "Too late," I said.

"In the morning?" she asked.

"I have to leave early."

A long pause. Unspoken understanding.

"Well," she said finally, "is there anything you can tell me now? Any ideas?"

"Only one," I said.

"Oh? What's that?"

"You and Nugent change parts," I said.

The silence that followed this thoughtless remark lasted for about eighteen months.

Another, shorter, bad time took place one early spring when she was visiting us in Connecticut. She and Ruth (two wildflower buffs) and I (not) went for a long walk in the woods.

With mounting excitement, they discovered and picked wildflowers. When we sat down to rest on a knoll, I told them what I had once heard about G. K. Chesterton thinking up his own names for wildflowers. One, he identified as "Sweet bigamy."

Kate studied me, coolly. We resumed our walk and I, bored with the oohing and aahing, began to play the Chesterton game.

"Look!" I cried. " 'Pink pudenda'!" Later: " 'Trailing thesaurus'!" Then: "You won't *believe* it—isn't it *early* for 'Queen Mab's clitoris'?"

Kate, picking flowers, rose from her knees and walked over to me, menacingly. I thought she was going to hit me with her bouquet. Instead, she pointed it at me and in a voice charged with deep meaning, said, "You'd better start learning some of the *real* names, my boy!"

But these were patches of bad weather that passed. For the most part our friendship flourished. First, Kate's and mine. Later, Spencer. Finally, Ruth, who married me in 1942. She had long been a great favorite of Kate's. In fact, Kate claims that in *Morning Glory,* for which she won the first of her three Oscars, she gave what she hoped was a good imitation of Ruth Gordon. That is what she says.

We became, all four, friends and friends.

When a bone is broken, if it is properly reset and allowed to heal, it is often stronger than it was before. There are those who believe a recovered heart to be more powerful than the original.

In the same way, a friendship that has had a history, that has been threatened, perhaps broken or damaged, is more meaningful than a bland relationship which has known only affirmative times.

I am thinking of the complex relationship in which Kate and Spencer and Ruth and I were involved.

I was indeed responsible for bringing Kate and Spencer together. Kate and Ruth had long been friends. Ruth and Spencer shared a mutual professional admiration.

World War II separated me, geographically and professionally, from Kate and Spencer and brought Ruth into my life.

My first postwar offer of a job came from Robert E. Sherwood and the Playwrights Company.

Bob had written a play called *The Rugged Path,* and had submitted it to Spencer Tracy. Spencer admired the play, and was attracted by the role. He was reluctant to accept, however, on several grounds. For one thing, he had not appeared on the stage in fifteen years. For another, he was under contract to Metro-Goldwyn-Mayer, and arrangements would be complicated. Most of all, there hung over him at this time the fear of losing so much as a single round in his continuing battle against alcohol.

A few days lost in the production of a film was no great matter. The discipline of the theater was far more stringent.

"You may be making a mistake with me," he said to Bob. "I could be good in this thing, all right. But then, who knows? I could fall off and maybe not show up."

Bob looked at him for a long time, and spoke in his slow and deliberate way.

"Spencer," he said, "all I want for myself is to see this play played once by you."

His words must have impressed Spencer, who agreed to do the play. I was invited to direct. The beginning of rehearsals was coordinated with my Army discharge.

Meetings began in New York. It was an extremely difficult production, with a large cast and multiple settings. Looking back, I see that the play went into production prematurely. No element of it was quite ready. Not the text, not I, not the physical production, and not the public.

We plunged in energetically, and throughout rehearsals Spencer was a revelation. Imaginative, resourceful, malleable. Kate was around, helping us all in the most self-effacing way.

It was only after the play opened out of town, in Providence, and did not go as it was meant to go, that the difficulties began. Desperate changes were put in for the Washington opening. We were improved, but still not right. The strain of simultaneously playing and rehearsing soon affected Spencer and he fell ill. This served only to increase the surrounding tension, especially Spencer's. Any other player with a temperature of a hundred and three degrees would stay off and let the understudy play. ("The show must go on" is no longer a fashionable dictum. Modern actors believe that *they,* and not the show, must go on.) Rightly or wrongly, Spencer believed there were those who were waiting for him to miss a performance, who were half expecting it, predicting it; so he struggled to the theater night after night, trembling with chills, sweating with fever, throwing up in the wings, but playing the play.

The Rugged Path was turning out to be a maddeningly prophetic title.

Washington. Further difficulties, strangely mixed with glamour.

A fractious rehearsal one morning, and, the same afternoon, a reception for Robert Sherwood, Spencer Tracy, and the members of the company at the White House, given by President and Mrs. Truman on the day when he had been President for exactly six months.

Although the atmosphere throughout the Washington engagement was volatile and exciting, a tentative decision to close there was made. It was apparent that there was more to do than could be done in the remaining time. As the date approached, Spencer found he could not bear the idea of such an ignominious failure, and asked that we go on to Boston as planned. We fared no better there, but continued to work. Spencer, on doctor's orders, finally had to cancel four performances. It served only to reinforce his determination. He was now Irish fighting mad. At the Fates.

The events surrounding the New York opening are understandably clouded in my memory. I do remember, however, arriving at the Plymouth Theatre on the morning the production was being taken in. (Rcturning to the Plymouth was a sentimental journey for Spencer. He had made an early appearance there, playing a detective bit in *A Royal Fandango,* starring Ethel Barrymore.)

Backstage, I went about with the stage manager, checking the dressing rooms.

In the star dressing room, a woman on her knees was scrubbing the bathroom floor. She looked up. Katharine, of course.

"Damn place is filthy," she said, grinned, and added, "—was."

In the ten days prior to the New York opening, all the important working relationships had deteriorated. Spencer was tense and unbending, could not, or would not, take direction, which amounted to the same thing. As a result of my own anxieties, I grew more unreasonable by the hour, asking the impossible and becoming furious at being refused. The management, sensing failure, was looking for the handiest scapegoat. The company was becoming increasingly demoralized. Kate was the only one who kept her head and made sensible suggestions. Alas, the rest of us were too panicked to listen. When I found she was coaching one of the actresses, Martha Sleeper, I foolishly made an issue of it. Spencer, rising to Kate's defense, blasted me powerfully.

The opening night was promising. It went far better than anyone had a right to expect. Spencer rose to the occasion and gave an overwhelmingly magnetic performance, but somewhere, about halfway through, the dramatic line failed to sustain. The play lost the audience and disintegrated. The reviews were mixed.

(Someone not connected with the theater once asked George S. Kaufman, "What does that mean exactly, Mr. Kaufman, when you theater people say 'mixed notices'?" "It means good and lousy," said George.)

Spencer's presence in the cast assured sold-out houses for a time, but we had not made it, and after about ten weeks, the play quietly expired.

Our opening night handshake had been meaningful. Spencer and I had stood there for a moment. I had tried to convey confidence, but his resentful gray eyes rejected me. Ruth and Kate looked on. We had all tried to behave well, but knew that the circumstances had sullied our fine friendship.

Our relationship, during the weeks of the run, was cordial but perfunctory. There were meetings, a few cast replacements, some rehearsals, but the closing notice seemed to refer to us as well as to the production.

It is not always so. There are times when mutual failure draws the participants closer, but, in this instance, the result was wreckage.

Spencer and Kate returned to California and Metro-Goldwyn-Mayer. I plunged immediately into the production of my own play, *Born Yesterday,* which turned out to be an even more horrendous experience. Eventual success somewhat mitigated the agony of revisions, re-revisions, cast replacements, and the physical collapse and resignation of the star, Jean Arthur, two weeks before the New York opening.

It was followed immediately by a production of my wife's

autobiographical play, *Years Ago*. This one proved to be more difficult than the preceding two combined. It was produced, closed out of town, recast, and produced again before it found success. Its final cast starred Fredric March and his wife, Florence Eldridge, both excellent players as individuals, but, as a team, too complicated for me. I could not understand why it was necessary to give her a direction every time I gave him one; or why, if a line of hers was cut, matters did not run smoothly until one of his was cut. There were other tensions as well, since it became increasingly apparent that the leading part was that of Ruth. (The Marches were playing her parents.) Matters were further complicated by the fact that the actual Ruth, some forty years older, was sitting out front and watching critically.

Difficulties proliferated.

In Boston (again!) on the night when *Life* magazine came up to do a story on the play, an explosion occurred. Patricia Kirkland, the young actress playing Ruth, had been (by chance) included in more of the shots than the Marches. We had discreetly absented ourselves from the session, but were summoned to the theater at one in the morning to be told that because of the photographic imbalance, the Marches were quitting the production. It did no good—at that hour and in that emotional climate—to point out that the final layout would not reflect the same ratio; and that, in any case, we had had nothing whatever to do with the photographers. It was all temperament and we were dealing, not with stars, but with exposed nerves.

It took a week to put Humpty Dumpty together again, but, by then, the mood was such that even the triumph of the play in New York brought no more than small comfort.

Following a short collapse, euphemistically called "a holiday," Ruth and I went to California to work on *A Double Life,* a film we had written for Universal-International.

We had neither seen nor spoken to Kate or Spencer for a year and a half. What the hell. They were doing fine and so were we, and our lives appeared to have no need of intertwining.

Our only point of contact was Abe Lastfogel, head of the William Morris Agency, the agent for all four of us. It was from him that we had, now and then, news of Spencer and Kate, always warmly delivered and stonily received. I assumed he was having the same experience at the other end.

"Spencer feels bad," he said to us one afternoon.

"How do you mean?" I asked.

"Well, he knows he didn't behave right every minute, and he's sorry not to be friends. Kate, too."

"Well," I said, "I don't suppose I behaved perfectly either."

"Can I tell them that?" asked Abe eagerly.

"Tell them what?"

"What you said. That you're sorry you behaved so badly."

"Wait a second," I said. "That's not exactly what I said."

"Sure it is," said Abe. "At least, that's what you meant. At least, that's what it sounded like to me."

At length, we agreed to have dinner one night with Abe and his wife, and Spencer.

Kate did not come only because, as has been noted, she does not go to restaurants.

We assembled at Romanoff's. The five of us sat in a booth for four. The physical proximity was unconducive to coolness. After twenty minutes of stiff small talk, we suddenly laughed heartily at a small joke, and began to find our way back to old conversational roads, such as complaining about our agency. The fact that Abe was sitting there added a piquant note and before long, we were relating easily.

"What really upset me," said Spencer, "was you doing this play with Freddie March, and everything going so smoothly and opening in New York and being a hit and no agony and no bloodshed, and I kept thinking, God damn it, if Freddie March could get through it all so beautifully, why the hell couldn't *I?*"

Ruth and I exchanged a long, pregnant look. Will you tell him, or shall I? She nodded. I looked at Spencer and said, "Spence, let me tell you something. Five weeks ago tonight. It must have been about four in the morning. Ruth woke up and whispered to me, 'Are you sleeping?' And I said, 'No, I can't.' And she said, 'Why not? What are you thinking about?' And I said to her, 'I'm just lying here thinking how I wish to hell I had Kate and Spence back, instead of these two.' "

Spencer's jaw dropped, and his fork fell. He left the booth and went to the floor. I thought he was retrieving the fork. Not so. He remained on his knees in front of the booth, clasped his hands, looked at Ruth and pleaded, "Tell me it's true. Promise me this little son-of-a-bitch isn't lying. Is he just saying that for me now? No, *don't* tell me! . . . Ruth, did he really say that?"

"Yes," said Ruth. "I swear to you he did, and not only did he say it, but what's more, he *meant* it."

Spencer, on his knees in front of the booth, had suddenly become the floor show. He rose, resumed his seat, and called out to Mike Romanoff, "Your Highness, bring me a phone, will you?" To us, "I've got to call Kate and tell her. No, you tell her."

The phone arrived and he said, "No, hell with it. We'll go on up there and see her." He glanced at his watch. "We can make it if we go pretty soon. She's staying up later these days. I understand she doesn't go to bed sometimes until nine-thirty. Come on. Finish your coffee. You don't need dessert. Let's go."

The Lastfogels stayed behind to finish dinner. The three of us went up to see Kate at her house. We stayed up until after two, an unheard of hour for all of us, reliving the whole ghastly experience, but, this time, finding it possible to joke about it.

I even related one of the wildest moments. It had happened in Boston in the period when it looked as though the play was going to close.

Every member of the Playwrights Company was present: Robert E. Sherwood, Maxwell Anderson, S. N. Behrman, Elmer Rice, Kurt Weill, and John F. Wharton. In addition: Victor Samrock, the general manager; and Bill Fields, the press representative. Possibly to keep up Bob's spirits, the focus of the discussion was on the projected reopening, rather than on the imminent closing.

"I think you have to face the fact," I had said, "that when we do it again, Spencer won't."

Max agreed, as did the others.

"I wonder if we could get Freddie March," mused Bob.

"Ask him."

"Who's his agent?"

"Could Ray Massey do it?"

"Yes."

"No."

"Sure he could."

"I don't think so."

"How about Ralph Bellamy?"

"Well . . ."

At this point, there was a knock at the door. A messenger had arrived from the advertising agency in New York, carrying a large portfolio.

In all the excitement we had forgotten that Norman Rockwell had been commissioned, months earlier, to do a definitive portrait of Spencer Tracy, to be used as the principal advertising logo for *The Rugged Path*. Bill Fields undid the strings, opened the portfolio, and brought forth an impressive Norman Rockwell portrait of Spencer Tracy.

Using an armchair as an easel, he set it up. We formed a semicircle around it.

"Beautiful."

"Excellent."

"Terrific likeness."

"Rockwell," said Bill, "he's something."

Now Bob spoke. "Ask him how much he'll charge to make it look like Freddie March."

On hearing this account, Spencer fell apart.

It was at that moment that the damaged friendship was mended.

It was not always smooth sailing. We were, after all, four difficult people, critical of one another, and demanding; but by and large, the friendship flourished and nourished. It took death to end it a second time.

Spencer's decision in Washington to continue in the play and go on to Boston had a significant, residual result.

He could not have foreseen it, nor could anyone, but it provided a considerable length of what is sometimes called "the gossamer thread of circumstance."

Washington, D.C., is, by tradition, a Southern city. In 1945, no legitimate theater there admitted Negroes.

Today, I find it difficult to believe the rule was never questioned. It was not—in all the years all of us used the theater.

Think of it. The capital city of The United States of America, hosting a permanent congregation of thousands of foreign visitors from virtually every country in the world, the diplomatic corps ("the Dips," as they are known in Washington), was willing to present this portrait of our free society.

Added to this was an unfortunate semantic point. Because the theater happened to be named the National Theatre, most of the city's guests took it for granted that this was, in fact, our national theater. There was no truth to this, but it was always difficult to explain that we have no national theater, since most foreign countries do.

The National Theatre in Washington was privately owned, booked by the Shuberts, and changed hands several times through the years. At no time, however, was any Negro admitted. Not during the years of World War I, nor in the years between the wars; not during the enlightened and progressive Roosevelt administration, nor through the open, free-wheeling years of World War II, and not during the period immediately following World War II.

In the topsy-turvy, Alice in Wonderland, nonsense world of racial discrimination, Negroes were permitted on the stage of the National, but never in the auditorium. In other words, they were permitted to be performers, but not spectators. Paul Robeson was permitted to star there, but would not have been allowed to come and see an Ethel Waters appearance.

Then came Spencer Tracy in *The Rugged Path.*

Because of the nature of the play—a World War II saga; and because Sherwood had been a member of President Roosevelt's staff—the White House requested the special matinee performance for President Truman, his family, and staff; the Cabinet and staffs; the Justices of the Supreme Court and their staffs; certain members of Congress, and, to fill the rest of the house, wounded veterans from some of the nearby hospitals. The President would sit in the seldom-used Presidential box. (A rash of John Wilkes Booth remarks and sick jokes when this news was announced.) Secret Service men began clambering all over the theater, arranging guard posts inside and out, and certain revisions were ordered in the performance. All prop guns and rifles had to be replaced with wooden simulations.

A more serious problem arose. Three members of our company, themselves veterans, heard that the wounded soldiers being invited were being carefully screened as to race. They mentioned this to Spencer who, in his characteristic phrase, "burst into song." He sent for Sherwood and for me, began by complaining, and ended by flatly refusing to play the special performance.

Sherwood had not known about the planned segregation. As for myself, I confess that, preoccupied with worries about the production, I had given the matter little thought.

Sherwood, of course, agreed with Spencer and took up the question with the members of the White House staff who were arranging the performance. He was able to report, within a few hours, that the house rules would be suspended for the special performance, and that wounded veterans of all races would be invited.

The performance took place in an eerie atmosphere. Limousines brought the brass, while buses transported the soldiers, all of them looking pressed and shiny, as though for inspection, many of them in wheel chairs, on crutches, or with artificial limbs.

Sherwood and I watched the performance, as we frequently did, from the back of the house. When it ended, we stayed there, chatting and comparing notes for some time. The audience was slow to leave since some had to wait for wheel chairs, crutches, and assistance.

Among the last to leave was a handsome young black Tech Sergeant, with a missing right leg. He was experiencing some difficulty getting up the steep aisle, but a white Air Force major with a bandaged ear was helping him. For some reason, the off-balance struggle made them laugh together. They reached the top of the aisle and stood there for a moment, out of breath. The sergeant bounced about on his single leg for a time before regaining his equilibrium. He reached into his belt, got out his overseas cap, and began to adjust it on his head.

He nodded to me (because I was still in uniform, I expect).

Sherwood said, "Hello."

"Hi," said the sergeant.

There was an awkward moment. Sherwood said, "How did you like the play?" Then added quickly, "I think I should tell you I'm the author."

"Excellent, Mr. Sherwood," said the major. "Really outstanding. I was in the ETO myself, so the Pacific stuff was especially interesting."

We all put our attention on the black sergeant because it seemed, somehow, his turn to speak.

"Yeah, fine," he said, eventually. *"Real* fine. I enjoyed it a lot." He looked down between his crutches, then back up again and smiled wryly, as he added, "Pretty stiff admission price, though."

I heard myself emit a hollow, meaningless laugh. Sherwood and the major were silent. The soldiers left. Sherwood and I started backstage. When, finally, I managed to look up at him, I saw that he was shaken. At the pass door, he stopped and looked back into the empty auditorium.

"Jesus," he said.

An hour later, we were all at the White House, drinking tea.

Margaret Truman, the President's daughter, was having a good time, mingling with the show folk. As an ambitious singer, she felt much in her element.

"Yes," she said disconsolately to a group of us, "that's how things happen. Luck. They were doing *Roberta* at school and of course I went out for it, and auditioned and auditioned. I can't remember how many times, but finally—I *got* it! Not just in it. I got the *lead*." She looked around the Oval Room, adding with a wave and a sigh, "And then all *this* had to go and happen."

Sherwood stepped over and led me away.

"Listen," he said. "I want you to tell it to the President."

"Tell what?"

"About what happened at the theater. About the colored sergeant. What he said."

"Oh, that."

"Yes," said Sherwood. "Go on."

"Wait a minute," I stalled. "I've never *met* the President."

"I'll introduce you."

"You tell it, Bob."

"I don't think I could."

"Some other time?" I suggested.

Sherwood looked down at me. "What do you mean, 'some other time'? Do you expect to get asked here every day?"

He was too much for me, and within a few minutes I found myself, dry-tongued and tense, attempting to describe the incident to President Truman.

I was telling it so badly, that halfway through, Sherwood began to help, which is never a help. At last we reached the end, with me repeating what the sergeant had said.

There was no perceptible reaction from the President. He looked at his watch. We moved away.

A few days later, Sherwood explained to me that he had talked the matter over with the President and several members of his staff. The reason our story had failed was that President Truman was not aware of the fact that Negroes were prohibited from entering the National Theatre.

We returned to New York. The event haunted Sherwood, and he talked of it each time we met. Out of these meetings, and subsequent ones with members of the Playwrights Company, a course of action was planned.

The matter was taken up at the Dramatists Guild, at Actors' Equity, at the League of New York Theatres.

Finally, an open meeting was held at the Lyceum Theatre, and the battle was joined.

The management of the National Theatre objected strenuously. It felt that it, in turn, was being discriminated against. Why the National Theatre they asked? Why not every motion-picture theater in Washington as well? Why not every restaurant and hotel and facility? Why pick on the National Theatre?

Admittedly, they had a point, but campaigns are won by winning one battle at a time, and the pressure to end racial discrimination at the National Theatre increased. The stubborn management would not give in and eventually closed the theater. It later reopened as a movie house and failed. The theater was sold. The new owners announced that they would pursue a program of nondiscrimination. It was the opening wedge. Plays began to play again at the National Theatre in Washington without incident. So, although *The Rugged Path* was a failure as a play, it made, indirectly, a small contribution to social progress.

I went once with Kate to look at a house she was thinking of renting.

She walked through the entire place twice. The first time, swiftly; the second time, slowly.

The rental agent and I waited in the downstairs hall. The wait stretched out.

"Where is she?" he asked.

"I don't know."

"Do you think she's all right?"

"Maybe she's lost," I offered.

He looked through the gardens, and I searched out front, thinking she might have left by another exit. Finally, she came down the stairs.

"Where were you?" I asked.

"Taking a shower," she replied.

"A shower?"

"Of course."

"You couldn't wait till you got home, or don't you have facilities there?"

"Listen, you ass," she said, with little patience. "If I'm thinking of renting a house, I've got to find out what it's like taking a shower in it, don't I?"

At that moment it seemed logical, even to me.

"Everything you own," says Spencer, "every possession, gets to be a burden. Nothing—that's my idea of heaven. The minute you own a car, you've got to take care of it, insure it, repair it, park it, worry about it. It can be rammed or wrecked or stolen. It's a pain in the ass. . . . I suppose I could have bought property out here, the way some did, as the years went by. I could've piled up a bundle. But then, what would I do with the bundle? This house. I love it but I'm damned glad I don't own it. I have to stay loose, as the kids say nowadays. . . . I don't own one damned thing I'd miss for more than five minutes if I lost it or if it were swiped. I like to check in and check out. A few years after we came out here—after I'd finished with Fox and moved over to Metro—we bought the ranch in Encino. Louise wanted it, the kids and all. And by that time I needed a goddam place for the ponies. We were still playing polo then, and I'd begun collecting ponies like an idiot. Possessions. The ranch was okay, though. I had some good days there. But what the hell. I'm not the squire type. Animals. Machinery. That's not what I should be thinking about. I used to get pretty lethargic out there. I'm lazy by nature and the rustic life seemed to encourage it."

In this connection, I tell him, "Oscar Hammerstein was once talking to George Kaufman and extolling the life on his Bucks County farm. 'You know, George,' he said. 'I sometimes sit out on that back terrace of mine and look off into the beautiful distance and for *hours,* think of absolutely *nothing.'*

" 'But Ockie,' said George. 'The idea is to think of *something!'* "

"That's it," says Spencer. "It was never the right life for me—getting weighted down with goddam things."

I tell him of an Army buddy I had shortly after my pre-war

draft. Red Rones, who became more and more morose as we queued up endlessly to be issued supplies and equipment.

"What do *you* care, Red?" I asked. "It's all free."

"Yeah, I know," he groaned, miserably. "But every damn time they give me somethin', I feel like I'm gettin' in deeper."

"I know what he means," said Spencer. "I never thought I was going to stay out here. My first deal with Fox . . . sure, it was a five-year contract, but all the options were on *their* side. Humphrey Bogart, he was in that first one with me for Jack Ford, *Up the River,* and they'd signed him and then dropped him after a year or so. So with me, it was just to pick up the dough I needed. After all, a thousand a week—not bad. . . . The Hill? Well, that was always important. Louise had to have a home for the kids. They've always loved it. It's a good house, and I paid for it, but I never think of it as mine. It's theirs."

Years ago, when Kate was living in the hilltop John Gilbert house, she invited my wife (who was not yet my wife) to visit her.

Ruth accepted, but then, remembering Kate's preference for odd hideaways, asked, "It's not one of those top-of-the-mountain places, is it?"

"Yes, it is," said Kate. "Way up on top of Tower Grove."

"Well, then," said Ruth, *"you'd* better come down and see *me.* I don't drive up those scary mountains."

Kate thought for a moment, and said, "Look here, I'll come down and get you Saturday morning, and we'll drive up and down several times, until you're used to it."

She was amazed when Ruth declined.

Kate owes her financial security to her father.

When, in 1932, she began earning large sums, her father insisted that the money be sent to him. He did the banking, paid her bills, and sent her a weekly allowance.

Had he been a business manager, she would doubtless have quarreled with him and perhaps discharged him, but since she was dealing with her father, neither of these things happened.

Dr. Hepburn shepherded her money, saved it, invested it, and handled it with care. Kate was a rich girl almost before she knew it. Her financial position would be otherwise had she been left to her own devices.

(As a matter of fact, her bills are still paid out of Hartford by a secretary.)

She is instinctively extravagant, blindly so, because she cannot recognize extravagance in herself. She constantly criticizes friends for *their* extravagances. She is madly generous. Her friends and family and staff and co-workers are the constant recipients of the most imaginative sorts of largesse.

In March, 1970, I directed a production of Robert E. Sherwood's *Idiot's Delight,* with Jack Lemmon and Rosemary Harris at the Ahmanson Theatre in Los Angeles. On opening night, there were the customary messages and telegrams, and small gifts from friends and well-wishers. There were some flowers and a few plants. Kate sent me an eight-foot apple tree.

Dr. Hepburn never consulted a stockbroker or a banker. There was no need. He considered himself something of a financial wizard. Apparently he was not far off, since he did extremely well for Kate, and was proud of it, in a New England way.

Felix Frankfurter once said that many Americans found living by the Ten Commandments strenuous. "But think of the New Englanders," he added, "who have an Eleventh to observe: 'Thou shalt not touch thy capital.' "

There are times when Kate turns curiously money-mean, economizes strangely, does without, makes do and mends. At such moments, she will explain, "Don't forget I'm Scottish—Hepburn—remember the chappie who had such a do with Mary Stuart? A Hepburn—The Earl of Bothwell—absolutely. When

I played Mary of Scotland it was a sort of incestuous experience."

Whatever the rationalization, it is perfectly true that on occasion she becomes stingy (New Englanders say "near with a dollar"), although she prefers to call it frugal.

I have known both these attitudes to obtain in the course of a single hour.

What it comes down to, actually, is an indifference to money.

After *As You Like It,* her first play with Michael Benthall, she was anxious to work with him again. They had grown fond of each other and found they worked well and interestingly together. After a number of considerations, *The Millionairess* by Bernard Shaw was suggested and Kate agreed to do it in London.

When the time came to leave, she wanted Constance Collier to accompany her. Constance was a valued friend, a confidante, and a mentor. Kate was certain that Constance could help her with the part of The Lady in *The Millionairess.* Constance agreed, but pointed out that she could not go without Phyllis Wilbourn, who was then her secretary-companion.

Kate did not feel she could ask the London management to pay *three* passages. In one of her Scottish moods, she decided to use the single first-class air-passage money to book herself and Miss Collier and Phyllis on a small, inexpensive ship. This would get them all there at no additional cost to anyone.

She chose a minor Dutch vessel. The voyage was scheduled to take eight days. A storm came up and it took eleven. The small ship rolled and pitched and tossed. The three travelers were sick a good deal of the time and arrived in London exhausted.

There, all thought of economy was forgotten. Kate installed Constance and Phyllis in the best suite at the Connaught, took the next-best suite for herself, arranged cars and chauffeurs for all, and put her full attention on the production of *The Millionairess.*

During the time when Kate and Howard Hughes were interested in each other, he came on a number of occasions to visit the family in Hartford, and a couple of times to Fenwick. He liked all the Hepburns, and they responded to him.

Once, after Hughes had departed, Dick went to his study and began to knock out a play about a handsome and attractive young multimillionaire who comes to visit the family of a girl who happens to be an actress, and so on, and so on.

When it was finished, Dick assembled the family and read the play to them. They were shocked and offended, not by its content, but by the notion that a member of the family had so blatantly invaded their privacy.

Dick saw it as a comedy and was stunned by their reaction. He held his ground and said he had every intention of producing his play. As it happened, it did not get on.

I have read it, and think highly of it. It seems to me a fascinating and entertaining portrait of a kind of American family. In style it is not unlike Noel Coward's classic *Hay Fever*. The character representing Hughes is sympathetically drawn, acting as a catalyst to reveal many things about the members of the family to themselves and to one another. It may have been written before its time.

There were Shubert Alley rumors about the play, and a false report that Kate had bought it to keep it from being produced.

"Food and conversation always seemed to go together at our house," said Kate. "With the French, it's food and wine; the Swedes, food and flowers; with some, food and love. With us, it was talk. Good talk. I wonder, now, why we didn't all get indigestion because the conversation was usually argument, although we liked to think it was debate."

"It was talk," said Spencer. "The Hepburns all love to talk.

Even when they look like they're listening, they're really only sitting there thinking what they're going to say next." He laughed and went on. "I remember a Sunday dinner one afternoon at Fenwick. It was back in the days when somebody—who was it? Henry Wallace? Well, whoever—had gotten up a description of the time as 'The Century of the Common Man.' Remember? Anyway, there I was, and nothing but Hepburns around this big table. . . ."

"Don't tell this, Spence," said Kate. She had gone beet-red and was suppressing laughter.

"Why not?" asked Spence, with his look of mock innocence.

"Because," Kate argued, "the way it happened isn't the way it sounds when you tell it."

"I'm a liar, is that it?" asked Spence.

"I didn't say that, but it was the whole *ambiance* and the suddenness—well, what I'm trying to say—"

"Yes, what *are* you trying to say?"

"That the facts," said Kate, "don't always convey the truth."

"Okay," said Spence. "Now go over there by the *ambiance* and try to make some sense out of that remark while I finish my story."

Kate laughed, as he continued.

"So there we were and the subject was The Century of the Common Man, and there was a lot about 'define your terms' and 'exactly what do you mean by the common man?' and tricky stuff like 'the common man is uncommon.' I think some of it they were spouting to impress *me,* or trying to. After all, I was the visitor. At one point Dr. Hepburn was off on a big tirade about how the rights of the common man had been violated and how he'd been exploited, how rent was immoral because a working man pays four times the value of his flat in his lifetime, and how, by God, it was about time this so-called democracy began to . . . And all of a sudden he stopped in the middle of a sentence, or maybe it was the middle of a *word,* and he looked out of the big dining-room window, across the porch, and way down to the edge of the beach, and there was a speck—a man walking along. Dr. Hepburn said, 'Who's that out there?' And the whole family looked, and nobody recognized the man and the next thing I knew, Dr. Hepburn had jumped up and rushed out on to the porch and was yelling, 'Hey, you! Get the hell off! This is private property!' And by this time Dick and Bob, and Emma Goldman here, and the whole slew of kids were all tear-assing after this poor brute on the beach. Well, he saw them coming and got his bones the hell out of there as soon as he could."

Spencer got his laugh, but he said, "Wait, wait. That's not the tag. . . . They all came back to the table, out of breath, and I'm a son-of-a-bitch if Dr. Hepburn didn't pick up right where he'd left off and went on for another five minutes about the rights of the common man!"

Another visitor to Fenwick has described another scene. The family is lunching merrily, when a small, hysterical boy bursts in, screaming and pointing. An accident! A brother! A boat capsized!

There is a rush for the shore. Dick kicks off his shoes and sheds his trousers as he approaches the water. Bob does the same and Kate follows suit. Her shoes go flying and her pants drop as she joins her brothers to effect the rescue.

Dr. Hepburn watches proudly as his three pantsless offspring bring in the boy's brother and his boat.

Many people have principles and know right from wrong, but only a few live by those principles—even when their application is inconvenient or uncomfortable.

Kate recalls, "We used to live on Hawthorne Street in Hartford—a red house—a beauty, and right next to it there was a big factory—In those days people brought their lunches in those tin boxes or in paper bags—no such thing as a union or anything to get them rights, so they had to sit out on the sidewalks or on the fences to eat their lunch. Mother was outraged. One day she walked over and told them they were welcome to use our place—the lawns or the porches or anything they wanted. Well, you can imagine what happened. They tore the place up—left all their garbage around—broke things, ruined the lawn. Dad said to her, 'Well, my dear, now you've learned something about the difference between having principles and acting on them.' "

New England girls are devoted to the weather. Windstorms, sunshine, tempests, breezes, and floods speak to them.

Kate, in New York, once received a telephone call from Spencer, in California.

"How are you?" he asked.

"Fine."

"How's the weather?"

"Oh, it's simply *beautiful,*" said Kate. They went on to talk of other things.

Half an hour later, Spence was talking to Abe Lastfogel in New York. The conversation began in the same way.

"How are you?"

"Fine."

"How's the weather?"

"Just *awful,*" said Abe. "I don't think we're going to be able to fly back this afternoon. I hear everything's grounded. There's the damndest blizzard—I guess you'd call it a blizzard. It's rain and hail and snow, all mixed together, and it looks like night already and it's only eleven o'clock in the morning. I never *saw* such a day."

Spencer called Katharine again and asked, "Are you all right?"

"Certainly. Why?"

"Abe just told me there's a blizzard going on where he is and that's only ten blocks from you."

"Oh, we're having it, too," she said, gaily.

"But you just now told me the weather's beautiful."

"It is," she said. "I call this beautiful. You ought to see it. It's thrilling. Yes, beautiful."

Spencer once told me about a fine director with whom he had worked in the early days—with whom, in fact, he had made one of his best pictures.

"The rumor was," said Spence, "that he couldn't read and couldn't write. The idea fascinated me. How does a guy get up there—where he was—and be literally illiterate? Is that what I mean? Yes. Could it be? So I watched him. I watched him all through the picture. Mind you, I'm not saying yes or no to the gossip. . . . But I *can* tell you that I never saw him write anything—never even jot a note. And the script girl would always be reading the scene to him. Or his wife would. And once, he said to me, 'Y'mind reading this speech out loud? I haven't got my reading glasses.' But then I watched for another three weeks and he never *did* have reading glasses. Can you believe it?"

"Certainly," I replied. "In fact, I know a fellow around right now. A big star. Marvelous actor. Now, he can read, all right, but he can't write. Somehow never learned, I guess."

To my surprise, Spencer took the bait and asked, "No kiddin'. Who is it?"

"Spencer Tracy," I answered.

He did one of his ever-surprising reactions: this one, an innocent-unjustly-accused-on-the-verge-of-tears face.

"I can write," he said, with a Jackie Cooper pout. "Maybe not Palmer method or like that, but *pretty* good."

"I think you can write your autograph," I said, "and that's all. That's all *I've* ever seen."

"I've written you," he said indignantly. "Plenty of times."

"Wires," I said. "And cables. That's not writing. That's wiring. Or cabling."

Kate came into the room and I asked, "Has he ever written you a letter?"

"No," said Kate. "I don't think so."

"Well," said Spencer, becoming another character, a crafty,

leering villain. "You know how we say in Wisconsin: 'Do right and fear no man; *don't* write and fear no woman!' "

Kate floated out without reacting.

My rib was based upon fact. After a thirty-year friendship, I have in my possession exactly one letter from Spencer which he wrote me after seeing *The Diary of Anne Frank*. Ruth has two, also of professional reference.

Very few have ever seen Spence's writing. It is, in fact, a lovely hand: flowing and highly expressive.

For necessary communication, he favored telegrams, appreciating the speed with which his message reached the recipient. The imposed brevity further pleased his sense of life-rhythm, for he was, basically, an impatient man. He treasured life, and revered time, and could not bear to see either frittered away. He often repeated Benjamin Franklin's admonition: "Don't waste time; that's the stuff life's made of."

Even more than wires and cables, Spencer loved the telephone. It is an instrument that suited his personality. He enjoyed the objectivity of it, as well as the ease with which a conversation could be terminated.

When Kate was away, his telephone bill was so high as to be comical.

When he was traveling, he would phone California often. He liked to feel a friend in his hand.

One evening, after a long walk in Paris, we returned to the Hotel Raphaël. Spencer began drinking Evian water even before taking off his hat and coat. He picked up the phone and placed a call to the M-G-M studios in Culver City, California. I heard:

"Mr. Mannix, please. . . . Spencer Tracy. I'm calling from Paris. . . . Fine. How are you? . . . Good. . . . Who's this? Peggy? . . . How are you, Peg? . . . Spencer Tracy. . . . Fine. . . . Hey, Eddie! What do you say? . . . Not much. . . . Listen, what's the weather there? . . . It is? . . . It's beautiful here. Just beautiful. Yeah, I just came in from walking. . . . I don't know. I'd say sixty-five, sixty-eight degrees. . . . What's it doing there? . . . It is, huh? Cloudy. . . . Yeah, maybe. . . . Okay, Eddie. Nice talkin' to you. . . . So long."

He turned to me and said, "Eddie says it's cloudy in L.A."

"Is that so?"

"You don't really care, do you?"

"No, I don't."

"Well, neither do I. Does that surprise you?"

There were periods when Spencer would hole up and refuse to go out. Those who came to visit him, during these retreats, were meant to bring news or tidbits of the outside world—the sort not found in the papers or on the newscasts.

I always felt called upon to provide entertainment of some kind and one evening, I came prepared with a report I knew would interest him.

"Guess who I ran into in the dining room of The Beverly Hills Hotel this morning?"

"Flora Finch and John Bunny."

"Wrong. Adolph Zukor."

"Well," said Spence, "I was close."

"Mr. Zukor was having breakfast in the dining room, all by himself. I think this is the year he's ninety-four, isn't it?"

"Something like that. And that's probably *why* he's ninety-four."

"Why?"

"Because he has breakfast by himself. . . . Think about it."

"I couldn't wait to see what he'd order," I said, "because I'd made up my mind to order exactly the same thing and have it and keep having it every morning until *I'm* ninety-four."

"And what did it turn out to be?"

"Well, the waitress came over, and Mr. Zukor ordered orange juice, soft scrambled eggs and crisp bacon, whole-wheat toast, and coffee. And he had it and read the L.A. *Times*. Financial first. Then front page, then theatrical."

"There you are," said Spence. "Every day you learn something. . . . My God, Adolph Zukor. You realize that when he started, there was no such *thing* as a motion-picture business, or studio or theater?"

"I know."

"And here he is, still around. Some of these guys who started it all, still doing it. It really is an infant art—isn't it?—compared to theater or music or painting."

"Of course."

"So how come there's so many think they know so much about it? Or all about it? You know what I think? I think *nobody* knows very much about it. We're all bluffing. . . . Go on about Zukor."

"Well," I continued, "after breakfast, on my way out, I stopped to pay my respects, and the old gentleman asked me to sit down and have a cup of coffee with him, and I did. He wanted to know all about Ruth—she's a favorite of his—and what was she doing, and he talked about her in *Ethan Frome* and *Serena Blandish* . . . I mean, alert as can be. Then he told me that he was all excited because he had just—a few days ago—become a great-great-grandfather. Of course I knew he'd made a blunder, and thrown in an extra 'great,' but at ninety-four, he's entitled. So I said nothing. But he said, with a mischievous little twinkle, 'I can see you're skeptical. Why is that? Everybody is when I tell them, but it's true. My granddaughter, Jane, in Phoenix? She just became a grandmother, so I'm a great-great. Isn't that right?' And I said, 'You're great-great all right, Mr. Zukor, in my book.' "

The idea hits Spencer hard.

"Good God," he says. "Let me get this straight. It means that little Joe, Johnny's boy, would have to grow up and have a kid, who would then have a kid of his own—and me still around!"

"Could be."

"Not a chance," said Spencer, "but human possibility. Isn't it fascinating? Of course, I don't know what the hell I'm so surprised about. When I first got out here, I was what? Thirty. And I used to see Adolph Zukor around some—and he was an old old man then."

"But that's not what I wanted to tell you, Spence. It's something else. Something he said at breakfast that made me think of you. Let me see if I can remember."

"Press on," he said.

"Well, I'd seen Mr. Zukor at the premiere last night, so naturally I asked him 'How'd you like it?' And he nodded, sort of benignly, and said, 'Nice. It was nice. A good picture of its kind. How commercial? Who knows? Nobody knows. Only the public. But it was good. Except—too long. It was too long.' And then he looked sort of pained, and took a sip of his coffee and went on. 'If you want the truth,' he said, 'all pictures are too long. Every single one.' And he held up his hand to keep me from speaking. 'You're going to tell me *Gone With the Wind* but I tell you too long. It was great, yes. But if it would have been shorter, it would have been even greater. Believe me. When we started making features, there were four reels, then five. Six. *Broken Blossoms,* six. *Queen Elizabeth,* four, even with Sarah Bernhardt. Take *Quo Vadis.* Metro. The original? Five reels. Now? Over three hours to tell the same story—and don't forget in the silent, the titles took up some footage too. And I'll give you a secret—don't repeat it, please—I liked the first one better. Shorter. Now they all go crazy. They think the longer the better. But they're wrong. The shorter the better. Look at that New York Sunday *Times?* The maid complains she can't even lift it.' He waved a disgusted hand in the air and then he said, 'Dinners. They go on too long. And meetings. And every speech I ever heard. Even me telling you *this,* is too long.' He had some more coffee, and then he looked me right in the eye. 'And my life? That's gone on too long, too. . . .' And then he got up and said, 'Nice to have seen you. Give my regards to Ruth,' and he walked out briskly."

"He's right," says Spence. "Thanks for telling me. It's a terrific story. A little too long, of course. Next time see if you can't cut it down to, say, as long as the *first Quo Vadis."*

I have no idea what a graphologist would make of Kate's swiftly written, difficult-to-read hand, but to me her letters are charming small portraits of herself.

A letter from Kate—always welcome—hard to read but no matter—interruptions—off the subject, back on—practically no punctuation, who needs it?—I said to her once, "Kate, I'm going to give you a fine present for Christmas. A box of commas, three sets of periods, and a few semicolons."

In Hollywood parlance, Tracy and Hepburn had what is called "he-she chemistry." It is a vague and largely meaningless phrase used to cloak a mystery. Certain pairs create interest, give off sparks, excite; others do not.

Yet, they had to make delicate adjustments to each other.

Spencer was a poor traveler. A break in his well-ordered routine was upsetting, and, in the end, he would rather stay than go. He loved to *plan* trips and journeys, but no more than one in twenty ever happened.

Conversely, Kate is a born traveler. She knows that the secret of successful travel lies in planning. Maps and timetables and air schedules and cable blanks are never far from her elbow. She moves about the world easily and makes herself perfectly at home anywhere. She has toured the country on several occasions, unusual, these days, for a great star. Her most recent coast-to-coast tour in *Coco* broke records everywhere.

Mrs. Patrick Campbell, coming round to see Lillian Braithwaite after a performance of Noel Coward's *Vortex* said, "You have a tour de force, my dear, a tour de force! while I—Well, I am forced to tour!"

Kate sees it otherwise, and finds great stimulation in new places and people. It is always an adventure.

She has played throughout the United States, in England, France, Africa, Spain, Australia, Italy, and her appetite for travel has only been whetted.

"Not me," said Spencer one evening. "I don't like to get too far away from my *props*."

The remark surprises me. It contradicts my understanding of his relationship to material things. I begin to see that during his years with Kate, he has begun to feel differently about possessions. He is surrounded now by imaginatively provided comforts: a great easy chair, a well-stocked, perfectly equipped kitchen, TV sets everywhere, a dream of a bath/dressing room; books, pictures, objects he has come to appreciate and understand and admire.

"I didn't know you were all that attached to stuff," I remarked.

"I'm not," he said. "I just would rather have it around than not."

"You want to watch that."

"Watch what?"

I had irritated him.

"Nothing. Forget it."

"No," he said hotly. "You've got something to say, say it."

I had stumbled into trouble and now there was no way out.

"Well, let me put it this way," I said. "And mind you, Spence, I'm talking to myself as well as to you."

"Just talk to *me,*" he said. "Talk to yourself on your own time."

I went on. "I once asked René Clair to define the word 'bourgeois'—I thought I knew, but I wasn't sure. It's a French word, after all, and he's a Frenchman, so I figured he ought to know. And that René! Did he ever lay it down. He said, 'For me, the "bourgeois" is a man who does not exist without his possessions. His everythings—no, his *all* his things—are parts of him, the same as legs and kidneys and balls.' " Spencer regarded me stonily. "I thought it was very neatly put," I added.

"So I'm a *bourgeois,*" said Spence, giving the word a fancy pronunciation.

"Now, come on. Did I say that?"

"Sure."

"No. What I said was that we have to be careful we don't move in that direction. Both of us. You and I."

"What are we?" he asked. "A team all of a sudden?"

"You know what I mean."

"I'm afraid I do."

I had touched a sensitive spot, invaded a private area. Could it be that he had inner misgivings about the shape his life had taken, was taking? Was it an idea he had brushed aside, and I had rudely brought forth again? I could not tell. I only knew that he was annoyed. He stuck his hand through the handle of his vibrator (I had bought it for him), clicked on the switch, and began to run it over his left wrist. I suspected that he was trying to calm himself down and not make more of the moment than it warranted.

"What's the *opposite* of bourgeois?" he asked quietly. (Too quietly?)

"I'm not sure."

"Why don't you call up René Clair and ask him?"

"He's in Paris," I said, thoroughly cowed.

"That's all right. Us *bourgeoises* use the long-distance all the time."

"I think the opposite varies. Depending on who you are. To a French aristocrat, I suppose it means someone upper class, or in finance. I don't know."

"Never mind French aristocrats. What is it to *us?"*

"I guess the opposite of bourgeois to us would be artist."

"Who ever told you you were an artist?"

"Nobody. Just a figure of speech. I mean, a word."

He shut off his vibrator, threw it onto his table, and got up.

"Listen," he said. "Let me tell you what's worse than thinking you're a bourgeois—thinking you're an *artist,* for Christ's sake. I'm an *actor*—it's a job, a trade. And what *you* do is, too —or ought to be. Don't start thinking of yourself as some kind of la-di-da member of the elite or you'll wind up on your ass."

The conversation was well out of hand now. There was nothing left to do but let it die away and hope for a better next time.

Next time turned out to be worse.

Spencer is talking seriously of his insomnia. It has plagued him throughout his life. When he was engaged on a project, it was bad. He had difficulty turning off his pulsating creative machinery. When he was idle, as he had now been for some time, it was even worse.

I suggest that if, perhaps, he could cut down his enormous coffee consumption . . . ?

"That hasn't got a goddam thing to *do* with it!" he snaps.

I had forgotten, momentarily, that in these nondrinking years, coffee was the important substitute. Whenever he and Ruth and I went out to dinner at Chasen's or Romanoff's or LaRue's, a waiter would bring him a pot of coffee as soon as he sat down.

We talk of hot milk and self-hypnosis and calcium tablets. He takes a sleeping pill now and then, but hates the idea. He is amazed when I tell him I have never taken a sleeping pill in my life.

"Why not?" he asks.

"Because I'm convinced that if I ever do, I won't wake up."

He studies me, gravely.

"I would be willing to bet," he says, "that you couldn't pass a sanity test even with me coaching you from the sidelines."

"How about hot, or warm baths?"

"Wake me up."

"Massage."

"Great," he says, "if you can get me Sophia Loren."

I tell him of a book that explains the necessity for preparation for sleep throughout the day, and particularly in the hours preceding bedtime.

"The hell with it," he says. "I'm not going to spend my waking hours worrying about the sleeping ones."

I tell him a doctor once suggested an electric blanket on a low reading, warm milk and a biscuit, and a massive dose of calcium. Also an eyeshade and earplugs.

Spencer shakes his head, miserably. "No, no," he says. "It wouldn't work. Any of it."

We share a depressed silence. And then—damn!—without forethought, a teasing quip escapes me.

"Have you ever tried a day's work?" I ask.

I regret it instantly, but it is too late. His fury is pouring over me and a few minutes later I find myself sitting alone in his living room. I leave quietly, ignominiously.

An hour later, I phoned him. Before I could begin to apologize, he said, "Jesus Christ, doctor. You sure hit a nerve."

"Listen, Flannel. . . ."

"Drop it," he said. "We were both wrong. But kidding aside, I may try some of that calcium crap, at that."

We cross the country with Kate by train, immediately after she has returned to New York from making *The African Queen*. She is carrying all sorts of souvenirs and mementos, masks, and crazy jewelry. Walking down the Grand Central platform laden with her stuff, she suggests an African tribeswoman on her way to a United Nations Security Council meeting.

There is a mix-up about her reservation. No drawing room, not even a compartment.

"Don't worry about it," she says airily. "I'll sit up."

"For three nights?"

"Oh, sure," she says. "I've done it hundreds of times."

The harried conductor comes through and tells her that a compartment has become available. She wants to know how. The conductor shrugs. She refuses to take it unless she has the details. She cannot bear the idea that someone has been displaced because a movie star might be discommoded.

The conductor explains that a gentleman on board, hearing that a lady was without accommodations, offered his space and agreed to double up with a friend.

This would have satisfied most people, but not Kate. She wants to know *which* man.

"I'll point him out to you at supper," says the conductor.

He is true to his word. While we are having dinner in the splendid 20th-Century Limited dining car, four men come in and are seated not far from us. One of them is a jolly, rotund, florid Irishman. The conductor points him out to Kate.

"That's the man," he says.

Napkin in hand and still chewing, Kate goes at once to the

nearby table and says, "Very nice of you to switch. Thank you so much. Appreciate it. Good of you. Yah."

The man rises, performs his version of a courtly bow and says loudly, "Think nothing of it, Miss Hepburn. I'm not so nice as you think. I'm on the Chicago *Daily News* and as soon as I get to the paper in the morning, I'm hoping to sell my editor one hell of a Sunday feature." His hand reaches into the air and limns a Sunday supplement headline: " 'WHY KATHARINE HEPBURN SLEPT IN MY BED ON THE NIGHT OF SEPTEMBER TWELVE.' " Kate blushes as the man's speech gets the expected reaction from the passengers. He continues, "That's worth a by-line, don't you think?"

"I don't want to tell you," says Kate, "what *I* think."

It is on this trip that she reads us an extraordinary document: a journal she kept during the making of *The African Queen.* It proves to be a thoroughly professional piece of writing containing freehand, intimate sketches of John Huston and Humphrey Bogart and Sam Spiegel. It offers a picture of the place and a description of the activity and a sense of life on location.

We urge her to publish it. She agrees.

A few months later, I asked her what had happened to it.

"Can you believe it?" she asked. "I've *lost* it!"

"Do you mean to tell me you managed to save all that maggoty junk and lost the only thing of value you brought back from Africa?"

"Yes."

In Beverly Hills and Hollywood, Bel Air, Holmby Hills, Brentwood, and Malibu, many houses, especially those which are offered for rent, are referred to less by street addresses than by celebrity appellation. "I'm living in the Paul Newman house," one will hear. Or, "They're tearing down the pink Judy Garland." "Is the Billy Wilder very expensive?" "I'm right next door to the new Jack Benny."

A few years ago we were searching for a house to rent. At

least five of them were identified as "the old Katharine Hepburn."

I thought we were being put on because, for reasons of her own, Kate, who has worked in Hollywood for almost forty years and frequently spent years at a stretch there, has never owned California property.

Perhaps she was heeding Harpo Marx's advice: "Never buy anything out here you can't put on the Chief and take home." He was thinking of the impermanence, in most cases, of film-world status.

Whatever her reasons, she always rented.

"We were looking at houses today," I said to her, "and five of them, they said, were old houses of *yours*."

"Probably were," she said. "God knows, I've rented dozens."

I went over the list with her. In every case, save one, the real-estate agent had reported accurately.

After her return from making *The African Queen,* she took a lease on the old Charles Boyer house. (There it is again!) It is a beautifully designed and executed hilltop structure that Boyer built to the specifications of his memory of a grand château somewhere in the South of France. (My wife has observed that in Beverly Hills one can see the replica of the finest house that exists in nearly every town in America.) Boyer added a number of splendid innovations of his own. A sliding ceiling in the circular dining room that opened to the sky at a push of a button. A spacious tennis court, multileveled stone terraces, and an exquisite miniature theater that served as his projection room.

Alas, it was something he could not put on the Chief and take away with him when, all at once, his popularity waned.

"One year," he told me, "I earned more than five hundred thousand dollars. The next year, I earned less than forty. It was not hard to tell something had changed, hey?"

As part of a contract settlement, RKO bought the house from Boyer. Some time later, Howard Hughes bought RKO.

There it stood, impressive but bereft, atop its hill. Kate knew the house. She had made a film with Charles—*Break of Hearts,* in 1935—while he was planning it.

The story of her one-time whirlwind romance with the enigmatic Mr. Hughes is well-known. What is less well-known is the fact that they have remained friends through the years.

(When Spencer's death was reported, the first call that came to Kate, at seven in the morning, was from Howard Hughes, offering, in addition to his condolences, any material assistance he might be able to give.)

With Hughes' help, she rented the Charles Boyer house. The real-estate department at RKO did not understand, pointing out that the house was absolutely empty.

It took Kate no more than two days to arrange matters. A trip to the RKO furniture and prop departments, to the homes of three or four friends, to the M-G-M studios, and her new house was beautifully, tastefully, and conveniently furnished. Linen, silver, china. Some she had in storage, some she went out and bought.

Of all the films Kate had ever made—twenty-eight up to that point—none had taken as much out of her, physically, as *The African Queen*. The travel, the climate, the rugged location, the adjustment to the tense and complex Humphrey Bogart, and to the erratic and whimsical John Huston. The small and large illnesses and infections. Following the location, flying back to London for studio work. All this combined to wear her out.

She is not a Christian Scientist but often behaves as though she were. She would not admit she looked drawn, was not functioning properly, and should rest. Eventually it hit her, and, once ensconced in the Boyer house on the hill, she stayed there, hardly ever leaving the property.

"In three months, I used half a tankful of gas in my car," was the way she put it.

There were some grand nights up there, in that grand house. She had brought home from Africa a boxful of color transparencies, and was anxious to show them—with a running commentary, of course.

She arranged for a screen and a slide projector, and having been assured by the gardener that he knew how to run it, engaged him.

The guests that night were Spencer, Cary Grant and his then-wife, Betsy Drake, Ruth, and I. After dinner, we settled down to the dubious pleasure of hearing about someone else's trip, with pictures.

The first slide came on. It might have been an out-of-focus tree in Central Park, or a swamp anywhere, or part of a Los Angeles golf course.

"Isn't it *fascinating?*" said Kate. "This is just to the north before we get to the AQ-two loading area."

"Oh," said someone.

She signaled the gardener. The next slide came on. A pastel-pale shot of a group of mission-like huts.

"It's overexposed," I said, and regretted the remark at once.

"It is *not!*" said Kate. "That's the way the colors *are* there. You've never *been* to Africa, have you?"

"No, ma'am."

"Well then, shut up."

The next slide came on, overexposed again, and still sort of nothing.

Silence.

The machine broke down. All efforts to repair it failed.

I did my best. Having been born and raised in Rochester, New York, I know my way around the various products of the Eastman Kodak Company, but I could not fix that one, that night.

Kate accused me of not trying. I swore and swear that I was.

The magic-lantern show was over but Kate doggedly continued the sound track, passing the tiny slides around. The commentary was wildly out-of-sync for most of us since she was generally describing a slide other than the one we were examining.

A few nights later, having acquired a new machine and an expert to run it, she decided to put the evening together again. She cannot bear loose ends. All was arranged.

At the last moment, Cary phoned to say Betsy had a migraine. How sad. They would not be able to come.

As we sat down before the screen, Spencer said, "I've got a migraine, too."

"You have *not,*" said Kate.

"I'm going to have," said Spencer.

The slides came and went endlessly, interminably.

Spencer began to improvise a voice-over of his own, describing what each shot looked like to him. Tension, until Kate began to see the comical side.

There was another occasion in the house that revealed a new facet of Kate's superlative artistic intelligence.

Charlie Chaplin had made *Monsieur Verdoux,* and it had failed. It had had poor reviews and had not found a public. This did not keep our bunch, Chaplin enthusiasts all, from wanting to see it. Kate arranged a screening. Only Chaplin lovers were allowed. This included the four of us, Irene Selznick, the Danny Kayes, Bill Tilden, and three or four others.

We settled into the charming little projection room in happy anticipation. The picture came on. The first two or three minutes gave great promise, and we all laughed it up even on the straight lines, but the laughter became more and more difficult to force, and it began to be apparent that even the great Chaplin could stumble. We hung on bravely to the end of the reel. Suddenly, the sound went dead. A minute passed, during which Kate buzzed the projection room frantically.

"You've lost your sound!" she shouted.

"I know! I know!" the projectionist shouted back on the intercom. "Just a moment."

"Stop it," she ordered. "Stop the picture!"

It was stopped, rewound, and a few minutes later, the explanation came over the intercom. "It's the frammis tube," he said. "Won't take the cronfair overload."

"I see," said Kate. "What do we do?"

"Well, this equipment hasn't been used in some time. We'll have to get another truran tomorrow."

"Tomorrow!" said Kate.

Everyone in the room was getting up, secretly relieved, when all at once, Kate said, "Sit down, everybody."

"What?"

"Come on, sit down." She spoke to the projectionist. "Rewind a couple hundred feet, then go ahead again."

"Go ahead?" he squawked.

"That's right."

She clicked off and addressed the little audience. "We are going to run it silent," she said. "After all, Chaplin is a silent picture actor, isn't he? Let's look at it silent. At least we'll see it, even if we can't hear it."

Spencer said, "But that makes no sense, Kate. The man made a picture that . . ."

"Shhhhh!" said Kate, as the room went dark and the picture began again. "Watch!"

We watched. And here is the wonder. *Monsieur Verdoux* without the sound track was infinitely better than it had been with it.

Kate was right. The only thing wrong with *Monsieur Verdoux* was that it talked. The attempt to make the actors speak and to play dialogue scenes was as awkward for Chaplin as it would be for a French playwright to write a play in English, even if he had acquired a working knowledge of the tongue. The acting, the staging, the organization of the scenes, and the comic points were effective, funny, and bitter. All that the great man had intended it to be. Film was his language.

Although Kate continues to rent, she often goes through the motions of looking for a property to buy. Sometimes a house (needs a lot of work!), sometimes a piece of land on which she plans to erect the perfect house. She clambers over hills, making discoveries; climbs fences; peers through windows of unoccupied houses.

She does not know it, but real-estate agents no longer take her seriously.

It may be that Kate, deeply attached to her New York house and her Connecticut family, finds it difficult to split her allegiance.

Whatever the reason, she has always been a transient in California.

On the other hand, she has genuine affection for the place. It is filled with good friends, nostalgic locations, memories of good work, and the great outdoors of which she is so fond.

She once took me on a drive all over Beverly Hills. A tour of the past, of all the houses she had lived in. The first house that she shared with Laura Harding when they came out by train in 1932; the second, jumping over the fence when she could not get in through the gate, recounting stories of the various adventures they had, the beaux, the excitements.

There is, however, a part of Beverly Hills, a large part, which Kate *thinks* she owns, although she does not. It is, in fact, not privately owned at all.

She discovered it during her early days in California. Beverly Hills and its environs have undergone great changes in the course of time, but Kate's spot has remained virtually unchanged. It is the city reservoir and surroundings.

Scarcely anyone goes there. The citizens of Beverly Hills are not noted for their interest in hiking or exploring. The reservoir is difficult to get to and there is nothing much there when you arrive. Kate has found it a haven and goes there for some part of almost every day she spends in Beverly Hills. She knows nearly every inch of it, its plants and shrubs and flowers and foliage, its paths, its entrances and exits. She has made friends with the long succession of custodians.

Most of her friends and co-stars and directors have been dragged through it, willingly or unwillingly.

"I do a lot of thinking up there," says Kate.

She takes her books there and her scripts and, lately, her dog.

On the rare occasions when she has agreed to talk for publication, she usually takes the interviewer there.

"I don't know why. I feel free up there, and not constrained."

She has special clothes for the place: boots and knee-length heavy socks.

"It's the damndest spot," she says. "I've left more blood on the brambles and bushes up there than anyone else, and ripped half my clothes to shreds, but who cares? It's worth it. This world of ours—it's getting harder and harder to find a piece of privacy in it, or an inch of peace." (Her wildly mixed metaphors serve only to underline her passionate feeling.) Kate often has a need to be alone, even if she happens to be with someone else at the time.

She tells of a long, long ago weekend trip to the country with a new beau. He is terribly attractive, but she does not realize what she is in for until they are driving along a back road and she finds he has not—for an hour—stopped talking about himself and his travels.

She begins to sing an invented little song to herself. The lyrics are:

Bore bore bore bore,
Bore bore
Bore bore bore bore
Bore bore bore!

The beau asks, "What's that you're singing?"

Caught, she stops and says, "Nothing. Just a song."

"It's pretty," he says, and goes on with his story of his canoe trip down the Ganges.

Her personal Beverly Hills reservoir supplies such outdoor peace and privacy as is available in those environs and she cherishes it.

There have been adventures there, too.

In a recent one, Kate was picnicking with Lobo and a script. She heard a noise in the clump of bushes at her side, jumped up and found herself confronted by a burly man with a pistol. He pointed it at her.

"Who are *you?"* he asked.

"Never mind that," said Kate, blazing. "Who the hell are *you?"*

The man whipped out his identification and flipped open a wallet to prove he was an L.A.P.D. detective. Two of his assistants made their appearance.

"There's been some trouble up here," said the detective. "A

man yelling for help. We got an emergency on it but we can't find the man and we can't find the people who called in."

"Who were they?" asked Kate.

"The superintendent," said the detective.

"Well, hell," said Kate, "I can take you to *him.*"

"You can?"

"Sure."

"Let's go."

They jumped into Kate's car. She took off down the dirt road at what was later reported to be about eighty miles an hour. She made two or three short cuts across fields. She described the detectives as being somewhat shook up.

"I was really ashamed of them," she said. "Law enforcement officers. Think of it."

"They were probably interested in remaining *live* law enforcement officers," I suggested.

"Just the same," said Kate. "I knew what I was doing and where I was going."

They arrived at the superintendent's cottage. He had indeed heard cries for help, and had called the police. The cries had developed into screams, but for the past half hour or so, silence.

He himself had not ventured forth because he was alone and unarmed and not certain of what lay out there.

He indicated the direction of the trouble. Kate joined the detectives in the beginnings of a search, stayed as long as she could, then had to leave for her singing lesson with Roger Edens. The superintendent said he would take the officers back to their car.

Late that afternoon, Kate told us the story, and asked, "What the hell do you suppose it could have been?"

We had no idea.

On the eleven o'clock news that night, there was revealed the story of a daring kidnap. Three armed men had abducted a resident of Beverly Hills from his home, taken him out to the reservoir area, bound him firmly to a tree, gagged him, and returned to begin negotiations for ransom. While these were in progress, the man managed to free the gag and call for help. As a result of Kate's assistance, he was found and freed. He was returned to his home in time to find his distraught family on the telephone with the kidnapers. The call was traced, the criminals easily apprehended.

I phoned Kate the following morning at seven (she is usually up at six) and said, "I've got a theory about that thing last night."

"Go ahead," she said. "What is it?"

"Well," I said. "I figure somebody kidnaped somebody, tied them to a tree out there, then went back to make a ransom deal. The super heard the yells, called the detectives, they got lost, found you. You took them to the place. They probably got the guy loose and so you helped to foil the whole thing."

"Have you been up all night?" she asked.

"No. Why?"

"Because that's the most *ridiculous* thing I ever heard!"

"Have you seen the *Times* this morning?" I asked.

"No. Not yet."

"Well, *read* it," I said, and hung up.

When Tracy and Hepburn made *State of the Union* in 1947, Adolphe Menjou was in the company. It was an ugly time, the Red Channels days. Menjou had become a militant, loud, right-wing leader; an overcooperative volunteer witness before the House Un-American Activities Committee, supplying innuendo, hearsay, speculation, and gossip under the heading of information.

However, they all managed to maintain a reasonable and professional relationship on the set throughout the making of the picture.

Some time later I tell Kate and Spence about a little squib I have read somewhere. Where was it? In *The New Yorker?* Probably. About Menjou down in Washington testifying before the Committee. He has been blowing the whistle shrilly and carelessly on all sorts of people with whom he has worked.

In a New York barbershop there is a discussion about it.

"Did you see where Menjou went down to Washington to testify for that Un-American Committee?"

"Well, sure," the barber says. "What the hell. Me, I can understand a thing like that. I've always liked that Adolphe *Menn*-joo. He was very suave, you know, with that mustache and everything, and I can feel for him. You know what I mean? Like, here's a guy, used to be a big star. A real big star, and had all the broads he wanted and everything. So the years go by. He gets a little older and some new guys come up and so then *they* get to be the big stars and guys like *Menn*-joo—well, they're not such big stars any more. They don't get the same kind of money and the same kind of good parts in the pictures, and so they're playing the small parts. And so what the hell? A guy like *Menn*-joo, it happens to him, he becomes bitter, you know what I mean? And from becoming bitter, the next thing you know—it's understandable—he becomes a *Communist!*"

The story goes well with Spence.

Dr. Hepburn and Kate were visiting us in the country.

After a long sweaty walk, I went up, showered, and changed my clothes.

When I returned, the doctor frowned and said, "You've changed your clothes."

"Yes, sir."

He regarded me carefully and asked, "How many suits do you own?"

"I don't know," I said honestly. "I haven't counted them."

"Good God!"

"What is it?"

"Any man who owns more than two suits is a *fop!*"

"Why two?" I said, bristling. "Why not one?"

He looked at me pityingly. "One at the cleaners, and one to wear," he said.

Kate assures me that, as a matter of principle, her father

never owned more than two suits or two pairs of shoes at any one time. "Don't clutter up your life with frivolities," was one of his often-repeated injunctions.

Although an intellectual, he retained remnants of truly old-fashioned Maryland and New England notions. One of them was that naughty children should be spanked. Both Dr. Hepburn and Mrs. Hepburn did the job when they deemed it necessary. Kate remembers, as a child, being cuffed around a good deal.

There is an antiquated bit of American doggerel that goes:

Father calls me William
Sister calls me Will
Mother calls me Willie
But the fellas call me Bill.

The rhymester was innocently beginning to come to grips with the notion that he, like everyone else, was many-sided, that his image was dependent on the eye of the beholder. He was coming to know that we exist in varying relationships and that what we are, finally, is the sum total of these empathies, leavened by self-estimate.

Since we are by no means all created equal (the Declaration of Independence notwithstanding) there are some who have more sides than others, including one of the two subjects at hand.

She is the respected Miss Hepburn to tradespeople, receptionists in doctors' offices, insurance agents, telephone operators, and so on. She is Kate to her friends: George Cukor, Irene Selznick, Laura Harding, Frances Rich, Sally and Chester Erskine, Michael Benthall, and Robert Helpmann, among many. I have never heard one of these refer to her as Katie. No, 'Katie' is the usage for taxi drivers, fans, stagehands, and certain members of the press.

Spencer Tracy usually called her Kathy; occasionally Kath, and sometimes Flora Finch; Olive Oyle; Laura La Plante;

Madame Curie; Molly Malone; Coo-Coo, the Bird Girl; Madame Defarge; Carrie Nation; Dr. Kronkheit; Miss America; or Mrs. Thomas Whiffen.

Her nieces and nephews call her Aunt Kath. I have also heard Kat, Miss H., Katerina, and Katinka.

Several times, I hear Laura call Kate "Max," whereupon they both giggle. I gather it is a private joke. When I know them well enough, I ask them what it is. Laura tells me. There used to be a cartoon character, a rabbit called Max Hare. One of the things he did was to play tennis with himself, running back and forth on the court, returning his own spectacular shots. Watching Kate play her energetic brand of tennis, Laura began to call her Max Hare. Eventually it was shortened to Max.

She has never been Kit, which is apparently reserved for Miss Cornell.

She remembers that her father, earlier on, called her Redtop; and later, Reddy. No one else ever did.

It would appear she thinks of herself as Katharine Houghton Hepburn. This is the name she uses when she writes for publication or when she orders stationery. The Houghton part is a matter of pride, in addition to providing a permanent link to the memory of her loved and loving mother.

She has been called other things as well. I was preparing a production of *Small War on Murray Hill,* by Robert E. Sherwood, and working on the designs with Boris Aronson. Boris is the sort of theater person who becomes creatively involved in every aspect of a show. The fact that I had, as yet, no leading lady troubled him. He looked out the window of his studio, across Central Park, frowning in thought. He turned to me and asked, wistfully, in his florid, coagulated Russian accent, "And you're sure *she* wouldn't do it for you? Your friend? Katharine *Halperin?"*

Kate: "Life's become too damned complicated—talk about 'Getting and spending, we lay waste our powers.'—it isn't only getting and spending; it's moving around from here to there, getting things clean, changing clothes, trying to shop, standing in queues, fooling around with all kinds of equipment—it's all so *complicated!* Walk into anybody's bathroom and look at the medicine chest—did you ever see such a mess?—powders and pills and lotions and gadgets—it doesn't take all that—our grandparents and great-grandparents did fine."

"Did they?" I ask. "I remember researching a story and coming across an item in a Binghamton, New York, newspaper of about 1860. And there was an obituary. 'Mr. Soandso enjoyed excellent health to the end,' it said, 'but succumbed to old age. He was fifty-one.' "

My account makes no impression.

"Oh, well, that's just—I don't know," says Kate. "What I'm getting at is, my grandfather used to brush his teeth with a washcloth—washcloths were always important around our house—that's why I'm still interested in them, I suppose, and so delighted when I find a good one—Dad used to say *his* father would buy a cake of soap and use it until it wore out—all he had—soap—took his bath with it and shaved with it—cleaned his teeth with it, too—and he was just about the healthiest specimen that ever happened—but look what goes on now—preshaving and shaving and aftershaving stuff by the buckets—depilatories and deodorants and every other kind of useless junk that people put on themselves and in themselves—it's all just to make someone else rich."

In 1939, she was living in the old John Barrymore house near the top of Tower Grove. One evening, at dinner, she squirmed uncomfortably.

"What's the matter?" I asked.

"I got too much sun today—sat out in the garden with no clothes on, like a fool."

Attempting to follow the explanation, I asked, "What do you mean, 'with no clothes on'?"

"I mean in the nude—what do you think I mean?"

"Nude," I repeated. "What did you want to do a thing like that for?"

"I had to," she explained reasonably. "I was posing."

"Uh huh."

"Bob McKnight is here—a sculptor friend of mine—an old beau, really—he wanted to do a little figure of me and so there we were—what are you looking so peculiar about?"

"Nothing."

Thinking it over later, I came to the conclusion that Kate had been teasing. I could hardly imagine a movie star sitting out in her garden, stark naked, posing for a sculptor.

A few weeks later, when the lovely little figure appeared on its plinth in her sitting room, I knew she had been telling the truth. The naked truth.

It has been said that each man has what might be called 'an ideal age,' a certain time of life that suits him more than other times. Some are best in youth, others in middle age, a few when old.

I did not know Spencer in his young days, but it would be hard to imagine a more satisfactory Tracy era than the final decade of his life.

Physically, he had made his peace with his body. He wore his bulk well, and—although he watched his weight and was prudent in his diet—the esthetics of the matter were no longer a concern.

Professionally, the wracking struggles of his early years were behind him at last. He was well off. He could relax.

He had come to know who he was and what. With Kate's help, rowdy pleasures had been replaced by richer ones. He knew what he knew, was resigned to his limitations, enjoyed his days and nights.

His work, too, was at its best. Spencer had never been a comfortable juvenile or leading man. He was always, essentially, a character actor and the characters he found to play later in his career were more interesting than they had been in the beginning.

We were both impressed, one evening, by Artur Rubinstein's reply to a question of mine.

"Am I right in thinking that you're playing better now than ever before?"

"I think so. Yes," he answered. "So that makes two of us. I hope there are a few more or we shall get lonely."

"Is it experience, practice, what?"

"No, no, no," said Artur. "Let me tell you. I am eighty. Isn't that so? So now I take chances I never took before. You see, the stakes are not so high. I can afford it. I used to be so much more careful. No wrong notes. Not too bold ideas. Watch tempi. Now, I let go and enjoy myself and to hell with everything except the music!"

Spencer listens and nods but makes no comment.

A few days later, however, he says to me, "That Artur thing. That's me. That's just how I feel now when I act. I've got damn little to lose and a whole lot to gain. I wish I'd had the guts in the beginning."

"That's not how it goes," I said.

I once asked Fanny Brice if she thought Spencer was a hypochondriac.

"No," she said. "He just *thinks* he is."

He was, indeed, tentative about signs and symptoms, aches and pains.

I said to him, "Spence, about most things like that, my Doctor Somach used to say, 'Live with it.' It's as good medical advice as I've ever had."

Spencer was unimpressed. He worried about the state of his physical being. There was a reason for this, but I was not to know it for some years.

In the fall of 1961, three young men—David Shaber, William Snyder, and Gene Wolsk—acquired the theatrical rights to *Death of a Man* by Lael Tucker Wertenbaker. Shortly thereafter, they brought it to me with a view toward dramatization. I had read excerpts of the book when they were published in *Look* magazine and had found them almost unbearably moving.

Moreover, I had known Charles and Lael Wertenbaker, briefly but warmly, in wartime London, where he was the chief of the Time-Life Bureau, and she, a member of his staff.

We lost touch after the war, but Bob Capa, a mutual friend, told me that Wert had done what all journalists dream of doing but never do. He had quit his job and gone off with his family to the village of Ciboure, in Southwest France, to write.

Later, I heard that he had fallen ill and died.

I was to learn the full details only after Lael recounted them in her extraordinary book which, although titled *Death of a Man,* I found to be about the value of life.

I considered the proposal carefully. I had never done anything in the way of dramatization, and was reluctant to put off work of my own. But the book and its meaning haunted me until it was no longer a matter of choice, but of compulsion.

I told the young producers I was willing to try. The job would necessitate a trip to Ciboure (near St. Jean-de Luz) and perhaps a stay. I told Spencer something about the project. He seemed noncommittal and reluctant to discuss it. We had been talking of a new screenplay for him. It would now have to wait. Perhaps, I thought, that is the reason for his coolness.

Many months later, when I had completed the play and returned to the United States, I called Spencer. The writing had proved to be an exalting experience.

"Boyo," I said, "it's finished and—what can I tell you?—it's great. You're going to be so proud of me. Wait and see. Look, I can say all this because the whole thing isn't strictly mine. After all, I didn't create the characters or invent the incidents. That was all there. But what I did come up with is a scheme—a way of telling this great story—that's far and away the best thing I've ever been near. I can't tell you how strong I feel."

"Good," he said.

It did not seem like much of a reaction to my explosive report. I went on.

"But here's the best part, Spence. I hadn't been on it a week before I realized I was writing you and Kate. I swear to God, Wertenbaker looked like you—not that that matters to anybody—but it was *very* helpful to me. And Lael . . . well, she's a real Hepburn type, although she's actually a Southern girl. Spence, listen. This can be the greatest thing any of us has ever done. Of course, I'd prefer to do it in the theater, the form it's in now, but if you're dead set against that—then, well, we'll do it as a film. I'll talk to the boys. We could do it right there—in the Basque country. *Tremendous* location—wait till you see it. By the way, the play is called *A Gift of Time.*"

"Yuh."

The lack of expected response began to dampen my enthusiasm.

"Well," I said, somewhat deflated, "the first thing is for both of you to read it. I'll put two copies in the Morris office pouch tonight. So you'll have them tomorrow. And we'll be out in a week or so."

"Fine."

A few more mumbles at either end, and our soggy talk was over.

We talked on the phone several times in the course of the week that followed, but he did not mention *A Gift of Time,* nor did I.

Ruth and I got to California and, as was our long-standing custom, went to dinner at Spencer's directly from the airport.

The same old jolly reunion took place, gifts offered, jokes made, splendid dinner consumed amidst happy noise.

After dinner, as subject after subject was ticked off, project after project considered, I became increasingly restive. The general reaction to my script had been excellent. Why was it taboo here?

I steeled myself and said, "I'd like to talk about *A Gift of Time.*"

"*I* wouldn't," said Spencer. "The scripts are back at the Morris office. Abe's office. Or somebody's. And let's say no more about it."

"You didn't like it?" I asked.

"I didn't read it," he said and walked out of the room.

"I read it," said Kate quietly. "You'll have to understand—it's the subject matter—impossible for him—upsetting. Please don't pursue the subject."

"Very well," I said.

Spencer returned. "It's going to rain," he said.

Conversation went on, but I took no part in it. I was sunk. I was not listening. My thoughts and feelings were elsewhere.

I heard Spencer's voice, looked up, and found he was addressing me, angrily.

". . . must be sick in your *mind,* for God's sake. Where do you get the gall to inflict punishment like that on an audience?"

"You said you didn't even read it, so how do you . . ."

"I know more about it than I *want* to know," he said, pale. "Of all the cruel, tasteless, crackbrained notions. . . ."

I got up and started out but could not resist making an attempt at a defense.

"If you'd read the play, pal . . . you'd see that it's not about death. It's about life. Reverence for life. The whole story *inspires* me and if you'd . . ."

"It inspires me, too," said Spencer. "It inspires me to ram it down your throat. And where the hell do you come off sending stuff like that to *me?* Don't you realize . . ."

"Hold it," I said. There was a long pause, after which I added, "I'm beginning to suspect that—I mean, reading between the lines—that you're not going to *do* this play. Am I right?"

And Spencer laughed. And we all laughed. And thank fortune that this time, a joke worked.

The play was done eventually, with Henry Fonda and Olivia de Havilland as the Wertenbakers. The press reception was predominantly favorable and I have proud memories of the production—but the play failed. I was not able to induce the audience to see it my way. They found it harrowing, as Spencer had found the idea.

On one of our Paris walks, a couple of years later, Spencer surprised me by bringing up the subject. It was a quiet autumn evening, and we were walking in the Bois de Boulogne dusk.

"I read that play of yours not long ago," he said.

"What play?"

"A Gift of Time," he said.

"Oh?" I masked my amazement.

"You did a good job. I still think an insane part of you chose it. It's a wrong subject, but you did it well."

"Thank you."

"Also. It's been on my mind for some time—that night I berserked on you. Let me see if I can explain it."

"No need, Spence."

"For *me,*" he said. "Not for *you.*" He slowed down and we moved at underwater pace along the rustling path. "My father—" he began, "John Edward Tracy—was a powerful man. In every way. Body and mind. He was in the trucking business most of his life—and he was kind of a truck himself. A hell of a worker . . . enterprising. Things got slow once in Milwaukee. He picked us up and moved us all to Kansas City. . . . That didn't pan out—so, back to Milwaukee. He was never a butt man. He was always in action. Even coming to New York, late in life—for General Motors—never fazed him for a minute. He was always in charge. I think he thought I was soft-headed to want to go on the stage, but he never made a move to stop me or even interfere. . . . Gave me the dough in the beginning and plenty of times after that. Whatever happened, I always knew there was *one* guy on my side all the way. What worried him most was that I didn't have the *looks.* He never said so, mind you, but I could read him pretty good, especially one day when he looked at me—full of worry—and said, 'Son, always be sure you keep a fine wardrobe!' I guess he thought that somehow might make up for my pan. The first time I ever played Milwaukee—it was for Cohan and that week he switched the billing and put my name up first over the title, that was Cohan—my father came to see the show and later, over a near-beer, he said to me, 'Spencer, you were fine. I never would've thought it. I could hear every word and the people liked you. But all through, son, I kept thinking, we just picked up a beautiful new five-ton truck. And I kept thinking that good as you looked up there on the stage, you'd look even better in the driver's seat of that five-ton beauty!' . . . He helped me whenever I needed help. Johnny was born in his house. . . . You know how people fade as they age? Not my father. Every year he became more vigorous—I think New York City did some of it—and louder . . . until . . ."

Spencer stopped talking and began to walk a little faster. We were out of the park now and on the Avenue Foch, heading for home. When he spoke again, it was without sadness, without sentiment or grief—but in a voice charged with anger.

"He got sick. And then he got sicker. Weak. And scared. He'd look at me beggingly—as though I could help if I wanted to. I'd see him wince. Once, visiting, I heard him crying out in the other room. Cancer. Nothing to do but wait and suffer and wait and wait. . . . I was working for Cohan in *Whispering Friends*. I was wrong for the part—Bill Harrigan had opened in it, and I was lousy besides—but Cohan knew I needed the work. I came off after the second act one night. . . . Went into my dressing room. . . . Cohan was sitting there. And he looked at me. And I knew. Then he said, 'You want to finish it? You don't have to.' And I said, 'No, but I want to.' And he said, 'I'll wait here.' After the show, he took me up there. . . . I looked at what was left—just practically nothing. I couldn't find that big, proud, Irish son-of-a-gun in the remains. And right then and there I made plans. Anything like that ever happened to me, I'd check out. And I will, too. . . . Can you see now why I couldn't stand your play?"

"Yes. I'm sorry."

"One more thing. I'm scared. It's a thing there's no prevention for. There's nothing you can do. We're helpless. Sitting ducks. If it hits, it hits. And when that's the way your father goes—or your mother—it's only natural to live with the specter of it. Or try. It's my cross."

I took his arm. It was tense. I said nothing.

Through the years we all exchanged many gifts. Opening nights, Christmases, holidays. Of all the gifts we ever gave Kate, what she most appreciated was a package of rough washcloths from England—called Vic, for some reason—which, when applied vigorously, damn near take one's epidermis off. They are just right for Kate. She turned up early one morning for a conference with a number of scraped bruises on her face. Some were bleeding. I was alarmed and thought she had fallen down, or been in an automobile accident.

"Your face, Kate," I said. "It's bleeding."

"I know," she said, smiling brightly. "It's those *wonderful* Vic *washcloths!*"

Nineteen fifty-nine. I am working on the musical version of *Do Re Mi.* Dinner at our house with Betty Comden and Adolph Green who are fascinated by the idea that Kate lives right next door.

Betty asks, "What kind of neighbor is she, anyway? I mean does she come in and borrow a cup of sugar once in a while or . . ."

She is interrupted by a sound from the kitchen. The swinging door slams open. There stands Kate wearing a wild wig and carrying two others.

She asks Ruth, "Look, what do you think of this? For Viola. Oh, hell, you can't see it in this silly candlelight. Put some lights on." She puts on all the bright lights in the room. She models the wig, drops to the floor, takes the wig off, puts on another one, stands up, swivels around, sits down, changes for a third time. *"Now* what do you think?" she asks. Ruth is about to speak when she says, "Well, *think* about it, will you, and let me know? I mean which one of the three do you think—?" She notices, for the first time, that there are other people in the room.

She smiles her most charming smile and says, "Nice to have met you all." She is gone.

Ruth turns to Betty and asks, "Does that answer your question?"

In Kate's piece about Lauren Bacall in Roddy McDowall's book, *Double Exposure,* I find the following sentence: "No zulac from the bazaar has a sharper knife."

"What does that mean?" I ask.

"What mean?"

" 'Zulac'?"

"Never mind 'zulac.' Do you know what the whole sentence means?"

"Yes, I guess so."

"Well, then," she says, triumphantly, "what's the difference?"

"No difference. I'd just like to know what a zulac is. I looked it up in every one of my sixty-seven dictionaries and couldn't find it."

"Of course not," she says. "I made it up."

"Why?"

"Sounded right."

"Maybe it's okay after all," I said. "Someone at Viking was telling me the other day that John Steinbeck was once going over a manuscript with a pedantic copy editor who said, 'But, Mr. Steinbeck, there's no such *word!'* And Steinbeck said, 'Don't worry about it, son. If the book's a success, there *will* be.' "

Kate says, "Damn right. Look up 'zulac' again in a few years."

Spencer Tracy loved the theater. He admired good acting, and responded to a fine play.

Whenever he came to New York, he wanted to go to the theater as much as possible.

He presented a problem, however, which was that he would only sit in the last row of the orchestra, on the aisle.

Great men must be permitted their idiosyncrasies and I never questioned this one. It might have been that he felt claustrophobic in a theater (many do), or that he felt the chances of his being recognized and pestered for autographs were less, or that he wanted to be in a position where he could leave discreetly if he felt like it. All very well, but getting a seat in the last row is difficult. The management normally holds out a number of house seats but these are usually in the fifth or sixth row, center. It would take no more than a single phone call to the management to say that Spencer Tracy would like to buy a pair of house seats for such and such an evening and the tickets would doubtless be forthcoming, but how to get the seats in the *last* row?

In time, we evolved a routine. I would call the management, explain the problem, and acquire a pair of the best seats. We would then go to the theater. Spencer would wait in the alley somewhere while I went to confer with the people sitting in the last two seats in the last row.

It is an odd commentary on the New York theatergoer that the situation was never simply resolved. In almost every case, the people did not want to move. I would patiently explain that the tickets I was offering them in exchange were infinitely more desirable than the ones they had. At this point they were sure that a strange racket was involved, that they were going to be asked to pay a supplement, or that I was a scalper of some sort. Invariably, it was necessary for me to tell the whole story and often bring Spencer in before they would leave their poor seats and go to their fine ones. Again, they would almost always take the position that they were doing us a great favor. In fact, they were.

Kate has been quoted as saying, "I feel that man himself is so remarkable. That the potentiality for men to be thrilling and adorable and noble is so great that it's enough for me. I believe in the example of Jesus Christ, that if one leads a completely unselfish life, one cannot be unhappy in life. Jesus slept well, I'm sure."

As a long-time listener to the lady I cannot feel that the words are correct. Kate is seldom syntactical when passionate, but the feeling and sentiment express her perfectly.

In the largest sense, Katharine Hepburn's popularity has never waned because people know (magically, intuitively) that she stands for something, even if many of them have no clear idea as to what that something is. They recognize that in a time of dangerous conformity, and the fear of being different, here is one who stands up gallantly to the killing wave.

The death of Kate's mother in 1950 hit her hard. Her mother had been a friend and a confidante, a person to whom Kate often turned for advice of the most intimate sort. She had complete faith in her mother's wisdom and in her original, progressive thought.

It was also an early sign of the beginning of the disintegration of family, and, in the case of the Hepburns, was serious. The family had long been Kate's island, where she felt safe, even when the weather was stormy.

Within a short time, Dr. Hepburn married Madelaine Santa Croce, the nurse who had worked with him for many years and was close to the family.

Kate, with her mother's great common sense, shrugged and said, "Well, when you've had a wife for forty-five years, I suppose it's pretty hard to get along without one. I like Santa—she'll be fine for Dad—we all should be damned grateful to her—she's taking on quite a handful."

One of the things that made our long-running friendship unique and interesting was the fact that we learned to talk to one another. More important, we learned to listen.

E. M. Forster may have been right when he said, "How can I tell what I think till I see what I say?"

In the course of our thousands of hours I discovered similarities between Kate and Ruth. On the face of it, they are different. Kate is tall, Ruth is not. Kate, a great beauty; Ruth has never claimed to be. Kate, college; Ruth, no. Kate, a movie superstar. Not so Ruth. As I came to know them better, significant congruities began to appear: determination, strength of purpose, will, won't-be-downed, fight back, built-in confidence, don't-tell-me-what-to-do-I-know-what-I'm-doing, discipline beyond discipline.

Later, I began to perceive that these two were typical products of New England upbringing, particularly as they related to their New England fathers. True, Dr. Thomas Norval Hepburn of Maryland became a New England father by adoption. Captain Clinton Jones, although he had spent the early part of his life at sea, retained the traditional attitudes.

When, in the late nineteenth century, Horace Greeley exhorted, "Go West, young man!" a good many did. They were generally the second, third, or fourth sons who felt their opportunities were greater away from home, where the eldest son enjoyed the major familial privileges by seniority. (New England aping Old England.) Those who stayed behind were the less adventurous, the more settled, and disciplined. They believed in a bird in hand, even though that bird inhabited tough, rocky, difficult-to-farm terrain. They learned to live through bitter winters. (I once heard a Quincy matriarch say, "But up here, we *enjoy* being uncomfortable in the winter time!") They became strong and, by example and custom, taught their children to be strong. They are still doing so.

When women began to emerge as individuals and as a class, the situation became more complex.

The background of Kate's home provides a case history. Her mother, realizing that she was challenging the authority of a patriarchy, was nevertheless unable to suppress her own instincts toward social progress. Dr. Hepburn, who loved her deeply, understood that he had to make way.

In Ruth's family, her mother remained subservient to the end.

Echoes of the rigorous training seasoned our many talks.

I have never been part of a discussion with Kate during which she did not quote her father or her mother. It usually came at the peak, as though to sum it all up.

For example:

"Well, Dad always used to say, 'If there's too long a pause in any conversation—jump in. Everybody will love you for it.' "

Whatever it was, it was delivered as a dictum, in the manner of quoting a decision of the Supreme Court of the United States.

Ruth and Kate constantly recalled the words of their fathers.

Dr. Hepburn: "Don't clutter up your life."

Captain Jones: "Be prepared. If you're in the Straits of Gibraltar and you want a can of lard, there's just two things you can do. You can have it with you or you can go without."

Dr. Hepburn (at eighty-one, deplaning in Greece after a five-thousand-mile flight): "Hello, Kate, you're looking fine. Now, where's the Parthenon?" Kate: "Don't you want to come to the hotel first and freshen up?" Dr. Hepburn: "Hell, no. I came all this way to see the Parthenon, so why wait? Let's go."

Captain Jones: "I never been in no situation where havin' money made it any *worse*!"

Dr. Hepburn: "If you want to get somewhere, don't write letters. Go over to where you want to go and appear personally. They can throw a letter into the wastepaper basket, but they can't do that to *you*."

Captain Jones: "God damn it! What could be better than being a physical-culture instructress?"

Dr. Hepburn: "Don't wait for things to happen to you. *Make* them happen!"

Captain Jones: "I want you to promise me one thing, Ruth. Don't ever act in no place where they serve hard liquor."

Dr. Hepburn: "If you must drink, drink when you're happy. It'll make you happier. If you drink when you're miserable, it'll only make you more so. Drinkers are people who're looking for easy solutions to their problems. The short cuts. There aren't any. Problems have to be faced and solved. You don't do anything with them by getting besotted, and pretending they don't exist."

A somewhat irresponsible friend makes an appeal for financial assistance. Kate writes to her father, and asks him to issue a check. He does so and says, "I sent the check to Soandso. As to your response to this appeal—I think it does great credit to your heart, and none at all to your head."

One drizzly Friday afternoon in the winter of 1947, Ruth and I were driving up to our place in Sandy Hook, Connecticut, for the weekend. The rain held intimations of snow, and the murky Merritt Parkway was beginning to have slippery spots.

Ruth is nervous in a car, and the worsening storm was adding to her unease. I sang her the entire score of *The Cat and the Fiddle* by Jerome Kern and Otto Harbach, but failed to relieve the tension.

I decided it would be best if I could get her to talk. She is always at her most relaxed when she is on.

"Tell me something fascinating," I suggested.

"I was once in a terrible wreck," she said.

"More fascinating than that."

"It was in France," she said. "Rain mixed with snow, just like this, and the car slid right off the road."

A passing sign read, "Entering Connecticut."

"Tell me something interesting about Connecticut," I persisted.

She thought for a moment and said, "Well, the story of the Whitneys and the Masseys. That's pretty interesting."

"Tell it."

She did, and it was, indeed, engrossing.

Raymond Massey and his wife, Adrianne Allen, were a successful theatrical couple. William Dwight Whitney and his wife, Dorothy, of New Haven, Connecticut, were both brilliant lawyers and close friends of the Masseys. Trouble in the Massey marriage. Adrianne confidentially consults Bill for advice on the mechanics of separation and divorce. At the same time, Ray confides in Dorothy. The next steps in the developing farrago are known only to the participants. The climax, however, was that after simultaneous divorces, Bill Whitney married Adrianne Allen and Ray Massey married Dorothy Whitney. Both the new marriages are still in happy existence after some thirty years.

Ruth's account of this, and my interpolated questions, succeeded in getting her mind off the road. Unfortunately, it also succeeded in taking *my* mind off the road and I missed our turnoff. Attempting to find my way back to it, I got lost and we blundered about on the back roads for an hour before finding our way home. No matter. One point in the account turned out to be as powerful as that one potent spermatozoon penetrating the ovum. The idea of a pair of married lawyers as adversaries in a case was instantly promising from a dramatic point of view.

Shortly after dinner, we began to talk it out and did not stop until almost four in the morning.

We awoke to find that the idea still seemed good, and we continued to amplify it during the weekend. In development, it seemed that the contest should involve some sort of male-female dispute, such as an application of the double standard.

Automatically, we found ourselves referring to the husband of our pair as "Spence," while "Kate" became the name for his spouse.

By the end of the weekend, we had decided to drop our individual projects, and get to work together on the screenplay of this one.

After a short stay in New York, we holed up in the country and in due course emerged with the script of what was later to be made as *Adam's Rib*. (Our original title, *Man and Wife,* was quickly vetoed by the Metro-Goldwyn-Mayer front office as being dangerously indiscreet.)

We sent it at once to Spencer and Kate, who responded affirmatively. It was submitted to Dore Schary, then head of the studio. He read it and phoned me.

"Hello," I said.

"Doll nose?" he asked.

When I heard this greeting, I knew all was well.

By general agreement, George Cukor was engaged to direct. Our project was under way.

I believe that casting—the right player in the right part—is the most vital element of theatrical or film production. To this end, we attempted to acquire the best players for every part, no matter how small.

In those days, Metro had no less than eighty players under permanent contract and the danger was that they might load the cast with their regulars who, although perfectly able, tended to make every Metro picture seem like every other Metro picture.

We suggested several bright young players from New York who had not yet appeared in films, such as Tom Ewell, David Wayne, Jean Hagen, and others.

One other project, at another studio, was simultaneously occupying my attention. Columbia Pictures had bought the film rights to my play, *Born Yesterday,* and production plans were under way. I was urging Harry Cohn, the dynamic and didactic president of Columbia, to use Judy Holliday and Paul Douglas in the roles they had so stunningly created.

Cohn would have none of it.

He had an actor, Broderick Crawford, under contract who was, in his opinion, perfect for the part. Moreover, Crawford had recently won an Academy Award for his performance in *All the King's Men.*

As to the girl, he owned Rita Hayworth (a big star). Also Kim Novak, also Lucille Ball. There was even a little dark (blonde?) horse, a contract bit player named Marilyn Monroe. (In fact, she made a test for the part, but Cohn did not take the trouble to step into the projection room adjoining his office to look at it.)

I urged Cohn to make a test of Judy Holliday.

"Don't waste my money," he said. "You don't seem to understand. On the stage you can get away with a broad looks like that, because the audience sits far enough away, but with the camera movin' in she'd drive people out."

I left one of these conferences with Cohn one morning and drove across the city to the Metro-Goldwyn-Mayer studio, trying to get my mind off this problem and on to the ones which lay waiting at Metro. I was unable to do so, and when I joined Ruth and Spencer and Kate and George, I was still full of the frustrated resentment I had accumulated at Columbia. I reported my most recent conversation with Harry Cohn.

Kate spoke. "Wait a minute. Listen to this. Wouldn't she be simply marvelous as the wife?"

"Who?" I asked. "What wife?"

"The wife in our picture. Tom Ewell's wife. The one who shoots him."

There she goes again, I thought. Impractical as ever.

"It's quite a small part, Kate," I pointed out. "Judy Holliday is a Broadway star. Why *should* she play it? I couldn't in good faith ask her to."

"You could build it up, couldn't you?" said Spencer.

I looked at Ruth, who shrugged noncommittally.

"Well, I suppose so," I said. "Yes. But it could never be anything more than a pretty good supporting part."

"She could score in it, all right," said Ruth.

Kate looked at me. "But don't you see? God, you're dumb sometimes. Cohn won't make a test of her, but *this* could be her test. It would be *better* than a test."

"Especially if she makes a hit," said Ruth.

"She will," said George.

For the next few days, Ruth and I put our attention on the script and attempted to improve that particular part. Visualizing and hearing Judy Holliday in it made the revision interesting and, finally, exciting. In the end, we honestly believed we had achieved one of those sure-fire supporting roles, in which the right actress could score decisively.

We submitted the script to Judy Holliday, who promptly turned it down.

We were all amazed. I discussed it with her, pointed out the strategy we had in mind, reminded her that I would have to let her out of the stage production of *Born Yesterday* to make it possible—a sacrifice on my part—but Judy continued to decline. Kate phoned her. No. Finally, George happened to be in New York a few days before shooting was to begin, and he looked her up. He had known her a few years earlier when she had played a bit for him in the movie of *Winged Victory*. She trusted him and seemed tempted but the answer was still in the negative.

George reported to Kate, who phoned Judy again and said, in that imperious way that usually flushes out the truth, "Why won't you do it, Judy? Tell me the real reason. The ones up to now don't make sense. You can tell me. Come on. The truth."

"Well," Judy blurted out, "I don't want to play a part where somebody calls me 'Fatso.' "

"Good God!" said Kate. "Is that all? One word! It happens *once.*"

"But it happens," said Judy.

(It was her sensitive point. She had gone into a spin a few weeks earlier when one of her costumes had come apart at the seams onstage, and a clowning assistant stage manager had begun to sing "Ju-dy's bustin' out all over!")

"They'll take the word out," said Kate. "They'll think of another word."

"They will?" asked Judy, in honest surprise.

"Of course," said Kate. "They're writers. They know lots of words."

A few days later the word was excised and Judy Holliday signed to play the role.

(This may be the place to record that the word later went back into the scene—at Miss Holliday's insistence.)

In the course of the shooting of *Adam's Rib,* Kate and Spencer involved everyone necessary in our master plan: the costume designer, Orry-Kelly; the hairdressers; the make-up people; the cameraman, Joe Ruttenberg; the supporting players; everyone and everything was aimed toward Judy's making a hit.

Judy's principal opening scene was shot in New York City, at Police Headquarters.

It involved Kate, as the lady lawyer, going down with her secretary to take a deposition from her client, Judy Holliday.

It was a long scene lasting about seven and a half minutes. Kate and George worked it out so that the shot was made in one continuous take, over Kate's back and onto Judy Holliday, as she makes her long statement.

The scene in the final picture is this take, because nothing else was ever shot for it. Kate convinced George to omit the customary answer shot (which would have been on her, over Judy), because she felt that nothing should distract from the impact of Judy's important introductory scene.

Incidentally, it tells something more about Kate to mention that Eve March, who played her secretary in this shot, played her secretary in *Coco* twenty-one years later.

The rest of the story is that the strategy worked perfectly. Judy Holliday made a standout hit in *Adam's Rib*. When Harry Cohn saw her in it, he was won over instantly and completely. He was, as a rule, stubborn and intractable and obdurate, but had an instinctive, almost religious appreciation of talent. "I kiss the feet of talent," was one of his continuing declarations.

He signed Judy for *Born Yesterday* without further testing. He engaged George Cukor to direct. The result won Judy the Academy Award for 1950 as Best Actress, as well as a film career that lasted until her death in 1965, at the age of forty-three.

We sat around, the four of us and George, the night of the day she died. I could not help recalling the generosity and unselfishness she had known from Kate and Spencer.

Kate brushed it aside. "Oh, hell," she said, "that was nothing. It was fun. It was the kind of thing you do because people have done it for you. My God, the help I got in the beginning from

Jane Cowl and Arthur Hopkins and John Barrymore. Phil Merivale and Mary Boland."

"And me," said George.

"And you, George. And so many others. You never get a chance to repay them, really, so what you do is repay them by doing what you can for someone *else* when the opportunity comes up."

When we were preparing the production of *Adam's Rib* the question of a song came up. I had done one I thought had the sought-for tone and fitted the situation: A songwriter neighbor (played by David Wayne) writes a name-song for the leading lady—"Madeline." My song was demonstrated.

"It's lousy," said Spencer. "I like it."

Cukor and Kate agreed with only the first part of his statement.

"Well," I bristled, "if you can get a better one, *use* it!"

Kate suddenly and surprisingly said: "Cole Porter!"

We all looked at her.

"What?"

"Let's get Cole Porter to do the song."

"Agreed," I said. "And how about Dwight D. Eisenhower to police the locations?"

"Cole Porter could do it," she said.

"We know that, honey," said George, a model of patience. "But how do we get him to?"

Kate considered the question for a long minute, and answered, "Ask him!"

That evening, when Kate turned up twenty minutes late for dinner, I suspected something had gone wrong. (Punctuality is a fetish with her.) I was in error. Something had gone right.

"Am I late?" she asked, and answered, "Yes. Sorry. Cole says you can't have a song called 'Madeline.' "

"When?" I asked, naturally bewildered.

"Just now. If you want to go over there after we eat, he'll tell you why. Why not, that is. My God!" she said, "I'm *famished.*"

"I don't see how," said Spencer. "You've been eating *people* all day."

Kate smiled and proceeded to give us one of her celebrated eating demonstrations. That girl can eat. A distinguished knife-and-fork expert of the old school. Two of everything, as a rule; and desserts like wildfire. Weight-watchers who observe her often go into shock, or demand a saliva test, or a recount. They cannot fathom how she puts it away at that rate and remains her reedlike self. Where does she put it? Is it possible to burn off that amount of food, even playing daily singles? The books say no. Here is the answer: Whatever she eats is consumed in the flame of tiptoe enthusiasm; correlated action of body, mind, and spirit; an appetite for life and living; and continuing excitement in every waking hour.

So she ate, while I regaled the table with two choruses of "Madelon" (one in English, one in French) and, shifting into an up-tempo, a chorus of "Paddlin' Madeline Home."

During a short pause, Kate explained that she had driven over to Cole's, given him a script and asked a favor.

"I think it's *fascinating,"* I said, "if you'll lend me that word of yours for a second, Kate, the ways people have of turning things down. I once actually had a slightly long-in-the-tooth actress turn down a youngish part. The way she put it was, 'I think that part is too young for me.' Get it? She wasn't too old for the part. The part was too young for her. And then there's the standard, 'It's great, but not for me.' And the marvelously disarming, 'I'm not *good* enough to play *that* part.' One I've been using lately with great success is, 'I love your play but feel it's a few years ahead of its time.' I must say Cole's come up with a pip, 'You can't have a song called "Madeline." ' Holy smoke!"

As we were finishing dinner, the phone rang. I picked it up.

"Amanda," said a voice.

"There's nobody here by that name."

"Amanda," the voice insisted. "This is Cole. Who's this?"

"This is Amanda," I said.

An hour later, we were all up at Cole's on Rockingham Drive, sitting in his glass room. (No, that is not a typo. *Glass room:* walls, doors, ceiling, fireplace; all done in shimmering glass. And it was raining hard. Imagine that.) He had read the script and had a notion for the song. Would we change the leading lady's name to Amanda?

Of course. Even though it went against the grain to give our Adam an alliterative wife. Still . . . Cole.

Eight days later, Cole Porter came to the studio, played and sang "Farewell, Amanda," and knocked us all sideways.

There remained the matter of the deal. A Cole Porter song came high and there was no provision for it in the budget. Cole, no slouch when it came to business, solved everything by taking no fee, and having Metro-Goldwyn-Mayer make a sizeable contribution (deductible) to the Red Cross.

The song worked wonderfully in the picture. . . .

Farewell, Amanda
Adios, addio, adieu. . . .

The orchestra at Maxim's in Paris used to go into it every time Spencer came in. I still hear it once in a while on the radio.

People seldom say "no" to Katharine Hepburn, which I suppose is the reason it breaks her heart when they do.

Consider the case of *The Millionairess* by George Bernard Shaw. He wrote it in 1938 expressly for Edith Evans, who had played brilliantly for him in *The Apple Cart.*

Miss Evans (now Dame Edith) recalls that GBS gave her a valuable piece of theater advice on that occasion.

"Go to Paris and buy your wardrobe there," he said. "You do see, my dear—don't you?—that when you play an intellectual part in an intellectual play it is imperative that you dress *beautifully.*"

But Miss Evans rejected the new play.

"Too icy for now," she said. "One wants warmth and feeling

in the theater these days." It was an old story to Shaw. He had written *Pygmalion* for Mrs. Patrick Campbell, who, for years, turned it down flatly; *Captain Brassbound's Conversion* for Ellen Terry, who would not hear of it; and now this. He would wait. This time he was wrong. He was never to see his play on the London stage.

The Millionairess was played by Sybil Thorndike to an indifferent reception at the Malvern Festival and for one reason or another did not come to London. Shaw's popularity in his homeland waxed and waned throughout his long and remarkable life.

In 1952, Hugh Beaumont of H. M. Tennent, Ltd., agreed that Katharine Hepburn and *The Millionairess* were meant for each other.

Kate was living in Irene Selznick's Beverly Hills mansion. We called one afternoon and heard peals of wild laughter coming from upstairs. A party, no doubt. We would join it. We went up and found Kate, script in hand, quite alone, sitting on the floor and laughing uproariously.

"Do you know this play?" she asked. *"The Millionairess?* Funniest goddam thing I've ever read."

"I've played it," said Ruth, "in summer stock. You'd be terrific in it."

"Listen to this line," said Kate, and read us the whole of Act Two.

She was an over-the-moon success in *The Millionairess* in London. Robert Helpmann was her leading man and Michael Benthall the director—the merry beginning of a trio of great friends, who have since worked and traveled and picnicked together joyfully.

Following London, the Theatre Guild and especially Lawrence Langner, for whom Kate had admiration and affection, insisted she play the play in New York—for a limited engagement, at least.

The magic of Broadway had by this time lost much of its power over Kate, and she was uncertain. In the end, she did it—

for Lawrence. Again, she triumphed and the Shubert Theatre sold out for the run.

The next stop, logically, was to transfer the success to film. Kate took charge. First there was the difficult matter of the rights—still controlled by Gabriel Pascal, that last great practical joke GBS played on the world. Eventually, who knows how, she achieved the rights, using her own money since she could not interest a motion-picture company. After a number of dead ends and wrong turns, she found her way to Preston Sturges, as fine a comic intelligence and as able a film director as America has produced. The play and the player enchanted him. Together they set to work. He moved into her house in New York and they emerged, months later, with a beautifully conceived, hilariously written shooting script. Sturges, the wild, erratic genius; and Kate, the practical disciplinarian, had formed an ideal working pair.

At last it was what is called "a package." Shaw, Sturges, Hepburn. The story, the screenplay, the director, and star—plus a pre-tested smash hit on two continents.

The turndowns began. Schedule and budget were revised downward. Still no takers. Hollywood, New York, London. Kate said she would take a large cut and gamble. Later, Sturges said he would, too. The answer was no. Personal friends, close contacts. No, no, no. Finally, Kate offered to forego reimbursement of her considerable expenditures, work for nothing, and pay Sturges. No.

A year or more of this and Kate surrendered to fate. In all our years, I had never seen her downed.

"I'm licked," she said one night, looking drawn. "It's gone on too long. I'm going to stop. I don't think I could bear one more—" That was as far as she got.

We sat around, sharing the comfort of the silence. The fire was roaring in her grate, but seemed to be giving off damned little heat.

I looked at that face and thought of all it had meant to millions; of her accomplishments; of her contributions; of how much so many had gained because of her. Now she faced closed minds and deaf ears.

I remembered what a wise old Broadway failure had once said to me, "If you're looking for justice, you might as well start by skipping Shubert Alley and the movie company front offices. There's more justice in any meat market in town."

Years later, a film version of *The Millionairess* was released. It was without wit, style, or pace. There was in it no more than a hint of Shaw, and unhappily, no Katharine Hepburn.

When she had put it all into perspective, she said, "Hell, I shouldn't have carried on so—it's happened to me plenty of times before, but of course I'd forgotten them—who was it talked about that lovely trick our memory plays and lets us remember mainly the good things?—Good Lord, I can remember being absolutely besotted by O'Neill's *Mourning Becomes Electra.* I wanted to do it at Metro with Garbo—wouldn't that have been *ravishing?*—me in the Alice Brady part and Garbo in Nazimova's?—perfect for it—her Swedish background and all the sea stuff going back to Leif Ericson—me, New England to the core—never worked so hard on a project in all my life. I got Lilly Messenger on my side—she was Mayer's Scheherazade in those days, you remember—used to tell him the stories. Well, *Mourning Becomes Electra* is a pretty hard story to tell—in the theater it played from five o'clock in the afternoon until after eleven at night—the audience had to have a dinner break—we finally got the great man's ear and it took Lilly almost two and a half hours to give him no more than a synopsis—L.B., remember, was very religious, and when she used the word 'incest'—that *did* it! He said no, and kept saying no and the whole thing cooled—definitely. . . . Then there was another time when Walter Huston—my God, what an actor he was!—asked me if I'd do a movie with him of *Desire Under the Elms*—he'd played it on Broadway and was an enormous success—but it all came to nothing. Amazing—isn't it?—how many things have been scotched by the know-nothings? Is it going to be better now, do you suppose? Now that the big studios are finished and we're all more or less independent?"

"In some ways, yes," I replied. "But now you don't have the advantage of build-up and follow-up and carefully designed careers. There was an advantage in having a big studio and its organization everywhere in the world on the lookout for stories and plays and novels and co-stars; certain creative producers developing combinations. Still, that soon degenerated into a sort of packaging and marketing. Sausage machines."

"Yah. Yah. I'm sure it's going to be better this way—more freedom of choice and risk and challenge—less money, of course, but that never seemed to help the pictures or the performances, did it?"

"No."

"But then—in some ways—I miss the old studios—your own dressing room—a kind of home, a headquarters, a great spirit of camaraderie."

"You remember, Kate, when you re-signed with Metro after a couple of bum years and I said to you, 'How can you stay with that studio? They're giving you such lousy parts and such stinking pictures.' And you said, 'Oh, yes, but they're *marvelous* when you come through Chicago and have to change trains.' "

In the summer of 1954, Ruth and I were living in the South of France at St. Jean-Cap Ferrat. There had been talk that Kate and Spence would join us there for a time.

One morning, she phones and explains that it is impossible for her to come, but asks us to urge Spencer to do so. She has to go to Hartford and will come along later. She lets us in on a secret. She has to have an operation—minor, but still. . . . She prefers Spencer far away to spare him any strain.

We follow her instructions. Ten days later, we meet the *U.S. Constitution* at Cannes and drive Spencer to our rented villa.

Les Rochers is run-down, but in its day must have been grand. It was built by Paris Singer for Isadora Duncan who, as a result of an ill-timed quarrel, never lived in it. Spencer thinks it a riot; not only the place itself, but the fact that we should be occupying it. Half an hour after his arrival, we are all swimming about in the bay in front of the house. It is a perfect day. Spencer is doing his spouting-whale act.

Ruth, floating (figuratively and literally), says, "Oh, Spence, isn't this wonderful?"

Spence, on his back, spouts and says, "Yup. And it's no more than what we deserve."

Our somnolent life goes on happily for a week, Spencer rising at five every morning to watch the sun come up and the fishing boats go out; reading, napping, resting, going to Mass every morning. Ruth and I are at work. We all meet each day for the first time at lunch. Spencer reads and reads and reads. We walk and explore.

He is on the phone daily with Kate. Secrets cannot be kept from so sensitive a man. He discovers what is happening. It throws him into a controlled panic and I do not think he takes it kindly that we have kept a secret from him. Still, he understands the problems of divided loyalty.

As though some dramatic complication were needed, in the seventh or eighth reel, a general strike hits the area. There is no phone service, no telegraph. The railroads stop. There is no mail, incoming or outgoing. It is, in sum, nothing less than the terrifying paralysis of a general strike. Spencer goes to pieces. I offer to drive him to Italy to make a phone call and perhaps stay there. We pile into the car, all three, and drive the crowded roads across the border. We check into an Italian hotel, but the phones there are overloaded because of the French crisis and we cannot get a call through to Hartford. We try everything: bribery, corruption, rank pulling. Nothing works. I suggest we stay the night and keep trying the following day, but Spencer reveals that he does not feel well. We get him home and send for a doctor. An ugly and painful rash has developed around Spencer's middle. The doctor diagnoses it incorrectly as *une piqûre de méduse,* or jellyfish sting.

"Very common," he says, "in this season. Be more prudent in the water."

He leaves a salve. It is utterly ineffective. The condition

worsens. Spencer is in severe pain. In the middle of the night I go and find another doctor. This one correctly identifies the ailment as *un zona*—shingles. There is nothing to do, he says, but deaden the pain narcotically and wait for it to run its course.

Downstairs, he asks, "M'sieu Spansaire, he is in some emotional strain?"

"Yes."

"Ah, well, when it goes, the *zona* will go."

The next day, with the help of an influential friend, we are permitted to put through an overseas call. Before doing so, however, the operator asks us to verify that it is *"Urgent. Très urgent."*

We assure her it is a matter of life and death.

The call comes through. Kate insists she is fine, that all is going well. Spencer says nothing of his difficulty and they chat gaily for half an hour.

Five minutes later, the agitated chief operator is on the phone accusing me of fraud and corruption and treason. The call, she insists, was *"pas urgent,"* not at all *"urgent."* She accuses me of defrauding the country, betraying the strikers, of being a filthy, no-good *Amerloque* and assures me of a sentence to the guillotine, or perhaps she said that that was what *should* happen to me.

Later in the day, Spence wants to phone again. I tell him the story of the outraged operator. He insists I try again. Fortunately, I get another operator; but unfortunately, she has been briefed by the first one. Ruth helps. Spencer talks. At length, the new operator is cajoled and bullied into putting the call through. Waiting for it, we coach Spencer to make it—*please*—sound *urgent,* and not to talk for half an hour. The call comes through within two minutes. Reassured as to Kate's condition, he begins to tell her about the telephone situation, laughing, and making her laugh. All at once, he is cut off.

We try to re-establish the connection but this time the operator refuses to speak to us.

The next day, Spencer flies from Nice to London and a few days later, Kate joins him there.

Spencer has a new nose and throat man, Dr. Richard Thomas Barton.

"What happened to the other one?" I ask. "You used to swear by him."

"I don't want to go into it," says Spencer. "But he broke his shovel with me."

I understand but cannot relate the phrase.

I ask him what it means.

Spencer thinks hard and says, "Damned if I know. We've all said it for years. Wait a minute. I think I remember. Yeah. It was a hell of a lot of years ago. We were all working in this stock company . . . Baltimore, I think it was . . . and doing a new play every week and living on prunes and scotch. How the hell we ever learned our parts, I'll never know. It was a pretty informal bunch. We'd come wandering in and out. One day, Frank McHugh wasn't there when they needed him for a scene. Not all that important. Somebody read it in. But then, when he turned up, the director decided to raise hell with him, and poor little Frank had to stand there, with everybody watching, and the director bawling the living bejesus out of him. He tried not to give in but his nose got red and tears came to his eyes. After a while, the director stopped, and Frank went to his dressing room. Toward the end of the day, we were all standing around, the director came over and put his arm across Frank's shoulders and said, 'I'm sorry, Frank. I shouldn't have lost my temper like that. I want to apologize.' Frank stepped away and shook the guy's arm off and said, 'The hell with all that, mister. *You* broke your shovel with *me!*' Probably something passed down by hod-carrying ancestors, but we all knew what he meant, and we've said it ever since."

It may be that Kate's athletic skills have developed her superior resilience. She plays tennis daily and hard, swims constantly, walks and jogs and runs; rides her bike in Central Park, and although she can no longer spare the time for golf, she was (probably is) one of the best lady golfers in the country.

She is also one of its most accomplished sleepers, which may be why she is healthy, wealthy, and wise. Kate believes in sleep, in both its quantitative and qualitative aspects. She has been known to sleep fourteen hours out of twenty-four—but in those waking ten, look out.

She explains. "Dad believed health to be the most important factor in success, and exercise the most important in health. I can't remember when we didn't have a gym of one kind or another in our house—and he had all us kids working out all the time—running, jumping, swimming, golf, tennis—he inoculated us all with this idea and it's still there—in the blood—I die if I don't exercise."

Her athletic abilities led us, at the beginning of 1952, to a most enjoyable co-venture.

After the success of *Adam's Rib,* the studio was eager to have another picture from the same team: Spencer, Kate, George, Ruth, and me.

As I watched Kate playing tennis one day (she was taking a lesson from Bill Tilden) it occurred to me that her audience was missing a treat. She plays tennis like an actress, with a great sense of form and style. There is feeling in her game as well as skill. There is excitement.

(Recently, as she played her daily round on the courts of The Beverly Hills Hotel, a stranger crossed behind her. She yelled at him. When the game ended, she approached him, apologized, touched his arm and said, "Please try to understand. This game, you see, is my life." He asked me afterward what she had meant. I do not know.)

Ruth and I began to discuss a lady athlete as a part for Kate. Later a group of Lindy sports promoters I had known were hammered into a single such character for Spencer. Finally, *Pat and Mike* became a reality.

It has in it one of Spencer's most enchanting performances: a dark-shirted, full-blooded, no-nonsense sporting man.

I had written a line for Mike to say when he first encounters and appraises Pat, an outstanding amateur golfer. With an eye toward turning her pro and making her part of his stable, he hands her his card. She takes it and walks away. He speaks to his crony-assistant.

George shot it at a drinking fountain on the golf course. I drove out to watch because I particularly wanted to hear Spence say that line.

When the moment came, Kate walked away, Spencer got his cue and spoke. As he did so, he watched her leave (thus turning away from the camera), leaned over the drinking fountain, shot a stream of water into his mouth, and gave the operative word an extra twist of New Yorkese.

I was horrified. I felt that with all this the line would surely fail and that the moment would be wrecked. I mentioned it to George, who, in turn, spoke to Spencer. Take two. Exactly like the first, only more so. I left.

Months later, at the preview at the Capitol Theatre in New York, I tensed as the moment approached. I need not have troubled. The line came.

"Not much meat on 'er," Spence (as Mike) commented. "But what there *is* is *cherce!*"

The theater exploded.

I learned a lot from him. So did Kate. So did we all.

He claimed *he* had learned most from his idol, George M. Cohan, who once said to him, "Whatever you do, kid, always serve it with a little dressing."

Three

Paris, 1951. We are at the Raphaël again and Spencer has joined us.

It is difficult to get him to leave his suite. The only times he is willing to go out are at six in the morning and seven in the evening, or whatever time the light begins to fade.

For the rest, he is content to stay in. He is resourceful and imaginative and needs little outside stimulus.

We have taken him out several times to lunches, receptions, and a few dinners with friends, but it is always a strain.

I respect his eccentricities but they often get on my nerves, and I tell him so. The more I complain, the more he laughs. My discomfiture entertains and amuses him.

One night, as darkness fell, he put on his coat and his cap and his dark glasses, which meant that he was ready to go out and walk. This time, Ruth joined us. When we got downstairs, Spencer automatically headed for the Avenue Foch, but Ruth objected.

"Come on, Spence," she said. "You've done that enough. You're in a rut."

"Yes," he replied, "but it's a rut I happen to like."

"Let me show you a new one," she said. "It's a beautiful rut called the Champs-Elysées."

Spencer looked horrified. "What're you talking about?" he said. "It's full of people."

"That's exactly why, Spencer," I said. "Something to see. This is a city of life. That's its main attraction. Nobody's going to bother you. You've said so yourself."

"Said what so myself?"

"That people don't recognize you unless you want them to."

By this time, Ruth and I were firmly steering him toward the teeming avenue.

Once there, he appreciated it. He found something to enjoy every step of the way. The characters, the young, the types, the exotic hookers, the oddballs, the crowd.

His theory notwithstanding, many did recognize him, stopped, and looked back as he went by, pointing him out to others. He was not, however, disturbed in the least.

At the Rond-Point, we crossed the street carefully, heeding René Clair's admonition always to cross a Paris street in the company of nuns or children.

"They do not mind to hit the Premier," he had said, "or their own doctor, but never a nun and never a child. That is because France is actually run by its children. Sometimes under the supervision of the nuns."

We started back on the other side and soon approached the blazing neons advertising the attractions of the Lido.

"See that?" I asked.

"See what?"

"The Lido."

"What about it?"

"Nothing," I said. "Only that if you weren't so old and I wasn't so gutless, we'd be sitting inside there within the next five minutes, at a beautiful ringside table, having a whale of a time."

"A tourist trap," said Spence.

"That's how much you know," I said, scornfully. "It only has the most talented, skillful, accomplished, dazzling, night-club entertainment in the whole world. Everyone, everywhere copies it and that's what they wind up with. A copy. This is the real thing. Beauty, naked girls, sensational comedy, fantastic production."

Spencer stopped walking and asked, "Did you say 'naked girls'?"

"Certainly."

"You mean right out in front of everybody?"

"The most beautiful girls in the world," I said. "Not just French. These guys screen the globe."

"What makes you think we could get in?" he asked. "Look at the crowd."

"We can get in," I said confidently, "because I am Spencer Tracy."

I was right. Despite the long queues and the surging mass at the entry, a ringside table was provided a few minutes after I had approached the general manager and identified my guest.

The Lido was infinitely larger than I had expected it to be and more crowded. The moment we were seated, the lights dimmed and the floor beside us rose, hydraulically, to platform height. It was almost as though they had waited for Spencer before beginning.

Neither Ruth nor I nor Spence were prepared for what we saw. It was, indeed, as I had promised, spectacular. I ordered a bottle of champagne (since I thought it was expected of me), a Coke for Spencer, a ginger ale for Ruth, a bottle of Vichy for myself. Our table must have seemed a curious sight. Three filled, fluted champagne glasses and ranged in front of them: a Coke, a ginger ale, and a glass of mineral water.

Spencer was enjoying himself. I relaxed.

Midway through the performance, The Charlevilles were announced. I remembered them vaguely as a daring acrobatic act I had seen in Las Vegas. Americans. After they had performed five or six thrilling stunts, one of them came forward, and, in fractured French, began to make an announcement. I was only half listening until I heard him shout, "Spencer Tracy!" The spotlight began to play over our part of the audience, The

Charlevilles rushed to the edge of the platform and stood just above Spencer, pointing him out. The spotlight hit Spencer.

"Jesus," he muttered.

"Stand up," I said.

"No."

"And sit right down," said Ruth.

"All right," said Spencer, and slowly rose to his feet, as he waved a tentative salute. The ovation was deafening. Spencer blushed. One of The Charlevilles reached down to shake hands. Spencer took his hand and was suddenly, inexplicably, wafted up onto the stage. I could not imagine how it had been accomplished until I realized that it was a practiced trick of levitation, performed by all three partners.

What followed is not clear in my memory. I remember Spencer being lifted from the ground, held by two of the acrobats, becoming part of the act in the center of the stage. He was pale and clearly terrified. I pictured myself jumping up onto the stage and stopping it all by shouting at them that Spencer was not well, and to for God's sake leave him alone. Alas, I came to my friend's aid only in my head, having been shocked into frozen immobility. I saw the third member of the troupe begin a series of whirling back flips, moving toward the body tangle of which Spencer was a part. Flash bulbs began to go off—or was I only imagining them or was I about to faint? The drum roll increased in volume until, with a crash of cymbals, the whirler leaped high into the air and landed on Spencer's outstretched legs. I saw him wince. The audience cheered. The group, still entangled, scurried from the stage, suggesting a monstrous insect. The Charlevilles returned for their bows without, needless to say, Spencer. He appeared at our table two minutes later, following a backstage attendant. As he passed us he said, grimly, "Let's go."

We followed him out, threading our way through the tables. The audience applauded him, some rising to greet him and pat him on the shoulder as he passed.

In the foyer, the manager, all smiles, approached Spencer and regretted it at once. Spencer was raising hell. Our waiter appeared and handed me the check. I got out some money. Spencer yelled something at me, and "Shove it!" at the waiter. He grabbed the check, tore it up, and threw it at the manager, as he said, too quietly, "The William Morris Agency will bill you for my appearance here tonight and I hope you can *afford* it!"

We walked for twenty minutes in clouded silence. I could think of nothing to say.

As we parted, he said to me, "You look awful. What's the matter with you? Jesus, after all, *I'm* the one did the death-defying act at the Lido tonight."

"Good night, Spence," I said. "Sorry."

"Good night." He kissed Ruth, turned to me. "Oh, by the way, you better get me all those pictures, too. Boy! That's *all* I need. Night-club hi-jinks pictures plastered all over. They'll think Tracy's on the ol' heimerdeimer again. Good night, pal."

Troubled sleep, followed by a hectic morning. With the help of the M-G-M press department, most of the photographs were gathered, and a warning issued to the Lido regarding the use of any missing ones.

When Kate arrived that weekend, we told her what had happened. She did not believe a word of it until we showed her the photographs.

Spencer continued to display them with increasing pride in his feat until the day he left. Then he destroyed them all.

A few years later he said to me, wistfully, "Damn. I wish I had those shots of me doing my acrobatics with The Charlevilles. Remember? The Lido? There was one that was terrific. What'd you let me burn them for? You don't always use your noggin, do you?"

Kate does not read the trade papers, or *Variety,* or the theatrical columns. This detachment often leads to curious moments.

There was the time when we were preparing *Pat and Mike* at M-G-M. A young actor named Russell Nype had made a great success in *Call Me Madam* with Ethel Merman in New York, and had been signed by Metro to make a picture. He came to California, and for some reason it did not work out. He was wrong for the part, or the part was wrong for him. One of those unfortunate situations. After a few days of shooting, the studio realized he would have to be replaced at great expense and difficulty. They hoped to make a settlement with him but his agent, quite correctly, held out for the full amount. We were unable to see Dore Schary for several days because he was completely occupied with the Russell Nype situation. The town was buzzing with it. There were all sorts of items in the trade papers and on the Metro lot there was hardly anything else discussed except how Dore Schary was going to deal with the situation. He was new to the job of running a studio.

He had been a writer at Metro. At the writer's table someone had said, "Don't worry about Dore. He'll know how to handle that. After all, he's the new Irving Thalberg."

Harry Kurnitz said, "The new Irving *Thalberg?* He isn't even the old Dore *Schary!*"

Somehow the situation was resolved, and Russell Nype was replaced. A settlement was made, and the studio took a blow. When, finally, we did get in to see Dore Schary for a conference on *Pat and Mike,* the very first thing Kate said was, "Look, I've got a terrific idea for an actor to play my husband."

"Who?" said Dore.

Kate pulled a piece of paper out of her pocket and said, "He's just been in a show with Ethel Merman. Russell Nype."

The roof caved in.

Ruth and I went to the American Embassy in Paris to cast our absentee ballots in the Presidential election of 1952.

Leaving the stately building on that crisp October morning, I saw something in the corner of the garden which I had not seen before, although I had been to the embassy many times. A matter of light, I suppose. I walked over to look at the piece of statuary. It might easily have been a figure of Spencer Tracy but it was, of course, Paul Wayland Bartlett's remarkable rendering of Benjamin Franklin.

It started me thinking again about a long-dormant Franklin project, with the added impetus of perfect casting. And perhaps because this thinking was being done in Paris, the Parisian part of Franklin's life seemed to stand out as the most interesting.

In the course of the next year and a half, I worked on the subject intermittently and when I had what I thought was a workable plan for the film, I took it to Spencer.

It turned out he knew far more about Benjamin Franklin than I did, could quote from the *Autobiography* and from *Poor Richard's Almanack*.

"There's only one thing troubles me about playing Franklin in Paris," said Spencer.

"What's that?"

"You think I'm old enough?"

"More so every day, Flanagan."

And so we had a new subject, something to discuss endlessly.

Whenever Spencer and I were in Paris at the same time we took trips to Passy and found every spot, every hill, indicated in the research.

We submitted it to the front office at Metro, where the idea received a lukewarm reception.

"What do we care?" I said. "The thing to do is to get a script that's so sensational nobody will be able to turn it down."

Spencer nodded and flexed his jaw muscles. "There was a time," he said, "they'd have done anything I was willing to do. Why didn't you come up with the idea then?"

"You were too old then," I said.

"The trouble is," he said, "even if we both work for nothing, it would still be an expensive proposition, wouldn't it?"

"Well, maybe not if it could be done in Paris on natural locations, some special angle, keep it intimate, don't go for a great big superspectacle."

But no matter how confidently we talked, we understood it would not be an easy matter to achieve.

Once I mentioned the possibility of doing it in the theater.

Spencer looked at me for a full minute without saying anything.

"I've got something," he said to me on the phone one day, years later. "It's not Franklin but it's a little more practical. I'm sending it to you. Read it and let me know."

It was a novel called *Kotch* by Katharine Topkins, a charming and affecting story of an old man who befriends a pregnant teen-ager.

I saw it almost at once in the shape and style of the great Pagnol films of the early 1930s: *Harvest, Fanny, Marius, César.*

We met and talked and decided to do it.

Thus began an eight-month period of promises, rejections, maybes, cut-the-budget, still less, work for nothing, finally: All right. Whatever they say. A week later, they sent us a message: Sorry, we've changed our minds.

We did not discuss it at length but I could see Spencer was staggered by this one. He joked about it, bitterly.

"Well," he said, "I guess it's time to say yes to the television boys and go for the old getaway money."

He began to talk seriously of television and we considered a number of ideas. One that appealed to him was a series to be based on Joseph Mitchell's *McSorley's Wonderful Saloon* in which Spencer would play a New York bartender. Nothing came of it nor of a nearer-to-fruition plan for Spencer to narrate a documentary series based on American holidays.

A meeting with Georges Lourau, the French film producer, reactivated the Franklin project. I outlined it to him, and he responded with great enthusiasm, assuring me there would be no trouble whatever about financing it if it could be done as a French film in the English language, and if Spencer would commit himself.

I gave Spencer the first sixty pages of completed screenplay. He was interested but refused to believe the picture could be made. I decided to keep working on it, and I did, but nothing happened.

Long afterward, when he had finished *Guess Who's Coming to Dinner,* he announced at the dinner table that he had retired.

"One more," I said.

"No, I don't think so."

Kate said, "You always say that every time you finish a picture."

"This time I mean it," he said. Then, sensing my sudden gloom, added, "Unless Jasper can snow them into Franklin. I doubt it, though."

A few nights later, as we were ending our evening telephone chat, he said, "I'm sorry as hell about Franklin."

"What do you mean?"

"I'd have been good in that. Yup. That would've been a good one."

The next day he was dead.

Yes. That would have been a good one.

There is no doubt that Kate expanded Spencer's horizons and kept him alive in the last of his years.

She is a doctor's daughter, and knows a great deal about medicine and surgery and the men who practice it. Her extensive private list of physicians in New York, California, London, and Paris, is the result of years of careful investigation, triple-checking, and personal experience. No matter what goes wrong with her or her friends in whatever part of the world, she knows the man to deal with it.

She is not remotely hypochondriacal, but does seem to take pleasure in being a patient. It is her way of showing respect for the medical profession.

Her delicate skin was damaged by exposure to the violent Congo climate when she went there to make *The African Queen.* She correctly diagnosed the little rough spots as skin cancers, and lost no time in having them dealt with surgically. She became an expert on the subject, and for a year or two her friends were all subjected to squint-eyed scrutiny.

She searched my face tenderly one afternoon, reached out and touched my cheek. I was moved and surprised by what I thought a rare show of affection. Not at all. She was simply practicing medicine, looking for skin cancers on my face. She found none, but at the end of the examination, ordered sharply, "Stay out of the sun."

When Spencer began to experience some difficulty with his upper-respiratory system early in 1963, she undertook the supervision of his medical care. I recall his making light of it.

"Yup," he told me over the long-distance phone. "I'm on the blink. Well, hell, so would anybody be who once stayed drunk for twenty-five years!"

"What're you talking about, Spence?" I asked. "God damn, you just say any old thing, don't you? Twenty-five years."

"You heard me."

"But what do you mean?"

"I mean," said Spencer patiently, "that for twenty-five years, I wasn't sober. There was a time there I used to take two-week lunch hours. I wasn't the only one. There was that whole bunch of us. We managed okay. Fact is, I did some of my best work in those days. We even played polo."

"Drunk?" I asked.

"Well, maybe not drunk," he said. "Don't be so goddam district attorney. Say mulled. You know, always with a nice little bun on, just enough to cushion the shock of life. Naturally, the bigger the shock, the bigger the cushion a guy needed. And you know, considering the amount I put down, it's a damn wonder I didn't come unglued before this. But don't worry. Ol' Kathy's got it in hand. In fact, she's out now taking a treatment for what's the matter with me, and if it doesn't kill her, she's going to let *me* take it!"

Aspects of medicine, diet, and exercise were carefully handled in a way he could not have done himself. An oxygen tank appeared in the hallway of his house, an Exercycle in his room, a vibrator on his reading table. Water, water, everywhere. Spencer was being cared for.

The memory of a comical, scarifying, daffy time comes flooding back with pieces missing and parts of the sound track blurred.

It is early in the spring of 1961. Spencer has completed *Judgment at Nuremberg* and is preparing to leave Germany, totally fatigued but happy. Kate is with him.

Ruth and I are in Paris at the Hotel Raphaël. They phone, and I urge them to stop in Paris for a few days. It is out of season. The city is tranquil. The hotel is virtually deserted, and I think I can get them several of the small suites up on the roof—one with a terrace, maybe, for Spencer. All right, they say, try.

The arrangements work out so well that the days stretch into restful holiday weeks. Spencer rarely leaves the hotel, content on the roof with his terrace. He sits there at dawn watching the sun come up, and observing the minute details of the city coming to life.

In Paris, he finds one particular walk attractive: Leave the Hotel Raphaël, walk three blocks to the wide Avenue Foch, and all the way to the Bois de Boulogne. Into the park for a while and return on the other side of the Avenue Foch. We take this route many times, sometimes at seven in the morning, other times in the late afternoon.

I ask questions and he answers them. There are times when he says, "None of your business."

I ask for advice on the subject of insurance, explaining my adverse emotional reaction to it. He shows me my error and outlines exactly the sort of program I should have. I have it.

We talk of medicine and I confess that if I could begin again, I would become a doctor. I tell him I have been reading a biography of Harvey Cushing.

He stops walking and says, "We knew him. Louise and I."

"You did?"

"Sure. We went to see him through some personal connections after we'd had Johnny in several different places. Cushing was a great head surgeon and had done more ear operations than anyone. He examined Johnny and called us in and told us there was nothing that could be done. And he looked at Louise and said, 'Mrs. Tracy, you should consider yourself a very lucky woman. Just think of the opportunity this gives you to do something for your son.' He was quite a man."

We talk about drinking. He tells me he thinks I drink too much. We had been to a slow reception the previous afternoon and I certainly had taken more than my share. Ruth and Spencer and Kate had been amused by my post-party antics, but this was the morning after. The party was over and my good friend Spencer was speaking seriously.

"There's nothing wrong with a drink," he said, "and there's nothing right with a drunk. Booze kills brain cells. For good. You don't believe that, ask around. That's why big drinkers reach a point where it's too late to stop. Anyway, what the hell are you drinking about? I can understand it when some poor son-of-a-bitch whose life is empty and without hope wants to fuzz it all up for a few hours to give himself a rest. But what's *your* problem?"

"Nothing. I enjoy it."

He stops walking and turns me toward him. He is not joking now. His eyes burn into me as he says, "Enjoy something else!"

Everything during this time was fine, except that the food at the Raphaël was indifferent. Among other things, Paris means food, and it seemed a pity not to be able to partake of some of the superlative offerings. But restaurants were out. Kate and Spence had never been in a restaurant together.

Late one afternoon, during our stay at the Raphaël, Spencer began to hanker for a steak. We saw an opening and plunged in. We began to extol the wonders of the Cochon d'Or, a steak house situated in the slaughterhouse district, La Villette. Ruth is an outstanding food describer, and so effective was her dramatization of the dinner it was possible to have there, that by the time she had finished, my appetite was entirely satisfied. I felt as though I had already *had* my steak.

Not Spencer. He rose quietly and began putting on his necktie.

"Where you going?" asked Kate.

"Why," said Spence, turning French, "to ze Cosho Dior, hinky dinky parley-voo for ze steakey."

Kate, who had been lying on the floor was on her feet—as Spencer used to say—"in one frame."

They exchanged a look I shall not attempt to describe fully.

It had questions in it, and worries; time and deprivation; it had the kind of youth in it that comes only after age.

Spence said, "Let's go, Kathy."

Ruth and Spence out the front. Kate and I out the back. They in the Columbia Pictures car. We, in a taxi. The Cochon d'Or was virtually deserted when we got there, but as our glorious dinner progressed, five or six tables became occupied. No one bothered us, but the stars had been recognized by several new arrivals.

The atmosphere at our table became slightly tense, but Spencer was enjoying his perfect steak so much that it seemed well worth the difficulty. Kate ate heartily and swiftly—too swiftly, I thought, but said nothing, recognizing that in this situation any sort of faultfinding remark might easily trigger a scrap. Ruth worked hard to keep up the buoyant mood, and I talked too much.

I suggested we have no dessert, an idea which died stillborn. Spencer's sweet tooth was hollow and the Cochon d'Or had precisely the thing with which to fill it: a billowing container of floating island. Ruth joined him. Kate, perhaps because of my earlier suggestion, had *two* desserts—an order of chocolate mousse and a huge slice of hazelnut cake. I had only proposed the no-dessert idea because the place was filling up.

"Ate too much," said Kate, and took a slow, deep breath.

"No!" said Spence. "Have some dessert. Never mind what *he* said. Go ahead."

"Too much," she said. "Crikey, it was good though, wasn't it?"

"Superb."

She lit a cigarette.

"Okay to go now?" I asked.

"Okay with me," said Spence. He studied Kate. "But better check with Laura La Plante there. She may want another steak. Look at her. She looks hungry."

I looked at her. She did not look hungry, but she did look odd. Had she been a television image, I would have reached out and begun fiddling with the hue and color dials under her face. A blue-green tint suffused it as she sat there, smoking happily, and smiling beatifically. I looked about to see if something had happened to the lights in the room. Nothing. But now all the color had left her face. I glanced at Spencer, and, being nicely in wine, thought, There it is! Her color has gone over to *his* face. He was double pink.

I said to Kate, "Are you all right?"

"No," she replied gaily, tamping out her cigarette. "I'd better go." She surveyed the establishment swiftly. "Somewhere. I think. Yah."

"I'll come with you," said Ruth.

"No," said Kate. "I'm going to need *him*. Thanks though."

She and I rose. I assumed that since I had been chosen, we were going out into the air, but I heard her say to a passing waiter in lovely French, *"Où est le lavabo, s'il vous plaît?"*

"Là-bas, mademoiselle, là-bas," he pointed with a plate of asparagus vinaigrette.

Ruth and Spencer sat frozen. Kate strode toward the ladies' room. I followed ridiculously, thinking, What do I do when we get there? We went through the back room, mercifully deserted at this hour. As I continued after her, a resting *sous chef* jumped up and attempted to head me off.

"Non, non," he said, pointing to the other side of the room. *"Non, non, pas ici."*

When I failed to heed him, and continued to follow Kate, he started toward me. At the same moment, an attendant came out of the door marked *"Dames."*

I could sense a situation in the making. I was right, but I had the wrong situation.

Kate stopped suddenly, reached out, grasped a handful of air, and keeled over. Too much strain had led to too much food consumed too quickly.

Members of the restaurant staff went into effective action at once and assisted. We lifted her from the floor and put her onto a banquette. My Army first-aid training came in handy at long last. I loosened clothing, rubbed wrists. People were bringing things. An ice pack. I could smell vinegar. A window was opened. I leaned over, slapped her gently, and called her name—all her names. The *vestiaire* had removed her shoes and was massaging her ankles.

As my anxiety peaked, the color flooded back into her face with a rush. She opened her eyes. A moment.

"My-y-y Gg-o-d-d-dd!" she said.

"Are you all right?"

"Sure, sure. Stupid. Damn."

She sat up.

"Hold on a minute," I said. She was thanking the staff as I went back to the main room and found Ruth sitting at the table, alone, pale.

"She fainted," I explained. "Perfectly all right now."

"I've paid the check," said Ruth. "Tips and everything. Can we go?"

"In a minute," I said. "Where's our boy?"

"He left."

I went outside. Spencer was sitting in the front seat of the car, beside the driver. He looked grim in the way that only he could look grim. He seemed to be, at that moment, the inventor of grim, the copyright owner.

"She just fainted," I explained. "Perfectly all right now, though. Nothing to worry about. The excitement, I guess, huh?" No response. Grim to grimmer. I babbled on. "This going out bit—restaurants, Café Society—she's just not used to it. Don't you think that's it?" Silence. He stared straight ahead through the windshield as if the car were going ninety miles an hour, and not simply standing still. I plowed on. "Listen," I said. "What do you think? Should I phone both trade papers or give this one to *The Hollywood Reporter* exclusive?"

Spencer, usually a perfect audience for even the limpest of my jokes, sat there, carved on Mount Rushmore.

I was failing to communicate with him, but someone tapped me on the shoulder. I turned. There was no one within twenty feet. Odd. I turned back to Spencer, but before I could speak, was tapped on the shoulder again. This time I whirled about.

No one. Then I saw the white pigeon droppings on the shoulder of my dark suit.

I was not surprised. It seemed a natural, normal, fitting climax to the kind of evening it had turned out to be. I took off my jacket and started back into the restaurant, as Kate and Ruth came out, arm in arm.

I threw my jacket into the trunk of the car. We got in and started off.

Kate said, "I'm *so* sorry. I guess I'm not made for public life, that's all."

"It's a thing you've got to do more often," said Ruth, "or not at all."

Spencer remained stony, but at one point, I said something that made him turn to me. He started to say something, stopped, and asked, "What the hell happened to your jacket?"

When I told him, he laughed too hard.

Four days after the misadventure of the Cochon d'Or, we were sitting on the terrace atop the hotel, having tea. Spencer looked up at us and said, casually, "I'm taking everybody out to dinner tonight. Me."

"What?"

"That's right. What's everybody so surprised about? I know places. I hear things, y'know. I get around."

"Where we going?" I asked.

"Oh," he replied elegantly, "there's this *charming* little place in the Rue du Cherche-Midi. 'Châtaignier.' I understand they have great chicken, and *sensational ambiance.*"

Actually, some of his old Metro-Goldwyn-Mayer pals had been in to see him and had recommended it. He had driven over that afternoon and checked it out.

"The great thing is," he continued, "it's so small that when Kathy faints, there's no room for her to fall down." He looked at me and went on. "Also—extra added attraction—no trees, so no pigeon danger for *you,* Jasper."

"I won't faint," said Kate, indignantly. "Why should I?"

Before we left, I slipped a box of ammonia capsules into my pocket, just in case. A damned good thing I did, too, because

Spencer, having recommended the chicken, ordered a steak, bit hard on a piece of bone, broke a front tooth, and we all had to take off suddenly in search of a dentist. On a Sunday.

As a result of this excitement and despite her promise, Kate did faint again, but managed to wait until we were back in the car. The ammonia capsules came in handy.

I phoned friends for help for Spencer, but since it was Sunday evening, no one was available. The emergency, however, had to be dealt with.

"I think I'll call Christian," said Kate. "What time is it in New York?"

"Christian" is what she calls Dr. Carlisle C. Bastian, her close friend and dentist, who has long been responsible for protecting one of the celebrated features of that great face.

"What can he do on the transatlantic phone?" asked Spencer, reasonably.

"Recommend someone here," she replied.

"Hold it," I said. I had suddenly remembered that in the elevator of the apartment house at 70 Avenue Marceau, where our friends, the Seidmanns, lived, I had seen a little plaque that read:

> Dr. Somethingorother
> Dentiste
> 3ème étage

I reported my recollection.

"Let's go," said Kate. "It's worth a try."

The dentist was at dinner with his family when we arrived. He was understandably startled by the group in his hallway. He recognized Spencer and Kate, showed us into his reception room, and left.

He returned a few minutes later, wearing eyeglasses and a white smock. We were in luck. The dentist spoke English, had studied in New York, and, in fact, was acquainted with Dr. Bastian. The examination began.

Yes, the broken tooth could be repaired. The work could begin at once. The first step would be to kill the nerve.

"I don't think so," said Kate.

The dentist looked at her with no little surprise.

"You don't?" he asked.

"No," said Kate. "Christian doesn't like killing nerves."

"But I can assure you, Miss Hepburn, is no other way to make the work."

"Well, anyway," said Kate, "don't do it until we've talked to him. May I use your phone?"

The call went through swiftly, but Dr. Bastian was not at home.

"Damn," said Kate. "Now, what about right now? What can we do for the night? Does it hurt, Spence?"

"I can stand it."

"Well, then," she said, "just something to hold it till morning."

The dentist, now completely submissive to Kate's takecharge, saw himself as her assistant. Together they worked out a plan for the night, involving a temporary cap.

Dr. Bastian, when reached the following day, confirmed what Kate had said. He would prefer that the nerve be left intact. He held a long telephonic consultation with the French dentist. Kate and Spencer returned to New York, where Dr. Bastian did what was necessary.

Some months later, sitting in Dr. Bastian's chair myself, I asked, "That was something, wasn't it? About Spencer's tooth."

"Yup," said Dr. Bastian.

"Did you have to kill the nerve?"

"Nope."

"I'll be damned. Kate knows all about this stuff, doesn't she?"

"Yup."

Before Kate and Spencer left Paris, however, there were to be two more restaurant encounters.

Gilbert Miller, who knew about such things, had recommended an exceptional bistro, called Monteil, in Les Halles, the market place of vibrant memory. Obscure, out of the way, and we chanced it. It proved to be all Gilbert had said after we had, with some considerable difficulty, found it.

Through a passage with a cheese stall on one side and a fresh herb stand on the other, up a flight of back stairs, along a dark corridor to a room containing six tables.

Ours was ready.

The single *plat du jour*—a memorable *pot au feu*—was served and we relished it. Best of all, no one in the room paid any attention to the presence of Kate or Spencer. Obviously, they had not been recognized. We all relaxed. A single bad moment when we declined a carafe of *vin ordinaire*. At that time none of us drank much, and Spence had not had a drink of any kind for about ten years. (The prestigious Dr. de la Chappelle of New York City had finally convinced him—using plain talk and X rays—that continued indulgence might be fatal.)

A delicate salad with one cheese (Pont l'Évêque); finally, a small silver platter that held four perfect raspberry tarts and a bowl of freshly whipped cream.

Coffee, after which Spencer paid the check. All at once—a ceremony. The *patron,* a corpulent markety man, stood before us, making a speech. In one hand he held a capacious, bowl-like glass; in the other, an ancient bottle with a patina of crusted dust. Squinting, I made out the word "Marc" and it struck terror, since this is a brandy distilled from wine sediment and is known to be dangerously potent.

Applause, during which every person in the room rose. The speech, delivered in the Alexandrine rhythms of Racine, continued,but the boss's Marseilles accent made it sound to me as though I were listening with cotton-stuffed ears. I caught "*M'sieu Span-saire*" several times and "*Mam'selle Ka treen*" even more. "*Artistes du monde—honneur—p'tit établissement—très heureux—jour de fête pour toutes Les Halles—dans la manière habituelle.*"

Still talking, he poured a generous portion of Marc into the glass, set aside the bottle, raised the glass four times, once to each of us, as he repeated, "*A la vôtre!*"

Somewhere in here, one of the carried-away customers broke into song:

À la tienne
Étienne!
À la tienne
Mon vieux. . . .

That was as far as he got. I recognized the rude, men-only drinking song René Clair had taught me. The boss stepped over and pushed the hapless singer down the stairs. He returned, said *"Pardon,"* bowed, and continued the toast. He ended it, quaffed mightily, and handed the glass to Kate. She demurred, but the moment would not have it so. She took a small sip. Ruth's turn. She pretended. Me. I used it as an excuse to take a drink. As the boss handed the glass to Spencer, Kate and I exchanged a petrified look, but Ruth's hands shot out and grabbed the glass. She stood up, said something about not having had her fair share or some such obfuscation, and drained the glass. In the applause and excitement that followed, we made our getaway.

As we walked toward the spot where the car was waiting, I watched my wife with apprehension. Kate regarded her with awe, and Spencer enveloped her with his look of love.

Our restaurant life would thus have come to an end had not René taken me to lunch at a new place, only a few steps from the Raphaël, called Potel et Chabot. The firm had been, for a century, one of the great Parisian pastry shops, but the new owner had recently installed a restaurant upstairs, which René claimed was as fine as any in the city.

He urged me to have a specialty of the house: a napoleon.

I said, "I hate napoleons."

"You will like this one," he said.

He was right. This napoleon was unlike any other I had ever known. It was an individual piece of pastry, made to order, and took a worth-waiting-for while.

René explained that it was not until a waiter had placed an order for this delicacy that the paper-thin sheets of pastry dough were placed in the oven. Meanwhile, the ingredients for the filling—called *crème frangipane*—were mixed and beaten in a great container set in ice.

At the proper moment (the choice of which, René said, was the art—like Henri Cartier-Bresson knowing precisely when to click the shutter of his camera) the pastry came out of the oven, was cut and combined with the *crème frangipane* to build a fresh hot-cold masterpiece.

I had only to describe the above process to Spencer to make him forget all our unfortunate restaurant visits. When I explained that there was a private room up there, and that we could walk over—the evening was joined and we went.

We ate lightly and sparingly to leave room for what we had come for. When it came it did not disappoint. I had one, Spencer and Ruth had one each and split a second. Kate had two of her own and did not faint. She toyed with the idea of a third until she was shouted down.

"All right," she said, "all right. I won't. But I'm going to order one to take back to Phyllis. I want her to have one. She *loves* French pastry."

"Nothing doing," said Spencer.

"How will you get it to the hotel?" asked Ruth.

"Garçon!" called Kate.

I said, "I don't think it's any good if you don't have it here and hot."

"Don't do it," said Spence.

Kate ordered.

(Waiting for Phyllis's napoleon seems as good a time as any to tell about Phyllis. It is not possible to write about the Katharine Hepburn of the past nineteen years, without including Phyllis Wilbourn. For that length of time, Phyllis has been inextricably woven into the fabric of Kate's life as secretary-companion-assistant-indispensable. She is more than a treasure; she is an extension—in the McLuhan sense—of Kate. She is a gentle gentlewoman, who, for many years, was companion to Constance Collier. When Miss Collier died in 1951, the demands for Phyllis's services were clamorous. She chose to go with Miss Collier's great friend Kate, and she has never regretted it, although she did have some thorny moments with Spencer. He was fond of her and grateful for her help to him and Kate. Yet such was the wayward nature of his complexly structured personality that he would often nag or hector or tease her. He did it to us all, but with Phyllis it was different. She was, after all, part of the working *ménage à trois*. Among other things, Spencer, the greatest American film actor of his time, had achieved an imitation of her that was devastating. He found the precise tone and pitch of her voice, the lovely lilt of her speech, the beat of her upper-class British accent, and when the mood struck him, would reply to her questions in her own voice. She would blush and he would continue. Games People Play. Spencer's with Phyllis was to twit her, mainly because she reacted so sharply. He was, however, deeply attached to her and . . . Here comes her napoleon.)

As the astonished waiter and the *maître d'hôtel* watched, Kate carefully wrapped the napoleon in a napkin, as though it were the most normal thing in the world to do.

We rose to leave.

"I'll return this," she said airily. "Probably."

"She means the napkin," explained Spencer. "Not the napoleon, although she may bring *that* back, too."

Back at the Raphaël, we ensconced ourselves in Spencer's suite to digest dinner and to talk it over.

Kate went to Phyllis's room next door to deliver the treat.

She returned a few minutes later, flushed and pleased.

"She was *thrilled,*" said Kate, lying down on the floor.

Spencer went into his act. "Aeeeeoh! Miss Hepp-bunn. Yeeou shouldn't hev," he said, becoming Phyllis. "Hahow viddy viddy kind!"

We began to make plans for the following day, Sunday. A trip to Chartres? Why not? The cathedral, and the drive. What time?

And then. All at once. The explosive sound of French hotel plumbing gone berserk. Worse than ever, here on the topmost floor. Wild whooshing sounds and gurgles which crescendoed into ear-splitting shattering splatterings and hissing exhalations like sighing monsters and high whining whistles reminiscent of bombs from B–52's on their screaming way to earth.

The volume and intensity of these ungodly sounds increased.

Ruth started out of the room. Kate sat up. I was on my feet, good and scared.

"My God!" I yelled. "What the hell is that?"

Spencer looked at us all calmly and said quietly, "Nothing, nothing. Sit down. It's just Phyllis, eating her napoleon."

We went, after all, to Chartres. We studied the cathedral, exclaimed, lunched at the Henri IV, and were glad we came.

We joined the stream of sightseers as we walked back to the car. Suddenly Kate ran ahead, into the middle of the road. She picked up a small object she had spotted. She turned back, held it aloft, and shouted, "Look! Look at this!" (I cannot remember what it was.) As she rejoined us, Spencer said, "You better go back and do that again, honey. I think there's a guy over there—the one with the beard—who didn't see you."

Kate blushed and threw away the object.

Driving back to Paris, we discussed the phenomenon of instant recognition. Spencer again maintained that even well-known figures are not spotted unless they want to be. Kate said it was true only some of the time.

I recalled walking down Madison Avenue with Jean Arthur and mentioning my surprise that no one was recognizing her.

"That's because I don't want them to," said Jean.

"I don't understand," I said.

"Watch."

Almost at once, oncoming strollers began to stop and point. Two greeted her and one asked for an autograph as we waited for a traffic light to change.

We crossed the street and proceeded downtown. Again, because she willed it, she went unrecognized.

"Sure," said Spence. "I've done it myself. Nothing to it."
Kate said, "Well . . ."

Dinner time. Kate orders dinner for everyone, and for herself.

"I want some soup—what do you have? Yah. . . . Yah. . . . Yah. No, none of those will do—what about consommé?—Do you have consommé?—No, I don't want it cold—no, not hot. Warm—Tepid—Does it have salt in it? Oh, well, never mind the consommé, I'll have a steak—grilled, please—rare—just grill it five minutes on each side, please—don't keep turning it over—sliced tomatoes—and berries, do you have any berries?—oh, good, strawberries—are they very fine?—good—I'll have strawberries—but, listen, don't wash them—I said, *'Don't wash* the berries, please!'—Thank you." She hung up.

We were all looking at her.

"What do you mean?" asked Spence. " 'Don't wash the berries.' "

"Ruins 'em," says Kate, sitting on the floor. "Any fool knows that."

I remembered the matter of the corn. I had never before seen anyone eat raw corn. At Faraway Meadows, in Connecticut, our farmer had planted a small cornfield. Kate wanted to see it. We walked through it. She examined the stalks carefully, admiringly, stopped, tore an ear of corn from a stalk, shucked it expertly, and began to eat it.

"What are you doing?" I asked.

"Eating corn," she said. "Why?"

"Like that?"

"Best way," she replied, "if it's fresh—ten minutes off the stalk and it's no good raw."

She prepared another ear and offered it to me.

"No, thanks."

"Why not?"

"No, thanks."

She ate it herself.

I had refused only because I was afraid she might be right.

The next morning I went out into the field by myself and tried it. She had been right.

I prefer not to name the celebrated playwright who lunched with Ruth and Spencer and me in Paris one afternoon at Maxim's.

He had been anxious to meet Spencer, who was honored to meet him, and the luncheon was a success from the outset.

Dawdling over coffee, reluctant to end the occasion, we continued our conversation.

"I'd love to see you in a play with Katharine Hepburn," said the celebrated playwright. "It would make history."

"It would if the play was any good," said Spencer. "And the parts."

"Of course," said the celebrated playwright, "that goes without saying. I'm damned if I'm not going to try to put something together."

"Very flattering," said Spencer.

"Not at all," said the celebrated playwright, "not at all."

It was almost possible to see his creative juices beginning to flow. His fingertips tapped the table and he lit a cigarette although he had a fresh one burning in the ashtray. His eyes darted about like minnows in a pool.

"I can see it," he said. "I mean, feel it. The sort of relationship it should be. And I'd want to tailor it very carefully. The acting, the big acting, would have to be in *your* part, of course. But use everything possible out of that delicious personality of hers, so that . . ."

Spencer frowned as he interrupted. "What do you mean? I'm not sure I follow."

Ruth looked worried.

"Well," said the celebrated playwright, "we all know that Kate is a tremendous personality but not what you'd call a real actress."

"Not what *who'd* call a real actress?" said Spencer in tones that vibrated the china and cutlery on our table and reverberated through the mirrored room.

The celebrated playwright was aware he had blundered.

"What I mean . . . mean to say," he began.

"I *know* what you mean to say, you stupid bastard," said Spencer. "I heard you. I understand English pretty goddam well. I've been studying it for years, and anybody who says . . . Where the hell do you come off calling her Kate? You don't even *know* her."

"No, but . . ."

"What in Christ's name does an actress have to do before she gets the big final okay from you supercilious pipsqueaks? She's only worked and studied and practiced and knocked herself out for thirty years and improved all the time—and she was pretty goddam good when she *started*—and taken chances, and challenges. Did you see her as Cleopatra or in the O'Neill? *The Merchant of Venice? The Taming of the Shrew? The Millionairess?* What about *The African Queen* or *As You Like It? The Philadelphia Story?* She was a *great* actress in *Morning Glory* and that was *1933,* God damn it! Look—don't talk to *me* about acting. Talk to me about plays and playwriting or, what was that you called it? Dramaturgy? Yeah, talk to me about that, or about history or about geography. But *don't* talk to me about acting. I *know* about acting and I've acted with this girl—a lot—and if she isn't a real actress, then there never *was* a real actress. Thanks for the lunch. It was delicious. I'm going home now to throw it up."

He was gone.

It took the celebrated playwright two double brandies to calm his nerves.

"Good Lord," he said. *"What* a *bêtise!* I seem to have touched his sensitive spot."

"You're lucky he didn't touch *your* sensitive spot," I said.

"I didn't mean anything disrespectful," he said. "You know that. There are simply different styles of acting. What I think about her would be true about Sarah Bernhardt, I suppose, or Ellen Terry. Mrs. Pat."

"Laurette Taylor?" Ruth suggested.

"No," he said. "Not Laurette Taylor. She was the other kind. A great actress who invented a personality for every part."

"Well, anyway, you can take comfort in one thing," she said.

"What's that?" he asked.

"You don't have to bother writing that play for Tracy and Hepburn."

"No," he said, "no, I don't," and ordered still another double brandy.

June 1954. We are in London. Ruth is preparing to go into rehearsal with *The Matchmaker,* under Tyrone Guthrie's direction.

Kate and Spencer arrive to discuss a British film production.

Spencer moves into Claridge's where we are staying, Kate goes to live at the homier Connaught.

Each of us loves his own hotel and attempts, whenever possible, to prove its superiority. Travelers are inclined to do that, in the way that we all laud our dentists. I have yet to meet a person whose dentist is not "the best in the world." We believe it because we want to. After all, we are entrusting our teeth to this man. In the case of our hotel, we are entrusting our daily life.

"When I die," says Spencer at lunch one day, "I don't want to go to heaven. I want to go to Claridge's!"

Kate comes to visit every day, sometimes more than once, and, often, Ruth, Spencer, and I walk over to the Connaught.

One morning, an early call from Spencer. I am immediately anxious because Spencer, knowing that we are always at work in the morning, never calls before lunchtime.

"I'd like to see you, Jasper," he says evenly. "Important. You got a minute?"

Since I am neither shaved nor dressed, I ask, "Can we do it on the phone?"

"No."

The tone of that tiny syllable is such that I say, "I'll be right up."

Moving as swiftly as I can, I shave and dress. Claridge's is a staid old institution, and it does not do to dash about its halls in a less than *comme il faut* state.

A few minutes later, I am with Spencer in his suite. The inevitable large pot of coffee is at his side.

"Where were you?" he asks, irritated. "I said 'important.' Or weren't you listening?"

"Of course I was listening. I'm here, ain't I?"

"Well, you sure in hell took your time."

This might be banter, I thought. As we exchanged a long, hard look, during which the color of his eyes changed, I decided I was wrong.

"I'm sorry, Spence. I had to get dressed. I don't think they like you running around in this hotel in your dressing gown."

"No, they don't," he said, gravely. "Well, as long as you're here, sit down."

I did so. Spence rubbed his face, round and round, and said morosely, "The manager called me. Or the assistant manager. I don't know. Anyway, he wants to see me."

"What about?"

He exploded. "How the hell do *I* know what about? That's why *you're* here."

I heard myself shouting back at him. "Well, how the hell do you expect *me* to know?"

"All right, all right," he said, soothingly. "Don't burst into song."

"Sorry."

He forgave me, magnanimously. "That's okay, pal."

"I don't know what we're so jumpy about. He probably wants your autograph."

"I'll give it to him," said Spence. "But that's not what he wants."

"How do you know?"

"I *know* when that's what they want."

I was not about to argue with his infallible instinct. I began to share his apprehension that there was indeed a problem in the offing.

"You got a clue?" I asked.

"No," he said, "but I don't want it to be anything about Kath, that's all."

"Why would it be?"

"I don't know. That's what it feels like."

"Where?"

"On my skin."

"Do you think it could be this? . . ." I suggested. "Maybe they want to know how long you're planning to stay. Maybe they need this suite. Or want it. Did you tell them how long you're staying or did you just make one of those open-end reservations?"

"I don't know," he said. "You made it."

"Open-end," I said. "That's it. They want to know how long you're going to stay."

I rose.

"How did you develop such confidence in your judgment?" he asked. "It's usually lousy."

"What else *could* it be? We've been paying our bills, haven't we?"

Spencer bit his lip, and said, "It's not that. They could've asked that on the phone." He sighed and added, "Get him up here."

I went to the phone, called the manager's office and found that it was one of the assistant managers who had made the original call. I felt greatly relieved, reasoning that any matter of real importance would be handled by the manager.

We said nothing more while we waited. Spencer drank coffee. I paced until he told me to sit down. As I did so, there was a professionally discreet knock at the door.

I went to it and opened it. A distressingly tall assistant manager entered, wearing striped trousers and morning coat.

"Good morning, Mr. Tracy," he said.

"Good morning."

The assistant manager looked at me, and back at Spencer. "You will forgive me, sir," he said, "but I wonder if I might have a word with you in private?"

"Sure," said Spencer. "Sure."

The assistant manager looked at me again.

"Oh," said Spencer. "Perfectly all right. Say anything. That's my friend."

The assistant manager was about to say something more when Spencer said, "Go ahead. Sit down."

"No, thank you, sir. That won't be necessary. I shan't be a moment."

"Good," said Spencer.

I tried to make myself invisible.

The assistant manager, all at once ill at ease, said, "Well, sir. I've been asked by the management if it would be possible—you *do* understand, Mr. Tracy, this is not a *personal* matter, merely one of policy. The management has asked me . . . that is to say, Mr. Van Thuyne has suggested . . ."

As the assistant manager's discomfiture grew, Spencer relaxed. "*What* matter?" he asked. "I still don't know what you're talking about."

A pause.

"It's about Miss Hepburn, sir," the assistant manager blurted out.

Spencer paled. His famous jaw did its eminent clench, and I was glad, at that moment, to be myself and not the assistant manager. It would not have surprised me to see him assaulted. He could not take the glare of Spencer's angry gray eyes, which had become off-white. He looked at me and went on.

"It's a matter of dress, you see, sir. We do have certain regulations. In our restaurant, for example, and the various public rooms . . ."

I smiled, because all at once, I saw what the problem was. Spencer was still confused.

"What?" he asked.

"Miss Hepburn," said the assistant manager, "wears trousers, sir."

"Slacks," I said.

"Yes, sir."

"What about it?" asked Spencer. "What about them?"

"Well, sir. It's only that she frequently comes through our main lobby."

"What's wrong with that?" asked Spencer.

"Nothing at all, sir. Merely a matter of dress."

"Dress," I said. "They want her to wear a dress."

"I don't know if she's got a dress," said Spencer.

The assistant manager had lost weight.

"I was instructed to mention it to you, sir," he said.

"Why *me?*" asked Spencer. "Why don't you mention it to *her?*"

"Well, sir, we consider that since *you* are our guest and since, in a manner of speaking, *she* is *your* guest, it might be more . . . seemly. . . ." He stopped. "It's nothing more than that, sir."

He had gone moist, and stood there looking so utterly wretched that Spencer took pity on him.

"Okay, son," he said softly. "Okay. Tell them to stop worrying about it. I'll take it up with her."

"Thank you, sir. Mr. Tracy."

He was out of the room so swiftly that it seemed to me he had not even opened and closed the door.

"Well," said Spencer. "Now all you've got to do is tell her."

"Me?"

"Certainly," he said, with convincing logic. "This is your joint, isn't it?"

"I've got it," I said. "Let's send her a telegram."

That afternoon we all went over and lunched with Kate in her rooms at the Connaught.

When lunch was over, Spencer said, "We've got something to talk to you about, Kath. It's pretty important."

"Oh. What?"

He waved a hand at me and said, "Tell her."

"You tell her."

"Go ahead. You got me in there. I never should've listened to you."

"In where?" asked Kate. "What is all this?"

A look from Spencer started me off.

"The management of Claridge's," I said, "takes a dim view of you coming through the lobby wearing trousers. I mean slacks."

"Good *God!"* she said. "I've never *heard* anything so *idiotic!"*

"All right now, Kathy. All right," said Spencer, pacifyingly.

"I think we should all move over *here,"* said Ruth.

"No," said Spencer. "That's no good. A better idea is do what we're doing now. We'll come over here, instead of you over there."

"Oh, no," said Kate. "That's a bore for you."

"I've got it," I said, brightly. "How about Kate wearing a dress?"

The look she gave me was withering. "Haven't got a dress," she mumbled.

"Buy one," I said. "We'll all chip in and buy you one."

Her eyes were thinking. "Never mind," she said. "I know what to do."

Later that day, we met for tea. Kate came bounding in, flushed, carrying a bagful of scones and tarts she had bought at Shepherd's Market. We all looked at once to see how she was dressed. The same old slacks, of course.

"God damn it, Kath!" said Spencer. "Why do you want to . . ."

"Please," said Kate, grandly. "I can explain everything. I did not come through the main lobby, so there's no probb-lemm." (She always gives the two syllables of this word equal stress. "Probb-lemm." The trouble is it always makes the problem seem bigger when she says it that way.)

"How'd you get up here?" asked Spence.

"The service elevator," she replied. "In the back—freight elevator—I came up with the laundry and two beautiful Vuitton trunks—You'd have loved them, Ruth—and, of course, several of my new chums—Bert—wait till I tell you about Bert—his son's a racing driver—Le Mans, Indianapolis, everything. Isn't that thrilling? And little Dodie, a maid, an angel—I don't think she's on this floor—you'll all have to move to—*beautiful* elevator—sorry, *lift*—and they may not love me in the front of this hotel, but they *adore* me backstairs."

The probb-lemm was thus solved. Kate continued to call daily, to use the service lift, and to dress in her own way.

There is something to add. Not long ago, Ruth and I stayed at Claridge's. Late one afternoon, at the beginning of the cocktail hour, we came down the grand staircase to the main lobby. Half-way down, I stopped and said to Ruth, "Look."

"What?"

"All the women."

We both looked. At least fifteen of them were wearing the modish evening pants-suits now in vogue.

"Kate," said Ruth.

"Right," I said.

On the same trip, we lunched at Slim Inn, a popular health-food restaurant in South Moulton Street, frequented largely by photographers and their mod models. It is the sort of place where one gets one's own food, cafeteria style, on a tray, and looks for a seat. Ruth and I sat down at a table with two breathtakingly exquisite models. One of them was wearing a tricky make-up. As I studied it, I realized she had dotted false freckles across the middle of her face.

I smiled at her and said, "Those freckles. Are they fake?"

"Why, yes. Do you mind them?"

"Not at all. They make me think of Katharine Hepburn."

The model looked at me and said, "That's the idea, chum."

On her way from the Connaught to Claridge's one day, Kate stops in front of one of the many small galleries *en route*. A little painting of the Haymarket Theatre, where Ruth is scheduled to open soon, has caught her eye. She considers the painting as a possible gift.

The next day she looks at it again. It is beginning to grow on her. Another day and she decides it would be just the thing. For some reason, she delays. Early the following week, she walks by, looks in the window. The painting is gone. She goes in and, vexed, wants to know where it is. The dealer tells her it has been sold.

"That's impossible!" she says. "I'm buying it for Ruth Gordon."

"I'm afraid it's been sold, madam."

"But how could you *do* that, for heaven's sake? She's going to *open* at the Haymarket. It's a *painting* of the Haymarket. Who bought it?"

"I'm afraid I can't . . ."

"Oh, don't be idiotic."

The power of her outburst springs the information.

She gets the buyer on the phone and, provoked, takes the position that he has somehow behaved in a tricky way. In her excitement she forgets to identify herself and is given a firm brush-off.

At this point, most people would give up, but Kate is not most people.

She plans a strategy and executes it. She phones again, this time identifies herself and asks for a meeting. She calls on the buyer and charms him, but for a reason he does not disclose, he needs the picture, too. When she reveals it is a gift for someone else, her case is weakened. She offers to replace it, to give him a profit. None of this interests him, but he says he will think about it. She leaves, frustrated.

Later that afternoon, a package arrives at the Connaught by messenger, with a note.

> "My dear Miss Hepburn,
>
> It was an honor to meet you and your persuasive determination.
>
> I believe you left this behind. I take pleasure in returning it.
>
> Faithfully yours," etcetera.

Kate is a confirmed gift-giver and paintings are among her favorites.

For one of his birthdays, she gave Spencer a large, overwhelming Vlaminck that seemed to change the size and color and shape of the room. Spencer responded emotionally to the canvas.

"I love it," he said. "God *damn,* I love it."

"No wonder," I said. "It's a lot *like* you."

"What do you mean by that?"

"I mean it's dark and mysterious and brooding, but strong and has in it the intimation that tomorrow's going to be a fine day."

"And why is that like me?"

"No, Spence. What I meant was, it's a picture I can imagine *you* painting. That's what I meant."

"That's *not* what you meant," he insisted, "is it?"

"No," I confessed.

We talk of painting. I know that Spencer paints but I have never seen a single example of his work. He is secretive about it and ostensibly paints to express himself, not to impress others.

"How'd you happen to get into it?" I ask.

"I don't know," he replies. "I always used to noodle around with sketches, the way everyone does. But once I was visiting Fanny Brice. It was a nervous time for me and she caught it right away. There never was a more sensitive lady. And she told me I ought to start painting. She was doing a lot of it herself at the time because the Baby Snooks thing on the radio once a week wasn't exactly using all her juice. She explained how much it had done for her and pressed it on me. After a while, she dropped the subject and went on to something else. But the next day, she sent me a whole outfit. Paint, oil, brushes, palette, canvases, and a how-to book. That got me started. I can never thank her enough. It's been a great thing for me. Of course, she didn't do as well with me as she did with her son. Isn't that Bill Brice a fantastic story? She got Billy interested in art and in painting when he was a little boy. Imagine it! At his age Fanny was a slum kid on the East Side, cadging pennies from people, uneducated, practically illiterate, and she turns into this amazing woman with as much common wisdom as it's possible for a single person to have. And tremendous taste. Real elegance in so many things. Painting, architecture, clothing, food—and look what she did with Bill. He's one of the finest, most interesting painters in America today. His work hangs everywhere and he's teaching at UCLA. And it all came out of Fanny."

"Do you think you'll ever let us see any of your work, Spence?"

"No."

"Why not?"

"Because I don't want to."

"It's excellent," says Kate.

"And believe me," says Spencer, "there's a girl who speaks without any prejudice whatsoever."

"How did *you* happen to start painting, Kate?" asks Ruth.

"It was back in the thirties—the late thirties—I was having man trouble."

"That'll do it every time," says Spencer.

"And I wanted to find a way of distracting myself for a few hours a day—so I started drawing and painting—I did it for quite a while, but then, you know, there never seems to be enough time to do all the things one is meant to do so it was a pleasure I had to abandon—Then, just lately, time came up and I was glad to start smudging my clothes again."

"Man trouble again," says Spencer. "We've both got man trouble. With the same man."

"That's what we do mostly when we go out to the beach," says Kate. "We eat and paint."

"And I sleep," adds Spencer. "There's nothing like the old folderoo by the seashore."

Ruth was playing in Thornton Wilder's *The Matchmaker* in New York following its London success. Kate and Spencer came to see it. Afterward we went up to Spencer's suite at the Waldorf, where all the right things were said over club sandwiches and coffee.

On the next free Sunday we all had dinner at our house and after dinner, shoes off.

Spencer looked at Ruth for a long time and said, "We've been talking about you and about what you do in this part down there. It's a kind of classic performance."

"Spence," said Ruth, touched.

"Why don't you do it as a movie?" said Spencer, casually.

"I certainly would love to, but who'd do it with me? It's bound to be an expensive picture and I'm not a movie star."

"I am," said Spencer, "and so is Zasu Pitts here, and we've got an idea. We'd like to do it with you. How about that?"

Ruth's lips parted, her eyes widened. She could not speak. Spencer went on.

"I could play that guy, couldn't I? Vandergelder? And she'd be marvelous as the milliner. And you play your part. Why not? It would be great. Who'd turn it down?"

What made the proposal so astonishing was the fact that two great stars were offering to play supporting roles for someone they admired.

Ruth was in tears.

I said I had never heard anything more generous but that in addition to a cast it also needed a concept and asked if anyone had a notion of how it could be done. We began to talk out various angles.

As it happened, René Clair was in New York at the time. I imposed on his kindness. We walked in Central Park for hours trying to come up with a way. In the end, René said that if only it could be done as a silent picture, he would know how to do it.

One day we learned that the film rights had been sold to Paramount. The people there had their own ideas about what to do and they did it. It turned out to be a mediocre film.

Despite the fact that it never came about, there is a private version of the film that we play in our imaginations, and the fact that it is unreal does not in the least mitigate the depth of Ruth's appreciation for the gesture made by Tracy and Hepburn.

In 1964, Kate was asked for her views on privacy by the editors of the *Virginia Law Weekly*.

They had, inadvertently, touched the right button. Instead of simply replying, she sat down and wrote an article.

The circulation of this publication being what it is, few people ever got to read it, which matters not at all to her. It was merely a question of getting it off her chest.

Researchers are asked to cite her comments, as "THE RIGHT OF PRIVACY, Hepburn, 16 *Va. Law Weekly,* DICTA Comp. 18 (1965)."

THE RIGHT OF PRIVACY
THE PREDICAMENT OF THE PUBLIC FIGURE
By Katharine Houghton Hepburn

1890—*Boston—Samuel D. Warren and Louis D. Brandeis —The right to life—the right to enjoy life—the right to be let alone—Earliest Common Law—that the individual should have full protection in person and in property*—BUT THE DEFINITION OF PROTECTION WAS ALTERABLE ACCORDING TO THE DEMANDS OF SOCIETY. It came to recognize man's spiritual nature—his feelings—his intellect as well as his person and his property. The principle which protects is the principle of an inviolate personality—

If then the decisions indicate a general right to *privacy for thoughts—emotions—sensations—these should receive the same protection whether expressed in writing—conduct—conversations—attitudes—or in facial expression—*

The right to one's personality—The right not merely to prevent inaccurate portrayal of private life—but to prevent its being depicted at all—BUT THE DEFINITION OF PROTECTION WAS ALTERABLE ACCORDING TO THE DEMANDS OF SOCIETY.

The right to privacy—Fifty years from now this word as we have understood it—will have no meaning at all—if our world continues in its present direction—and it must or it will cease to exist—So it is probably necessary that we sacrifice privacy—

In the beginning of my career—in 1932—I had a right to consider privacy my right—and so I fought for it—a wild and vigorous battle—Quite successful—I thought—I went to a great deal of trouble—I went way—way out of my way—the few people I knew could keep their mouths shut—it was thirty-five years ago—and the opposition accepted a limit—

Today it is extremely difficult to control one's privacy—even if one is not a public figure—Who are you—How old are you—Who are your father—mother—sisters—brothers—grandparents—Of what did they die—what were they when they lived—What diseases have you had—What is your religion—have you ever been a communist—What is your income—Whom do you support—How much did your house cost—the furnishings—Your wife's clothes—her jewels—fur coats—how much do you spend on your children's schools—Travel—Entertaining—Books—Liquor—Flowers—Teeth—Do you wear glasses—Do you still menstruate—Are your periods regular—your bowels—What operations have you had—do you sleep in the room with your wife—and how long has that been going on—Have you ever been involved with the law—do you drink—Let's just have a fingerprint now—How much—These are among the questions which must be answered—if—you are insured by your employer—(an actor is)—drive a car—pay an income tax—get social security—etc.—

The greatest "bugaboo" against privacy—and the idea of privacy in this country is insurance—You can be protected against anything, but for it you must sacrifice your privacy—If a friend is injured in your house—let the company pay—If you can't save enough money to live on in your old age—if you are ill—if you are hospitalized—if an actor is ill—Now all this is progress—these things are necessary—They are things which an individual can no longer be responsible for—The Government or the Company must step in and bear the burden—but with the loss of responsibility—we have also lost our privacy—Privacy in the sense that it was used thirty years ago has almost ceased to exist—the individual has become a pretty well documented punch card—"There can be no privacy in that which is already public—"

Now let us take a public figure—an actor—We are worse off than the politician—the politician is selling his brain—supposedly—whereas—the actor is selling his body—and/or his own peculiar personality and this does not command high esteem—There is always a "Well what can you expect" back of derogatory comment—Both the public and press feel that they have an absolute right of access to the most intimate details of your life—and by life you must read largely sex life—for this is the department of an actor's life which is most titillating to press and public—

At the appropriate age for this sort of thing—I used to go through the most elaborate schemes to avoid the press—I felt that nothing of my private life was any of their business—By the same token I did not feel that I could then appear in a public place—or in their territory so to speak—railroad stations—airports—restaurants—bars—theatres—games—These places were their territory—My territory was my own home—a friend's house—a private club—This is all very well—but then you have the public place on a private matter—the hospital—the church—the cemetery—where a public character is forced by illness or death to use a public facility—It would seem that in such a case he or she should have a right to be protected from the peering eye of the outsider—a courtroom—But even here—or should I say especially here—the taste of the public has been geared to a diet of such extravagance—that the magazines and press—so called respectable ones—must continue to feed it—cater to it—in the manner to which they have accustomed it—Polite pornography is no longer interesting—No more subterfuge—The naked fact—Tell it—Do it—There it is—That is the fact—The truth—The four letter word—The naked body—Nothing withheld—You feel sad—low—take a benzedrine—You feel too lively—take a sparine—you want to sleep—take a secanol—you feel pain—take some codeine—you are confused—go to a psychoanalyst—Don't hide it—Talk—tell it—It is never your fault—We'll fix the blame—Mama—Papa—Uncle Sam—Teacher—Employer—They are responsible—I would seem to wander—but if you have a public feed on these intimate details—if you have a public geared to listen—read—speak—about the most intimate details of another's life (to say nothing of their own) and geared to "understand" any vagary—because nothing is either right or wrong—and geared to the divine right of life—to joy—to freedom—Run—Jump—Go—Go—Go—Happy—Happy—Happy—

Well—how hard should you try—Give us the responsibility—We are responsible—don't worry about anything—This is a tough atmosphere in which to establish the fact of privacy—let alone the right—Keep out of my life—I will be responsible—I have a right to be let alone—It is not a part of our lives anymore—Too many people—and people who have been too poor to be very interested in privacy anyway—

Bobby Kennedy wants to climb his brother's Canadian Mountain—to be the first to get to the top—leave a token there—This was warm and thrilling and mysterious—until he sold or gave it to *Life* magazine—and the television went along—the act had to lose a lot of its meaning to him by being publicized—or at least it would have to me—Who am of another generation—I pick him—because he is a fellow whom I greatly admire—behaving in the manner of today.

Their bosoms—their secrets—their loves—their sex theories—their sins—thrills were titillating when you only got a peek—But now in magazines you're not even ashamed to buy—Down in black and white—THE TRUTH—in words and pictures—Stolen or sold—a curiously literal world—The magazine—the ephemeral—what *can't* be caught in this black and white arrangement—Maybe it's inside your own head—your imagination—which cannot lend itself to words—Our own individual "touch of the poet."

Everything has to be considered in relation to the world we are living in—I do not know how you can relate privacy to this world—they would seem to contradict each other—

The above is a motion picture of her mind in action. The rushes, so to speak.

Kate is unpredictable and eminently changeable.

"I'm terribly set in my ways," she often says, but she is wrong. She moves with the times, with the days, with the weather.

I have found her, through the years, constantly surprising.

In 1954, when Ruth and I stopped smoking, we became as boring about it as anyone else who has ever stopped smoking.

For one thing, people who stop do not want to stop talking about it. They develop a smug, holier-than-thou attitude that makes those around them smoke even more. They feel the need to proselytize, to gain converts. It seems altruistic, but as one of the offenders, I can report it is no such thing. It is merely that having abandoned one of life's great pleasures, we cannot bear to see others enjoying it. We are miserable. We want others to share our misery.

We were talking about it one evening, Kate puffing away.

"I don't know a single person," I said, "with what I call full intelligence, who still smokes."

"Is that so?" said Kate. "And precisely what do *you* call full intelligence?"

"I call 'full intelligence,' " I replied, "knowing what's right and doing what's right. I mean, if you don't know that something is harmful—a certain mushroom, for instance—you're not necessarily lacking in full intelligence if you eat it. But if you *know* it's poisonous, and go ahead and eat it, I claim you're *not* fully intelligent. It's like not knowing enough to get in out of the rain."

Kate looked at Spencer. "Do you know what he's talking about?"

"Certainly," said Spencer, "and what's more, he's right. He's so right that one of these days, *I'm* going to stop smoking. You know why? Because I want to be fully intelligent, the way he is."

I was astonished.

"How can *you* give up smoking?" I asked. "You don't smoke."

Kate smiled.

"I don't, huh?" said Spencer.

"I've never seen you smoke," I said.

"Nor have I," said Ruth.

"I limit myself, though," said Spencer. "A pack and a half a day. No more. I wouldn't smoke that thirty-first cigarette if my life depended on it."

"I don't get it," I said.

"That's because you're not fully intelligent," said Spencer.

He smiled.

"Cutie McHugh, Frank's father, used to have a gag in the turn he did. The guy says, 'I haven't slept a wink in ten days.' 'Why's that?' the other guy asks him. 'Because,' he says, 'I sleep *nights!*' " He laughed, savoring the old chestnut. "That's me. I don't smoke in the daytime. Only at night, after I go to bed, while I read."

He went on to outline his singular routine. Some time after watching the eleven o'clock news, he prepared for the night, got into bed, arranged his cigarettes, ashtray, and matches, took a book off the pile that was always provided for him, and began to read. He was a strangely eclectic reader; the only man I know, for example, who had read through the fourteen volumes of Thoreau's journals. He read current fiction, admired Cardinal Newman, Thomas Merton, and Dickens. "But not at night," he said. At night, smoking, he read only mystery novels, thrillers. He read slowly, he explained, but smoked swiftly. After an hour or so, he would get up, walk about, get a drink of water and warm up a cup of coffee or have some tea, go back to bed, and continue to read and smoke until he had finished. He would then get up and walk about again, thinking over the story, digesting it, reviewing it in his mind to see if he could find any discrepancies or flaws, sometimes returning to the text in order to check. Finally, near dawn, he would return to the kitchen, make himself a fresh cup of coffee, drink it, go back to bed and to sleep.

A routine, a habit.

I remember a feat he performed on his sixty-fourth birthday.

It was difficult to buy him a gift, since he was not overly fond of things, as such. On this day, it occurred to me that a few books might be the answer. Browsing about at Hunter's, I conceived the idea of buying him sixty-four mystery books for his sixty-fourth birthday. I asked for the newest they had, including the British ones. I went over to Martindale's and bought what new ones *they* had. I continued downtown to the Pickwick Bookshop, went into their used-book department, and bought a number of old mystery books, until I had assembled sixty-four. I packed them carefully into one impressive bundle and delivered them.

Spencer was delighted. After dinner, we all sat down to coffee. Spencer looked at his gift stack of books, picked one off the top and said, "This one's terrific. You think all the time the daughter is nuts, but it turns out the father, who's trying to have her committed, is the one who's nuts." He tossed it aside, and picked up the next one. *"Not* so good. A phony. They ought to give you your money back. On page ten, I knew how it was coming out. The hippie." And so it went. He moved swiftly through the whole pile. Not only had he read all but three, but could tell the story of each in swift outline.

We were properly impressed, and said so.

"Smoking," said Spencer. "I couldn't do it if I didn't smoke."

After a time, Spencer did stop smoking. He was told to do so by his doctor and he did.

I would have wagered that Kate, out of deference to him, would have stopped as well. But, no. Unpredictable, as always, she continued. It was something she enjoyed. Therefore she would not give it up. Of course, she knew it was harmful. No matter.

"It's ruining my tennis game," she said, "I'll tell you that. I can't seem to make it out there the way I used to. But what the hell, I don't care so much about winning any more. I just like playing."

"And smoking," said Spencer.

But while she was in rehearsal for *Coco,* it struck her. Here she was, at sixty, dancing every day. Singing was proving to be more of a physical strain than she had anticipated. She was taking a singing lesson daily, rehearsing, fitting costumes, studying her part. It began to be apparent to her that she would be better prepared on the first night if she stopped smoking. She stopped. She no longer smokes. It was not her knowledge of medical research that convinced her, not fear, not logic, but simply her professional commitment.

In 1959, she went to London to play Mrs. Venable in the film version of Tennessee Williams' *Suddenly, Last Summer.* The project was difficult for her on many counts. For one thing, it meant a long separation from Spencer. For another, she was not entirely happy with the setup. Most important, there was something about the subject matter that made her uncomfortable.

However, she felt it necessary to work in films again. She had been off the screen for almost two years, involved in Shakespeare productions. Once she had made the decision, she moved into the project firmly and confidently.

Within a month, she had made a complete study of the work of Tennessee Williams, had read each of his plays, all his prose work, and poetry as well.

The organization in England left something to be desired from Kate's point of view. Sam Spiegel, with whom she had worked on *The African Queen,* is a strong producer of the old school. Joe Mankiewicz, who was directing, is an extremely personal and individual artist. The lines of authority were not always clear.

Elizabeth Taylor surprised her. She had expected to meet a glamour girl, a sexpot. Instead, she discovered a serious, cool, and competent professional with whom, however, it was not possible to become involved on a personal level.

"There seemed to be," says Kate, "no personal level at all."

Shooting commenced. Almost at once, the major problem of the production exploded. Montgomery Clift, playing the male lead, was in bad shape. Death (not far off) had already begun its flirtation.

This excellent young actor, once so full of promise, had been ill in mind and body for some time. The reunion with Elizabeth Taylor, with whom he had been deeply in love, was, to say the least, disturbing. He found it difficult to achieve a working balance, lost sleep, began to drink, had difficulty with memorization, and found it necessary to rely on artificial stimuli to get him going each day.

Elizabeth Taylor was compassionate but there was nothing she could do. Mankiewicz and Siegel, under great pressure of schedule and budget, were less sympathetic.

Kate began to hear rumors of a possible replacement.

She talked Mankiewicz and Spiegel out of this, and succeeded in bringing Monty through to the end of the picture. His performance was certainly satisfactory but had cost everyone a great price.

Kate felt that Spiegel and Mankiewicz might have had greater forbearance for an actor in trouble and resented the fact that they had not helped more.

She considered (rightly or wrongly) that they had been downright cruel.

On her last day of shooting, Mankiewicz came to her and said, "That's it."

She asked, "Are you sure?"

"Quite sure."

"There's nothing more you're going to need me for?" she asked. "No looping, no pick-up shots, no retakes?"

"I've got it all, Kate," said Mankiewicz, "and it's great. *You're* great."

"You're sure," she persisted, "that I'm absolutely finished in the picture?"

Mankiewicz grinned his characteristic grin, and said, "Absolutely, Kate. What *is* all this?"

"I just want to leave you," said Kate, "with this." Whereupon, she spat.

(Precisely where she spat and how she spat, depends on the version one hears. Hers, or Joe's, or one of the assorted onlookers'. There is no disagreement, however, as to the fact that she spat.)

She turned, picked up her belongings, and left the set. As she was packing in her dressing room, the phone rang. Sam Spiegel.

"May I see you for a few minutes, Katharine, please?" he asked.

"Certainly," said Kate. "I was coming over, anyway."

"Good."

In his office, she found a grim judge sitting behind the desk.

Spiegel looked at her gravely, and said, "I have heard that you have behaved very badly on the set to Joe."

"I behaved very well," said Kate, "while we were making the picture. This was later. If I behaved badly, it was on my own time. Not yours."

"Just the same," said Spiegel, "I'm shocked. I always thought you were a lady."

"You're going to be more shocked in a minute," she said. "I think *you* behaved very badly toward Monty. He's a tremendous young actor and he's in a jam and instead of helping him, you tortured him. He's been tortured enough. And this is what I think of you." And she spat again.

When she related this, I said, "Well, I don't know that *I'm* shocked. I find that hardly anything shocks me any more. What is that? A sign of age? But I must say, I am *surprised* to learn about that fishwifey side of you. Have you always had it?"

"Listen, my boy," she said. "It wasn't *all* about Monty. Yes, I'm interested in him—but in myself, too—I was really pent up—I wasn't going to go off feeling that pent up forever—I suppose I shouldn't have done what I did, but it helped me—gave me a most satisfactory feeling and released the tension—I wouldn't have done it if I hadn't had to, but I had to."

After this association with her, Tennessee Williams wrote, "Kate is a playwright's dream actress. She makes dialogue sound better than it is by a matchless beauty and clarity of diction, and by a fineness of intelligence and sensibility that illuminates every shade of meaning in every line she speaks. She invests every scene, each 'bit' with the intuition of an artist born into her part. Of the stars that belong to a generation preceding that of 'the method' Katharine Hepburn impresses me as having least needed that school of performance in depth. Like Laurette Taylor before her, she seems to do by instinct what years of 'method' training have taught her juniors to do."

Having met her and having worked with her, he did what almost every writer does after crossing her path. He set out to write a play for her. It turned out to be *The Night of the Iguana*. Kate was enormously flattered.

"I suppose he must be just about the best playwright we have, wouldn't you think?" she asked.

"I certainly would think," I said.

The play was delivered. She read it, studied it with care, and rejected it.

"It captures the wrong part of my imagination," she said. "I admire it, but I couldn't live in it."

She had many talks with Williams but remained unshakable in her conviction that the play was wrong for her and she for the play.

The following year when she saw it performed on Broadway at the Royale Theatre, starring Margaret Leighton and Bette Davis, she was even more impressed by it and said to Williams, "You're lucky. I would've ruined it."

He did not agree but nodded his head in that soft, gentle way of his and kissed her cheek.

In 1962, I directed Van Johnson in my play, *Come on Strong*. I believe Van accepted the assignment because he knew I was a friend of Spencer's. His reverence for Spencer approached awe.

"He actually discovered me," he said. "I was in the *Pal Joey* chorus and I had a little bit. And you know how it is, redheads notice each other. And he noticed me and told Billy Grady about me. So Metro offered me a test and of course I took it and they signed me. Bill told me what had happened and one day I walked over to Tracy's set and I found him and thanked him and all he said was, 'How'd you get on this set? It's supposed to be closed.' So I beat it. But I wrote him a letter and asked him if he would mind me coming onto his set. I didn't hear anything for quite a long time and one day an assistant director there called me up and he said, 'Tracy says any time.' That was all I needed. I haunted his damn set. I never talked to him. I just watched him go and learned everything I know. Then, during the war, he and Irene Dunne were going to do a big one called *A Guy Named Joe,* and can you imagine what I felt like when I heard I was going to be in it? That was when I had the smashup and busted my head open, so of course I was out of the picture. The first thing that happened when I got out of the hospital, though, was my agent called me up and told me I had to report to work on Monday. I said to him, 'Report Monday! for God's sake, I can hardly *walk.*' And he said to me, 'Well, you'd *better* walk because Tracy got them to wait for you and you can still play your part in *A Guy Named Joe.* I guess you can understand why I can't stay in a room where somebody even comes close to bad-mouthing Spencer Tracy."

In addition to her many accomplishments as a film actress, Kate has done, perhaps, more Shakespeare than any American actress of her time. She began with Rosalind in *As You Like It* under Michael Benthall's direction in New York, and, subsequently, on a long transcontinental tour. With the Old Vic Company she toured Australia playing Katharina in *The Taming of the Shrew,* Isabella in *Measure for Measure,* and Portia in *The Merchant of Venice.*

Two years later, in Stratford, Connecticut, she repeated her Portia, and played Beatrice in *Much Ado About Nothing.*

In 1960, she returned to Stratford to play Cleopatra in *Antony and Cleopatra,* and Viola in *Twelfth Night.*

She is one of the few actresses ever to succeed completely as

Shakespeare's Cleopatra. I have a theory as to one of the reasons.

In a long theatergoing life, I have seen a dozen or more Cleopatras (Edith Evans, Katharine Cornell, Tallulah Bankhead, Vivien Leigh, Claire Luce, Peggy Ashcroft, Margaret Leighton, Eugenie Leontovich, Zoe Caldwell, *et al.*) each with virtues, none without faults—but only of Kate's Cleopatra did one believe Enobarbus when he recounted:

> Age cannot wither her, nor custom stale
> Her infinite variety: other women cloy
> The appetites they feed, but she makes hungry
> When most she satisfies: for vilest things
> Become themselves in her, that the holy priests
> Bless her when she is riggish.

(I had to look up "riggish." It means "sexy.")

A tall order, and Kate filled it. As the speech is delivered, we are meant to think back to the Cleopatra of an earlier scene. Certain of the other actresses failed to suggest the embered eroticism of age, others had indeed withered, and only rarely was there the suggestive suggestion of "infinite variety."

When she first went to Stratford, in 1957, there were many speculations as to why an actress of her stature would be willing to work for minimum in a new theater, with a fresh company, and experimenting directors.

All sorts of reasons were given. One was that she was fond of Lawrence Langner, who had founded the theater, and was running it; that she felt indebted to him; and that he had asked her to come and do a season because the theater was having difficulty getting started.

Another explanation was that having succeeded in Australia as Portia, she was anxious to play the part in the United States.

Most of all, it was thought to be a patriotic gesture. Kate was a native daughter, having been born in Connecticut, and still maintaining a residence there.

We went out to see her one afternoon, and between performances, visited with her in the shack where she lived during her Stratford engagement.

It was ninety yards from the theater, on the banks of the Housatonic, hardly the sort of structure one would imagine to be the star's residence. It was more like a tool shed or a gardener's cottage.

In fact it had been, at one time, a bait house from which an old lady sold bait to the local fishermen.

Kate had fixed it up in her own way and, although she had been there only a few days, seemed to have been living there for years.

"It's perfect," she says, "simply perfect—I've never enjoyed living in a place more—Of course, it does have inconveniences—sometimes, when the tide comes in, if it's really *high* tide, it comes right up through the floor."

"What do you do then?" I ask.

"Why, we bail it out," she says.

"I see," I say.

She lights a cigarette and looks out the window, far off, as she continues. "I'm not much for fishing. It's too passive for me, but living in this shack and thinking about Bill Ingham and those days—the other day we got up very early and I decided to go out and fish." She shudders. "What a day *that* turned out to be—I'd forgotten it was a matinee day until we were far out and well becalmed—By the time we got some help, I was good and panicked and decided I could run back here once I got on land faster than any other way. So I did, staying close to the shore—fell into the mud a few times—when I got here to the theater area it was only about twenty minutes before curtain time—I dashed to the stage door—quickest way. Well, the quickest way happened to be right through the whole audience waiting around on the lawn—all dressed up in those white summer dresses—seersuckers for the men—and I threaded right through them, splattering them, I'm afraid—what remarks they made! Later on I couldn't help wondering how many of them realized that the muddy drenched cat that had streaked by, and Portia, were one and the same."

She was deeply fond of that cottage and of her life in it. When she returned, three summers later, to do *Twelfth Night* and *Antony and Cleopatra,* she explained, one sentimental evening: "I suppose this shack is really why I love to come and work here. Oh, sure, the theater's fine but a theater is a theater—the building doesn't matter—it's that audience out there that's terrifying, but living in this shack means a hell of a lot to me. First time I saw it, it reminded me of Bill's place—did I ever tell you about him?—he was the first man I ever loved—I haven't loved many—he was a fisherman. Once, when we were kids, Tom and I did something stupid out on the water, and he saved us—a real fisherman—how he made his living—We used to buy fish from him—his father before him had been a fisherman, too, and owned the fishing rights around there. Years later, Bill got into some trouble—the place became popular and it wasn't convenient for the sons-of-bitches to have the fishing rights owned by somebody else, so they tried to get them away—a few of us stood by him, but it was no use—they licked him—he was paid something, but that wasn't the point—the point was that they'd taken his life away from him—he became an iceman—Well, not really an iceman—it was quite a big ice business, and we all bought our ice from him, but it was tragic—he was never the same—I always think of Bill when I'm in this place—I suppose that's why I like to be here."

Dick once told me the Ingham thing was the reason they never had electric refrigeration at Fenwick, either in the old house or the new one that was built when the old one went down in the great storm of 1938.

From the time Ernest Hemingway's novella *The Old Man and the Sea* was published in its entirety in *Life* magazine, it seemed ordained that a film of it would be made and that Spencer Tracy would play the old man.

Among other things, his memorable performance in *Captains*

Courageous in 1937 suggested that this was a further development of the same strain.

The subject dominated our conversation for months. I, for one, did not see how a film could be made of the book, but it was already being hailed as a classic and Leland Hayward had made a deal to produce it for Warner Brothers. The project was under way.

Spence, who hated flying, had to tank up before he could get into the plane to Havana. The plane ran into a storm and fell all over the sky. Spence arrived nervous and shaken. Hemingway met him and for some reason began at once to bully him.

"Have a drink!"

"No, thanks," said Spence.

"Go on, have a drink."

"I'd just as soon not."

"What are you? A rummy? Can't you just have a drink or two? Do you have to go till you're insensible? Is that your problem?" And so on.

Making a motion picture is a communal effort and although a certain amount of friction can be absorbed, the chances of success are greater if the atmosphere is congenial. The important thing is to create an atmosphere in which creative work can take place.

Fred Zinnemann was the director. He and Spencer simply did not hit it off. There is no explaining this. A matter of temperament and chemistry. Strange, because in 1944 they worked well together on *The Seventh Cross*. Tracy had said at that time, "Watch this young Zinnemann. He's going places." Time and success and failure had combined to damage the relationship.

Hayward, with Kate's powerful assistance, tried to correct the untenable situation with no success.

It might have worked out had Spencer and Hemingway found a rapport but this was not to be. Hemingway seemed interested only in going out to catch and photograph The Fish and in putting Spencer down. In addition, the intense heat and the sketchy plan for filming made Spencer aware he was in the middle of trouble. He wanted to resign, but it was too late. Zinnemann quit. John Sturges took over. The concept changed. The production moved back to Hollywood, and work continued. Spencer held on, still hoping, loving the book even though he did not love its author. Kate had one of her toughest times, holding it all together.

The tanks, rubber sharks, trick effects, and process shooting were elements diametrically opposed to Spencer's notion of the picture. He felt it should be semi-documentary in style. He stuck it out gallantly. His feeling had always been that some pictures go and others do not, and all you can do is your best. But he took the failure of *The Old Man and the Sea* hard. A dream had failed to materialize because of pettiness.

For a time Spencer seriously considered the idea of becoming a film director. He talked to me about it on several occasions. I encouraged the idea.

"I'll tell you when it all started," he said. "I was making that goddam *Plymouth Adventure* and the ulcer was kicking up. I looked lousy and I felt worse and one day I found myself out there in front of a great big process screen. I felt particularly fat that morning, and about ninety-four. I'd seen myself in the mirror and thought I was like an old beat-up barn door. My face looked like it could hold three days of rain. Anyway, there we stood playing the scene and this lovely kid, Gene Tierney, had to look up and say to me, 'I love you, John. I love you.' And all of a sudden, I was embarrassed. I don't mean for myself. I was embarrassed for *her*. Here was this beautiful young actress trying to make her way, playing the parts she could get to play, and now they'd got her standing up against me making no sense at all. Later on I began to think, What the hell will the audience make of this idiocy? This sensational young beauty looking up at this cranky old man and saying all this bullshit. It just didn't make any sense. The only reason she was saying it to me was because I was a big Metro star playing the lead in the picture. That was the moment I decided I ought to begin to think of packing it in as an actor."

"Well, I'm not going to try to talk you out of becoming a director, Spence, because you know I think you should, but that's no reason. I can understand the Tierney trouble but that was only a question of bad casting. It wasn't a good idea for them to expose you to a leading lady that much younger."

"No, no," said Spencer, impatiently. "It wasn't so much a question of age. It's more that I can't stand any kind of stuff like that involving me, the way I am today."

"But Spence," I protested, "listen. Max Gordon, who's one of the sharpest theater minds I've ever encountered, points out that the greatest stars, the lasting stars of the American theater, have always been the character men, not the leading men. Edwin Booth, Richard Mansfield, Holbrook Blinn, Arthur Byron, George M. Cohan, Paul Muni, Walter Huston."

The argument impressed Spencer and he said, "Yuh, he's got a point there, but the parts don't always come along."

"Right," I said. "So in between, direct a picture. Or you can do both. It's been done. Larry. Orson Welles."

"Oh, Jesus, no," he said. "I never meant direct *myself*. Holy God, you gave me a fright. If I ever did anything like that I'd have to look at myself up there, wouldn't I? At the rushes? That's something I've never done. Anyway, those guys are geniuses and I'm not. No, if I'm going to direct, I'll direct other people." He looked at me seriously. "I honest to God think I could help some actors, some I've seen." He grins. "I guess most of them I'd just keep telling what you said to Pepi Schildkraut, huh?"

(He was referring to the opening night on Broadway of *The Diary of Anne Frank*. As the director of the production, I had gone backstage to wish the cast good fortune. When I reached Joseph Schildkraut's room, I found him in a highly nervous and agitated state although he had been giving a superlative performance during the course of the road tour and had nothing to worry about except a tendency to overact, or, rather, over*feel*. He grabbed me and said desperately, "Say something to me.

Say something to me that will help me. Say one thing. Please." And I said, "Less." Then left.

Schildkraut had later repeated this widely. When Spence heard it, he phoned to ask me if it were true. He reveled in actor stories.)

He must have continued to consider the directorial career seriously because when his friend Stanley Kramer began shooting *Ship of Fools,* Spencer became a daily observer on the set.

He explained. "Lord knows I've spent enough hours of my life on enough sets, but I hardly ever knew what the hell was going on, to tell you the truth. I was usually pretty involved with what *I* had to do and with what was expected of *me*. So to see how they organize it to get the whole thing together is fascinating. Stanley has a fine bunch of people. Vivien, Simone Signoret, a big interesting cowboy named Lee Marvin, or something like that, and of course, Max Schell. It's fascinating. Absolutely fascinating."

We talked a good deal about directing in those days. He seemed interested when I told him that after many years of practicing the craft, I had learned that the best direction was the least direction; that it was usually inexperienced or insecure directors who wanted to handle the players as though they were puppets.

I believe that had Spencer not fallen ill shortly after that time and become discouraged about his waning energy, he would have pursued this idea. Moreover, I believe that as a director, he would have made a significant contribution to the screen. It would have been only a question of translating his acting genius and storytelling gifts into the techniques of directing.

Kate's great good friend Lawrence Langner died on the day after Christmas, 1962. Kate was unable to attend either his funeral or the memorial service held at The Anta Theatre on January 10, 1963. She sent the following message, and it was read by Cyril Ritchard:

To identify myself in Lawrence Langner's life—let me say that since 1935 I have not worked for any one else in the theater. *Jane Eyre:* We toured about, doing great business, but we could not get the script right. Finally I told Terry and Lawrence that I would prefer not to take it into New York, that I had been roasted in *The Lake* unmercifully and deservedly, and that the next time I went to New York I wanted to feel, at least from my own point of view, that I was as good as I could be. There never was any argument. Going into New York was never mentioned again. We toured, got our investment back, and we closed. Lawrence and Terry thereby earned my undying gratitude. As management, they had looked at the situation from an actor's point of view.

Nineteen thirty-eight: Philip Barry brought me *The Philadelphia Story*. I told him I must take it to Lawrence. Phil did not want to because he'd done his last one with the Guild, and he hadn't been too happy. I said that I had no choice, that I must take it to them, that they had been very decent about *Jane Eyre,* and that I felt obligated. Phil said "Okay." Now, Phil did not know at that time that I could not get a job. I did not know that Phil hadn't had anything done for several years. Neither of us knew the Guild was absolutely broke. The Guild did not know about Phil or about me. Phil's play was a smash! It had to be.

After we'd run a bit, Lawrence came backstage one night and said, "Kate, what are you going to do next?"

"Good God, Lawrence, I'm doing *this!*"

"Yes, but what sort of thing are you aiming at?" and he began to talk about Shakespeare. "I think you should do Rosalind."

"Good God, Lawrence, I can't play Shakespeare!"

"How do you know?" he persisted. "Try, or learn."

Well, I went so far as to read *As You Like It.* Lawrence and his notions! Then two years later we did Phil Barry's *Without Love*. Lawrence again: "Kate, what are you going to do in the future? Why don't you play Rosalind? You know I'm thinking of building a Shakespeare theater? Don't you think that would be interesting?"

"Good God, Lawrence!"

Five years later, 1949, Lawrence called me and said,

"Kate, I want to talk to you. Now, where are you going? You are repeating yourself. You can't just travel one road. Take a chance. I want to see you play Rosalind."

It had taken me ten years to catch on. He's right, I thought, do it. I did. What can I say? He sort of opened my doors and windows. I'm very, very grateful to Lawrence.

And you know something? Urging me he meant two things. One: he wanted to broaden out my career, for my own sake. And two: he really meant it, literally meant it, in the most naïve way he wanted to see me play Rosalind.

"You have such pretty legs, Kate," he'd say. "You really must." But I must say to you, he didn't necessarily say Kate when he talked to me. He might call me Lynn or Kit or Helen: Helen—Kit—Lynn—Kate—what he really meant was——ACTRESS!

"What are you going to do? Don't you think it would be interesting?"

GOOD GOD, LAWRENCE, HOW WE'LL MISS YOU!

Elaine May is my welcome dinner partner. The subject of Kate comes up. "I admire her," says Elaine. "What else can I say? I admire her more than any woman I've ever known or read about. And all I know about her is what I read and what I hear from others. I don't think I've ever seen her off the stage or screen. Everyone keeps telling me how they see her in the street or riding a bicycle in the park. I've never had such luck. I just admire her. From afar. The way she lives her life and does her work. There's no bull about it. She seems to understand what it's all about. The ups and downs. She doesn't take either direction too seriously. She isn't intoxicated by the ups and she isn't defeated by the downs. She thinks for herself. She really is about the only person who gives you the feeling that maybe it *could* be a woman's world. What I mean to say is that I *admire* her."

Listening to the late television news on Sunday evening, July 31, 1963, we are stunned by a fragmentary report that Spencer Tracy has collapsed. We phone the house, we phone the beach. No answer at either place. We call the Erskines. They are not in. Finally, Cukor, who has some information but not definitive.

"He's all right, I think," says George. "I guess Kate saved his life."

"How do you mean?"

"Well, by knowing what to do. They were having a picnic on the beach out there, and he collapsed. Slumped over. She didn't wait a second but called the Zuma Beach fire department and they got there in a few minutes with oxygen and that kept him going until the ambulance from St. Vincent's arrived."

"Is that where he is now?" I asked.

"I think so, yes."

I phone St. Vincent's and ask to speak to Mr. Tracy's nurse. A few minutes later, Mrs. Tracy comes on.

She tells me the doctor has now determined that it was definitely not a heart attack but merely some upper respiratory congestion. Spencer is sure to be all right in a few days.

"Give him our love, Louise, and I'll call again tomorrow."

"Thank you," she says.

We cannot help but marvel at Kate's behavior in this crisis. She gets Spencer into the hospital. As soon as she has done so, she informs his family of the situation and allows them to take over.

Fanny Brice had many friends. Friendship was her avocation. Old friends from Follies days were constantly staying with her—often for years at a time. Harry Pilcer, Ann Pennington, Lillian Lorraine. Then there were new friends, the crowd from the radio business. The art world. Interior decorators. Doctors. Gamblers and worse. And Kate and Spencer.

The three of them shared a private and intimate affection. Fanny, the Queen of Common Sense, often assisted Kate in difficult decisions. And with Spence, it was just this side of love.

When I undertook the job of staging *Funny Girl,* the Broadway musical based on Fanny's early life, I consulted everyone who knew her. My most valuable sources proved to be Kate and Spencer.

In doing the show, we were not going to attempt a true biographical work—the book was largely invention—but it seemed to me that Fanny Brice was a unique figure whose real personality would provide the materials for an engrossing character.

All of us on the show realized that the bulk of the audience would be composed of people to whom Fanny Brice would be no more than a dim remembrance of the past, and that there would be many who would not have known her at all.

Indeed, this was true of our very young, supremely gifted leading player—Barbra Streisand. Barbra had never laid eyes on Fanny Brice, nor seen her in films, nor heard her on the radio. In fact, prior to discussions of the show, she had never heard of Fanny Brice at all. Small wonder. Barbra was born in 1945. Fanny died in 1951.

Barbra took the instinctively correct position that she did not wish to study the real Fanny too precisely. "I'm no mimic," she said, "and if I was, it'd be *worse!* I've got to do it like *me.*"

Well and good, but what was *"it"?*

In an effort to capture the essence of Fanny and instill it into Barbra, I sought help from Kate and Spencer.

They talked endlessly to me about Fanny, and loved doing it. Her cooking. Her painting. Her language. Her sense of business, of motherhood, of love.

After days and nights of this, I asked them, "What single word would you use to describe her principal quality?"

"Elegance," said Spencer.

I was surprised, although I recognized the truth of it at once.

"Well done, Spence," said Kate. "I'd have said 'sexuality.' "

Another surprise. Another truth.

I thanked my friends.

During the preproduction conferences, I studied Barbra. The girl had everything—well, almost everything. She sang, of course, better than anyone around. She moved beautifully. She had true emotion. She could act. She was funny and intelligent and highly professional.

But as the days went on, I perceived that she lacked only two elements: elegance and sexuality.

The latter came easily after a few frank talks. She had it, all right, she simply was not using it. Moreover, it was written into the part.

Elegance, on the other hand, was less easy to come by. It is an ephemeral quality, difficult to describe, impossible to verbalize, ridiculous to demonstrate.

Still, I persisted. I would speak the word to her daily, more than once.

One day she said, "Elegance. Elegance. Jesus! All right, already. I'm not sure I know what you're talking about. Do *you?*"

I told her that an outstanding British film critic, Dilys Powell, had once argued with me about Norman Wisdom, a comedian I admired.

"He's less than top rank," she had said, "because he has no elegance. All *great* comedians have it."

Barbra frowned.

I talked to her of Laurel and Hardy, Chaplin, Harold Lloyd, W. C. Fields, Danny Kaye, Bert Lahr, Ed Wynn, and, of course, Fanny Brice. Alas, most of these were only names to her.

I tried another tack, explaining that a fat comedian who trades on his fatness is cheap. He must have elegance. Or if he is small, or homely, or skinny.

"You've got to have a vision of yourself that's different from what's obvious. Fanny had elegance. Taste. Style. Dignity. Class."

"Elegance," said Barbra, vaguely, then day by day began to acquire it.

It was my one contribution to her performance. She needed

nothing more. She was and is a *rara avis*. In the end, her Fanny Brice had true elegance, and so did she. She has it still, and uses it.

I must tell her one day of the anonymous parts Spencer and Kate played in bringing her through, in supplying her with two vital attributes.

Actors and actresses need to act. That is why they are actors and actresses.

During the period of Spencer's enforced inactivity, Kate, brilliantly recognizing the problem, would put Spencer on whenever she got a chance.

"Tell them about the time you and Pat O'Brien were in stock in Baltimore together." Or, "Do that speech from *Desire Under the Elms,* Spence. Come on, do it." Or, "Do your imitation of George M. Cohan." Or, one evening, "Do they know about Lynnie's potatoes?"

"Of course they do," said Spence. "They've heard it a thousand times."

"Not me," I lied. "Lynnie's potatoes? What's that?"

Kate looks at Ruth who goes along.

"I've never heard it."

"Go on, Spence," urges Kate.

Whether or not Spence is deceived by our act, I cannot say, but he warms to the cue and takes off.

"Well, you know that gang of ours that used to meet and eat all the time? Jesus, they were great. Everybody always had some goddam problem or other, and of course everybody always ate practically the same thing, or drank—when they were drinking. Like Pat. He always had Cutty Sark and plain water. Always. Claimed it was healthy. 'A lady's scotch,' he used to call it. Most of the rest of us were knocking on it pretty good in those days, too. Well, hell, everybody was thirty-two years old. I mean, everybody in the world. Polo, staying up late. It was a time. One of our guys—everybody's favorite—was Lynne Overman. A beautiful actor, a tremendous comedian. He was under contract to Paramount and *never* stopped working. The one thing *he* had every time we ate together was these Lyonnaise potatoes, but they had to be done exactly the way he wanted them done. The exact proportion of potatoes and onions, and the potatoes had to be boiled first before they were fried, and the onions put in a little later so they came out crisp and not soggy, and the whole thing had to be sort of browned over. Once in a while, somebody else would order them, too. They got to be known as Lynnie's potatoes. Well, Lynne died and that made one hell of a hole in our bunch. I remember we were so affected I don't think we met for a month or two. I guess we just couldn't bear the idea of sitting down around the table without ol' Lynne. But after a while there were a few phone calls back and forth, and we got together. Now, the first thing that happened was ordering the drinks, of course. Lynne always used to drink something called a Rob Roy. So Pat O'Brien, with tears in his eyes, ordered Rob Roys all around. And when they came he made a big thing of raising the glass and saying just one word, sort of hoarsely. He said, 'Lynnie.' And as he took a sip, he saw that only Allen Jenkins was sipping with him. I didn't have any of mine, I was on the wagon at the time. Frank was sick—little Frank that is, McHugh. And Morgan—big Frank—was playing an important part and had an early call. Well, the whole situation really burned Pat, and he kept saying, 'It's to *Lynnie!* We're drinking a *toast*. To Lynnie's *memory*. What's the matter with you guys?' So I explained how I was off the sauce, and little Frank went into about how he was sick. And big Frank told his problem. And Pat blew his stack and screamed: 'Well, it's just too goddam *bad* that everybody here can't take even one sip of one damn Rob Roy to honor the memory of one of their dearest friends lying cold and alone and ten feet under. No! His friends have to turn out to be either a *lush* or a *crack-up* or a big hambo and nobody can even *drink* to him.' I don't know what would've happened about now if the waiter hadn't come over and started passing out the menus and Frank Morgan—my God, what a guy he was—said, 'I have it, gentlemen.

Since we're not all in a position to booze it, let's all have an order of Lynnie's potatoes.' Well, let me tell you it was one of those perfect cases of a guy saying the right thing at the right time. And even Pat brightened up and he said, 'Okay. Great idea. Really great, Frank. Thanks!' Then he said to the waiter, 'Lynnie's potatoes all around.' After a while, when the food came, Pat took a big forkful of the potatoes, raised them above his head, and said, real solemnly, 'Come on, fellas. To Lynnie.' So we all pitched up a forkful of those Lyonnaise potatoes and raised them into the air and we all said, 'Lynnie,' and we ate the potatoes. And everybody felt fine. So it got to be a ritual. For the next few weeks, every time we met we'd order Lynnie's potatoes, and pass them around, and each one would take a forkful and raise it in the air and say, 'Lynnie.' It went on that way for quite a time. Then one night, the potatoes were being passed around and when they got to Frank McHugh, he said quietly, 'No, thank you,' and passed them on to me. I took mine. And all of a sudden, Pat was off again. He looked at Frank and his eyes—well, you could've knocked them off with a stick—and he said, his voice was trembling, 'What did you say?' And Frank said, 'I said, "No, thank you."' Pat said, '"*No,* thank you"? You're not going to toast Lynnie in Lynnie's *potatoes?*' They were looking at each other pretty hard, and Frank said, 'No, I'm not. So say no more!' And Pat said, 'Well, I'd like to know why the hell *not!*' And his hand was shaking so that his potatoes fell off his fork and he had to get a fresh forkful. And little Frank said, 'I'd rather not say.' Well, Pat went pale and said, 'Talk, Frank.' Frank said, 'It's personal.' Pat leaned over and said, 'I'm warning you. . . .' At this, little Frank leaned over and yelled, 'All *right!* It's because every time I have these goddam potatoes I get sick and go home and puke! And I loved Lynnie—I loved him just as much as *you* did but I'm a son-of-a-bitch if I love him so much that I want to *join* him!' And of course that ended the whole business of Lynnie's potatoes."

We all responded as we were meant to. Although I had heard him tell the story many times, it never failed to enchant me. Kate laughed, not putting it on, but because she so thoroughly enjoyed reliving that part of Spencer's life with him.

Television and especially the film showings on it became a great boon to him in these days.

Spencer saw most of his pictures for the first time. Apparently Kate had not been much of a moviegoer either, and many of the pictures were new to her.

"My God, but he's good!" she said to me one day, as though making a discovery. "Did you ever see him in *Libeled Lady?"*

"Of course."

"Funniest damned thing I've ever seen in my life, and what about *Boys Town?"*

"And *Captains Courageous?"*

"Yuh, well, I'd seen that, but so many of the others not."

One evening Spencer asked me, confidentially, "Do you ever find yourself talking back to it?"

"To what?"

"To the tube? I mean answering back. Having conversations with those little leaping tintypes?"

"Not very often," I said. "Sometimes listening to those guys reviewing plays."

"Well, at least you do it sometimes. I began to get the feeling, sitting here, talking back to it, that I was going bananas. I want to tell you it's a goddam eerie feeling to look at yourself the way you looked and sounded and acted twenty or thirty years ago. It's not hard to be objective. The stupid bastard up there isn't really you. He's some kind of a distant relative you remember but never really liked. And once in a while—I don't mind saying this—I think I'm pretty damned good." He went on. "I had an experience here the other night. I was sitting and watching *Boys Town* and there I am with this whole group and I realize that one of them a few days before—I'd seen in the paper—had been picked up for drunk driving, and one of them is off his rocker in an institution somewhere. Then there's two of them, they were friends back then, and somebody told me they'd been picked up for pushing dope, and then there was poor little Mickey, and I've got my arms around all these characters and the camera's rolling in and I say, 'There *are* no bad boys!' I want to tell you I nearly fell out of this chair. Nearly, hell. I *did*."

Stories that effectively dramatize the deep, uncommon love that can exist between two men are almost always successful: From Damon and Pythias through Quirt and Flagg to Butch Cassidy and the Sundance Kid.

How warming when we see them in the life around us. I believe that intermittently I shared such a relationship with Spencer. My love for him never varied, indeed, intensified without regard to the difficulties and vicissitudes of our relationship. It was this love that made the bad times so much harder to bear. He was, as a rule, highly critical of me and of my activities, often of my work, and frequently of my opinions, yet he once looked across the room in the midst of one of our evenings, and in the presence of Kate and Ruth, said, apropos of nothing, "You know, I don't think I'll ever marry again, but if I ever did, I think I'd like to marry *you,* Gar."

It remains in my memory as the most treasured of my compliments.

Another such pairing was Spencer and James Cagney. They met when they were knocking about in New York, trying to get a foot into the theater's door.

Spencer could never manage to tell, without choking back tears, the story of Cagney and *Broadway*. Jimmy had understudied Lee Tracy in this great success, and was finally, after dozens of auditions, engaged to play the part in the London production. The luggage was bought, the passport achieved, the boat reservations made, and the farewell party given. On the day before the boat was to sail, Jimmy Cagney was informed there had been a change in plans. He would not be going after all. No more reason than that. They had simply decided on someone else. Cagney was on the verge of giving up, which is frequently the first instinct at such a moment, but he went on. In the years to come, the one interruption did not seem to matter.

At the time Spencer made his sensational success in *The Last Mile,* Cagney also scored on Broadway as Little Red opposite Charles Bickford as Big Red in *Outside Looking In,* adapted from Jim Tully's novel of the hobo world, *Beggars of Life*.

Spencer was swiftly invited to Hollywood to play in *Up the River,* a prison picture, of course. It took Cagney a second hit (*Penny Arcade* with Joan Blondell) to bring him to Warner's.

("All you need to be a success in the movies," says Walter Matthau, "is forty good breaks.")

Jimmy Cagney said to me one evening, "Spence? He's the most difficult son-of-a-bitch I've ever known. And the best. Certainly the best actor. Have you ever noticed something? You go to a vaudeville show or a nightclub, watch those variety things on television, and guys are always coming on and doing imitations. Eddie Robinson, me, Bogie, Jimmie Stewart, John Wayne. Have you noticed how they never imitate Spence? Never try? You know why that is? It's because there's nothing to imitate except his genius and that can't be mimicked. He doesn't have any mannerisms of his own. Well, maybe that jaw clench but that's nerves, I think, more than anything. You know, *squeezing* the part out. With him every character he plays develops his *own* mannerisms and idiosyncrasies. I love the guy. I don't understand him, but I love him. We've had good times together, and rough ones, too. He's too demanding. Have you noticed that? Demanding of his friends and sometimes he sets standards nobody can meet. Hell, he doesn't meet them himself. Maybe that's why he's so miserable all the time."

"Not all the time," I say.

"Well, enough of the time. He wants to be perfect and he knows he isn't, and can't be, so he wants all his friends to be perfect and then he gets sore when he finds out *they* can't be. A hard man."

I remember a delicious moment at Spencer's house when Cagney invited Spence to see if he could remember the soft-shoe routine he taught him when they were both on their way to try out for a chorus job. Spencer rose grimly, moved to Jimmy's side and, to Jimmy's sung accompaniment, performed as charming a soft-shoe routine as can be imagined. Spencer had not done it in forty years.

The more tragic, then, to consider that in later years the friendship cooled; indeed, practically fell apart. Cagney had grown extremely rich as a result of unceasing work and judicious investments. ("No actor," Tracy said, "has a right to be *that* rich!") Spencer observed that the richer Jimmy became, the more right wing and intolerant he became politically. In their youth, Cagney had been more left wing than Spencer, who, throughout his life, steered a middle political course.

In the beginning, the crack in their relationship was a subject for jokes, such as the evening when their clan sat around talking sentimentally about the wonderful work done by the new Motion Picture Country House. Overheard, their dialogue usually sounded as though it had been written by Sean O'Casey.

"A grand thing, a great thing. Imagine it!"

"Wonderful, wonderful!"

"They're welcome to the one per cent of *my* pay. I wish it were more."

"Give them more."

"I *will,* by God!"

"It's a proud day for the actors, boys."

"I'll drink to that," said Cagney. "I wonder—I mean, when the time comes—how would a man go about getting into the place?"

"Buy it!" said Spencer.

Later, the matter became more serious. The war came, and McCarthyism, Red Channels and blacklisting, along with all the ugly apparatus of the superpatriots in vindictive action with questionable motives. On many issues, Tracy and Cagney found themselves seriously at odds. The phone calls grew shorter, the time between visits longer, and eventually they saw little or nothing of each other.

Spencer never gave up on Jimmy, and kept alive the memory of their great days. And each time I met Cagney anywhere, his first question would be, "How's ol' Spence?"

Jimmy sent a message to Kate when Spencer died, but did not attend the funeral.

"Don't let it hurt your feelings," I said to Kate.

"They're not my feelings," she snapped. "They're Spencer's."

Spencer Tracy's death on June 10, 1967, was, for Kate, an end and a beginning. It was the end of a meaningful personal and long professional association. In their twenty-six years they had done their finest work, together and individually. Playing as a team, they brought out the best in each other; and their separate projects had always the advantage of the other's advice and inspiration.

For a long time, before Spencer's illness, work came first. Thus, there were long separations: Kate in London for *The Millionairess;* in Africa for *The African Queen;* in Stratford, Connecticut, for *Antony and Cleopatra, The Merchant of Venice,* and *Twelfth Night;* in Australia for the Shakespeare tour with Robert Helpmann under Michael Benthall's direction; in London again for *Suddenly, Last Summer,* and still again for some nonsense with Bob Hope; in New York for *Long Day's Journey into Night.*

This last was a something in their life. Eugene O'Neill admired Spencer greatly and tempted him time and again; with *The Iceman Cometh,* with *A Touch of the Poet,* and finally, with *Long Day's Journey into Night.* Each time, Spencer would read, study, cerebrate, sweat, discuss, and finally decline. His given reasons were never the real ones. Those he kept locked within himself. Imagine him, if you will, in any one of those three plays!

When, however, *Long Day's Journey into Night* was to be made as a film, the condition changed. It was offered to them both and the prospect was a heady one: two of the most accomplished film players of all time in the spectacularly brilliant roles in O'Neill's greatest play.

But Spencer balked, and no amount of persuasion could move him. It had been decided to shoot the film on a low budget, which meant that fees would be small. I cannot believe that this would have affected his decision (any more than it did Kate's, who played the role she wanted to play for one *tenth* of her established salary), but it might have been that he was concerned about the over-all quality of a low-budget film. Tracy's orientation in films had entirely to do with important pictures at major studios. Artistically, he erred.

Still, one of the strengths of this partnership was the fact that each partner retained complete sovereignty.

Kate says, "Spence was the only *pure* person I ever met in all my life. I've encountered some fascinating ones, and some terribly attractive ones." She smiles a faraway smile. "I can't tell you how many times I've relived those ten seconds—and wondered where would I be and who—if she hadn't come out and called at that instant."

We wait, silently, for her to go on.

"Once, in Wales—touring all over it—fascinating—with a friend. We stopped in a little village. I got out of the car to stretch—I'd been driving—she went in to mail some postcards or buy some—I don't remember. And a wagon pulled up and stopped on the other side of the street—and the driver—a young man—the handsomest creature I'd ever seen—or have seen since. Dark—dark in every way—hair, skin, eyes, spirit. All at once, we were looking at each other—and it happened—you know—it happens to everyone at times—communication beyond words or action—complete clarity and understanding—as though there's been a past—and the future seems already to have happened. He smiled—my knees went funny—he made a movement with his head and hand—beckoning—an invitation to join him—I felt myself moving toward him—all lightheaded—

and my friend came out and yelled, 'Kate—where're you going? Come on—we're late.' And he stood up—I saw anger and power—and he made another sign—but the spell was broken—I was a proper New England girl again—and I turned away and we drove off—never looked back.

"I suppose," she goes on, "we've all had chance meetings like that—What are those lines? 'I did but see her passing by, and yet I'll love her till I die.' It's sweet, that idea. Then there are the ones we get entangled with—for better or worse—usually for worse—but when those things are over, you've got to try to remember the good parts—what was valuable about it and what you gained from the relationship and—well, Spence was simply *different*. No affectations—not a selfish bone in his body. I know sometimes it looked as though he were being selfish—wasn't—He just knew I loved doing things for him—and wasn't he *funny*—about everything?—even about himself—He took his work seriously—never himself—and such a good, clean brain—he really used it to think with—he didn't merely remember—he *invented* his own opinions—didn't have to wait to read in a book or a magazine what to think about something—made up his own mind—and sometimes he had no opinion at all on a subject—refreshing these days when everyone feels they have to have an opinion on *everything*—as if having no opinion is impotent or something—not so at all. Why does everyone have to have an opinion about everything? Spence. I'll miss him every day as long as I live."

A few minutes after we heard the dreadful news on that bleak Saturday morning, we were on our way to Spencer's cottage. I drove speedily at first, but began to slow down as I turned into Doheny Drive and started up the hill. Slower and slower. I did not want to reach the destination that had in it such awful finality. I pulled up to the curb and stopped.

"I think I'd like to wait a while."

"All right," said Ruth.

"I mean about an hour or so."

"No," she said. "Kate expects us."

I took a few minutes to collect myself, tried to think of what to say, how to behave on arrival—failed—found myself touching the doorbell, performing an act that had for such a long period presaged a good time.

Phyllis opened the door. We embraced.

"She okay?" I asked.

Phyllis nodded.

We went into the living room. Kate was there, already moving toward me. Before I could speak, she put her arms about me and said, "Oh, Gar. Oh, dear. I'm *so* sorry for you."

There was nothing more to say, not for a long time.

I spent the next few days thinking of my lost friend, fixing details in my memory, reviewing our years, remembering. . . .

. . . His full name was (is?) Spencer Bonaventure Tracy, but he was more commonly known simply as Spencer Tracy. He was also called Mr. Tracy, Spencer, Spence, M'sieu Spansaire (by French fans), The Gray Fox (by Frank Sinatra), Flannel (by me), The Pope (by other actors), and Ratty (allowed only to Kate). There were other appellations in other lives, because Spencer is (was?) many men. To me alone, he had been brother, father, son, teacher, confessor, adviser, adversary, collaborator, and friend.

On the phone with me, a few hours before his death, he had described himself as "Okay, but all in." Small wonder. He had packed a lot of living and loving and eating and drinking and reaching and working into his sixty-seven years. (He was fond of Joe E. Lewis's crack: "You only live once—but if you work it right, once is *enough!*")

I recall that in the course of that last year, I phoned Spence no less than two hundred fifty times. He phoned me once. That was on the night of the day he finished shooting *Guess Who's Coming to Dinner*. He was gleeful, excited, relieved, and slightly incredulous.

"Finished!" he cried. "Do you believe it? *I* don't. I was betting against myself all the way. I owe me a fortune. I may welsh. But *finished*. Are you impressed?"

"No," I replied. "What impressed me was you *starting*."

"I get it," he said. "Everybody's down at the party. Both Kathies—everybody."

"Why not you?"

"Hell, no. Too emotional. This is it. The Big Wrap-up. I've retired."

"You should've gone."

"I thought I might, but then right after the last shot today, Stanley said, 'That's the one!' And I knew it was over and we shook hands and he started to cry and so did I and I figured the hell with it and came home. I think I've got about five beers in me! But did you hear me, Jasper? I finished the picture."

The five beers may have been a happy exaggeration. It had been years since he had had even one. The subject interested and amused him now and he could talk with ease and gaiety about "the ol' heimerdeimer days." And even though he was through with it, there was always a full supply of booze in the cabinet in the living room.

I asked him once for his opinion on which airline to fly.

"Doesn't matter," he said. "They're all good. I've flown from here to New York on every one of them." He thought, then added, "And a couple of times, I flew there without any airline at all!"

In 1958, he was to read the eulogy at the funeral of Louis B. Mayer. Although he had admired L.B., it was a duty he did not relish. He sat alone in an antechamber of the Wilshire Temple, looking over the text. Rabbi Magnin came in, greeted him, and offered him a drink. Spencer declined.

The rabbi said, "Whenever Georgie Jessel has to do this, he always takes a drink first."

"I know," said Spencer, "but if *I* did, Rabbi, I might bury *you* instead of Mr. Mayer."

In a profession where backbiting, put-down, panning, jealousy, faultfinding, and blameputting are common coin, I have never heard or read a word against Spencer Tracy the actor, or the man. In this, too, he remains unique, since there is no other figure about whom this can be truly said. He was a no-nonsense man; focused, concentrated, dedicated. Never a moment of toadying, of currying favor, of preoccupation with image. His standards were high, his views often overcritical, sometimes harsh. There were many in his profession of whom he did not approve and when the occasion demanded, he said so.

Spencer was, indubitably, the finest screen actor of his generation. Acting can be good, accomplished, polished, skillful, or great. And there is a plateau beyond—to acting which has within it artless art, a touch of magic, an aura of the supernatural, a suggestion of extrasensory perception. Man creating man out of man. In acting on this level, the audience is made aware of what a character is thinking and feeling no matter what he is doing or saying. Players have accomplished this in the theater, but rarely on the screen. The living empathy of theater art makes the phenomenon understandable; on film it is a surpassing achievement.

In a long professional lifetime, during which acting has been an encompassing subject, I have had no experience more impressive than the one that took place one rainy evening in George Cukor's library: Spencer and Kate reading aloud the screenplay of *Pat and Mike*. Spencer sat in a corner of the room, his eyeglasses perched on his nose. He began to read, to act, to be. The man with whom we had dined a few minutes earlier was no longer there. Instead, we were confronted by Mike—a personality far more real and complex than the person we had imagined—with a way of breathing, thinking, smoking, coughing, speaking, and munching peanuts. For two hours and more, Spencer stayed in character. I saw the art of acting that night, plain.

Memories of this mesmeric man continued to crowd my consciousness, wanting to be remembered.

The time in Paris, in the Louvre, when I lost him, and came upon him half an hour later, the center of a singular sight: the celebrated "Venus de Milo"; Spence staring at it, transfixed; a crowd of fifty staring at Spencer Tracy. When I described the spectacle to him, he blushed and asked me not to repeat it.

I heard him make a speech only once—at a dinner honoring

the new head of M-G-M, Dore Schary. Spencer said: "Ladies and gentlemen: Many years ago, I starred in *The Last Mile* on Broadway. My part was Killer Mears and the scene was a death house. Toward the end of the first act, three reporters came in to interview me. One of them had six lines, another had two lines, and the third one had no lines. The play was a big hit and had a long run and at every single performance, when those three reporters left, I used to look at the third one—the one with no lines—and give him a little bow. Because, ladies and gentlemen, somehow I knew that some day he was going to be made the head of M-G-M!"

With middle age, his problems of overweight began. The polo-playing days were now behind him. He had been a fine player, slashing about regularly with Will Rogers, Darryl Zanuck, Tim Durant, and Tommy Hitchcock.

But now he fought the added pounds, especially before starting a picture. He asked me to read *The Seventh Cross,* a script about a World War II prison camp escape. I thought it excellent and told him so, but he sensed some small reservation.

"It's a fine part for you," I said, "but—well . . ."

"Don't worry about that," he interrupted.

"About what?"

"About what you're thinking."

"Oh."

"There's going to be a change in the rewrite," he explained. "In the new version I *eat* my way out!"

All great actors are larger than life when they are acting. Spencer was so, on and off. He was a man of size and dimension in spirit, intellect, and vision. If something or someone struck him funny, he did not laugh, he caved in. His was the slyest smile, the wickedest cut, the tenderest sympathy, the purplest rage, the firmest stand. Yet at no time was he out of control.

He was able, better than anyone I have ever known in any line, to concentrate, to focus, to put the blinders on. While making a picture, he brooked no distraction, recognized no other life. Playing a scene, his one-mindedness was so intense that it had a galvanizing effect on anyone and everyone who happened to be watching.

When he began to paint, I understand that his first subjects were: a single tree, a single flower, a single wave.

There are film stars who not only watch the rushes of each day's work, but study them carefully, often running them again and again; who attend the showing of the first rough cut; who see sneak previews; enter into editorial discussion; who go to their premieres. Not Spencer. He never saw a single day's work, never went to a preview or an opening; in fact, never looked at any of his pictures until, later in life, they began turning up on television.

It is to Stanley Kramer that we owe four of the last Tracy films: *Inherit the Wind, Judgment at Nuremberg, It's a Mad, Mad, Mad, Mad World,* and *Guess Who's Coming to Dinner.*

"Lots of people around here keep telling me how great I am," Spencer said one night, "but you notice how it's Stanley who puts me to work."

I recall that as plans for the final film moved toward completion, trouble arose. The insurance company declined to cover Tracy because of his illness four years earlier. Kramer, with an unprecedented display of courage, insisted on proceeding. Spencer pointed out the risk, tried to talk him out of it, without success. About two weeks before the starting date, Spencer had a minor setback. He sent for Kramer and explained his condition in detail.

"Well, Spence," said Kramer, "if you don't feel up to it, I'll call it off. I'm not going to do it without you, and that's that."

"Okay," said Spencer. "Let's go."

And go they did. Tracy's part was long and complex and delicate. Above and beyond the demands of the performance, he felt the heavy weight of responsibility because of Kramer's rare faith in him.

"The guy's got more moxie," he said to me one evening during this time, "than any six I've ever known. I tell him my life expectancy is about seven and a half minutes and he says 'Action!' He's some kind of a nut or saint. Or both."

Looking backward, it is increasingly clear that Spence was aware of his failing health, yet observe how this extraordinary disciplinarian marshaled his forces and husbanded his powers in order that he might finish his work, fulfill his contract. His final accomplishment is characteristic, the way of a professional. He did his job before he died.

With Spence one always experienced the inhale-exhale, give-and-take, yes-and-no, hot-and-cold, up-and-down, in-and-out of life which makes it bearable.

I find it significant that he, a devout Catholic, and I, a confirmed atheist, could have formed and continued and reveled in a thirty-year friendship. Long walks—Spencer patiently interpreting his faith. Long talks—during which he listened (as only he could listen) to the other side, with never a moment of pique or irritation. We reached no conclusions, changed no stands, but were both enriched by the exchange of nerve ends.

Now I had to come to grips with the fact that the walks and talks were ended.

Summing up, I see that if I am right, I must be content with the heritage of the memory of a nonesuch actor and a darlin' man and a rare friend. If *he* is right, I envy the angels.

And I remind myself that Goodadventure was (is?) his middle name.

Carroll Tracy had a difficult time after his brother's death. He had for years existed as a living part of Spencer. When Spencer died, Carroll began to deteriorate. Dorothy, his wife, died. He followed a year and a half later. In between, he suffered a loneliness he had never known.

He and Spencer had talked daily. Carroll was on Spencer's payroll. He had something to do with managing Spencer's affairs; an amiable man, much attached to his brother. He lunched every day at the Bistro. I came in one day and found him sitting there. I had recently returned to California and had not seen Spence for some time. I had phoned him but there was no answer. (Spencer would often not answer his phone for days on end.) I said casually to Carroll, "How's Spence?"

"Why," said Carroll, smiling broadly, "he's . . ." He could not go on, and burst into tears. It was thus I learned Spencer was ill. Not seriously ill but not himself.

When I saw Spencer later that evening I reported my encounter with Carroll. Spencer shook his head and said, "Poor son-of-a-bitch. He's part me."

After Dorothy's death, Carroll began to fade rapidly. They were childless. He was virtually alone now and had to be moved to a convalescent home. Kate went to see him every single day. When she found she was not pleased with the home he was in, she arranged, with great effort, to have him moved to another, a better one.

One day she turned up, sat down in his room with a script on her lap, read him the complete libretto of *Coco,* and sang the score from beginning to end. She attracted a good many of the other patients but did not mind and went on. A great ovation at the end. The first of many to come. This may be said to have been the first preview performance of Katharine Hepburn in *Coco.*

Kate and Spence were highly civilized people, who held firmly to the enlightened principle of live and let live.

Further, each practiced an extremely personal form of religious expression.

Spencer was a true believer, accepted in all faith the doctrine of his Church, went to Mass and to confession, but was often critical of certain activities and attitudes of the Church.

For example, he was offended when, on his first visit to Rome, a delegation from the Vatican came to call on him at his hotel.

"I'm an actor, for cryin' out loud," he said to us later. "A movie actor. All right, a star. Why the hell should a delegation from the Vatican come to see *me?* What's *that* got to do with what the Church is supposed to be about?"

I remind him of a joke long common around Rome. Automobiles registered in Vatican City bear the letters SCV preceding the number on their license plates. The letters stand for *Santa Cittá Vaticana* (Holy Vatican City). But waggish Romans insist that the letters stand for: *Se Cristo Vedesse* (If Christ could see!).

Spencer nods, clenches his jaw, shakes his head and says, "Yes. Yes."

Katharine, too, is of a special breed. Freethinkers are generally materialists, but she finds profound spirituality in nature, in weather, in flowers, in trees, and plants. She recognizes the oneness, the sense of organization in the scheme of things.

She exists in an unusual relationship to animals. She treats cats and dogs and horses as though they were fellow human beings. She practices the "reverence for life" propounded by Schweitzer. It is the reason she dislikes circuses and cannot understand why I am so taken with them. She understands that, in the words of Thornton Wilder, "Any man who does not realize that he is half an animal is only half a man."

Whatever they believed in, they believed in each other as well, and although she is an atheist, or agnostic, or a freethinker, depending on one's understanding of these labels, she placed in his coffin, before it was sealed, a little St. Christopher statue that he loved, a piece of Carrara marble he had found, and his rosary beads.

I step into the back of Kate's car one afternoon and go sliding upside down. I see her looking down at me from the driver's seat.

"I'm sorry," she says. "Give me that. I'll take care of it."

"Give you what?" I ask.

"Skate board. Isn't that what you slipped on?"

I retrieve it from beneath myself and hand it to her.

"What the hell're you doing with a skate board?" I inquire. "Isn't it pretty dangerous—for you?"

"It's only dangerous," she says, "if you're no good at it. I happen to be marvelous."

Her open confidence makes me laugh. Mistake.

She pulls the car sharply to the side of the street, hops out of the car, grabs her skate board and says, "Pick me up at the bottom."

I watch with no little apprehension as my middle-aged friend, playing a teen-agers' game, miraculously glides to the bottom of the hill with skill and grace. I drive down, pick her up, and we continue in silence.

Her close friend, Peter Viertel, is an expert surfer with years of experience.

For many summers, Kate maintained a small cottage at Trancas Beach, next door to the Erskines.

Watching a group of surfers one day, she wondered if she might not enjoy the experience.

She invited Peter to come out and bring his board. The surf was up and Peter demonstrated his skill.

After watching him for about half an hour, she said, "Here, let me try."

Peter attempted to reason with her. "Now wait a second, Kate. It's not as easy as it looks."

"Come on. Let me try. What can happen?"

"What can happen," Peter said, "is the wrong kind of wipeout where you get hit in the head."

"Yah. Well, I'll see I don't do that."

She took the board from him and started out. Peter reported that he watched, agape, as she fought the tide, unable to make progress, threw the board, swam after it, attempted to mount it, fell off, wrestled it, coaxed, pushed it, cajoled, and then, all at once was atop it, but only for a few seconds, tumbled off, remounted, fell again. Peter says it was the most impressive show of raw determination he has ever seen. After a time, there was no sport in it, no recreation. The sea no longer mattered nor did the board. All that mattered was the triumph of her will. She stayed with it for well over an hour and Peter swears that by the end of that time, she made three near-perfect runs in quick succession, came in, threw the board at him, and said, "Yah. Yah. I could get to do that just great if I wanted to, but I don't want to."

No matter what her age, Kate is young, which is why the young respond to her on every level.

As a rule an actress of her age draws the interest of only a diminishing circle of fans. Kate continues to generate powerful magnetism for the young. Her fan mail is preponderantly from young people. The crowds who wait outside the stage door to greet her each night are made up principally of the long-haired, bearded, Levi'd, poncho'd set.

They see in her—as an actress and as a woman—a courageous, outspoken, fearless individualist. They are right.

As the years go by she does not lose her old admirers, but goes on gaining new ones.

Four

We took Kate to see *Forty Carats.* At the end of the performance we all agreed that it was an extremely dull, meretricious effort, but that we ought to go backstage nevertheless.

We moved through the pass door and all at once were surrounded by the unmistakable atmosphere reserved for visiting royalty, the feeling one has backstage in a British theater when a member of the royal family goes back. I remember the night backstage at the Haymarket, when Ruth was playing in *The Matchmaker* there and the Queen Mother came backstage.

At the Morosco Theatre there was an echo of this event. The whole company stood about, waiting, charged-up, sensing that this was an important moment.

Kate was gracious and skillful in the way she was able to compliment Julie Harris whom she did admire, without committing herself as to the play. She did everything that needed to be done, said everything that wanted to be said, and left behind a memory of dignity and a reservoir of good will.

A few nights later we all went to see *The Great White Hope.* This time backstage it was easier as she was able to express honest admiration for every element of the evening. She went to

James Earl Jones's dressing room to compliment him, met his wife, and stayed for a long time talking about the play. When she left, the rest of the company was still waiting, assembled on the stage to greet her.

I find it droll that Kate, who is not only a democrat but a Democrat, should create (without attempting to do so) such a royalist atmosphere.

For several decades, New York, Washington, and Hollywood were the three great gossip centers of the nation, but only in the last was it raised to a form of popular art. The public's interest in the type of gossip that emanated from the West Coast was great. Further, many millions were expended on every variety of press agentry. Not only gossip, but innuendo, *on dit,* whispers behind trade papers, columns and columnists, and the high-ups who knew the low-down. Telephones never stopped buzzing. ("Are you alone?") Mimeograph machines never stopped whirling. (FOR IMMEDIATE RELEASE) The flacks gave the public what they thought the public wanted.

I find it surprising that the Tracy-Hepburn relationship was largely immune to all this. For one thing, they behaved discreetly and in a most civilized way, but more, even the scroungiest item-digger and planter respected these two, as individuals and as a pair. They lived and worked in the midst of this strange community, radiating a rare sort of warmth and dignity and good feeling.

So much for what ended with Spencer's death. What began was yet another career for Katharine, one which was to surpass those that had gone before.

Four and a half years of professional inactivity would in most cases spell the end. Actresses, unlike children, should be seen *and* heard. The public is fickle and swiftly forgets past joys. Each season brings new players with dash and promise. New toys so easily take the place of old ones and movie stars are indeed among our toys. In Kate's case, the moment it became clear she was again free to work, the offers began coming in; tentative at first, then bolder, until a torrent was loosed along with a clamor for her services.

She was unprepared for the onslaught and was soon dealing rustily with the matter of pressured decision. Which role in which work and with whom and under what circumstances? And when?

A week or so after Spencer's funeral, I received a call from Alan Jay Lerner.

"Don't get mad," he began, "but let me ask you something. Is it too early to talk to Katharine Hepburn about a show?"

"I would have thought so," I replied, "but the offers started the day after. There are others not so gentlemanly as you, Alan—so my guess is: get yours in fast. What is it?"

"Coco," he said.

"The musical?"

"Of course."

"What the hell makes you think Kate would want to do a Broadway musical, for God's sake?"

There was a pause, after which he said, "I've got to have her. That's all. I've just *got* to."

"So does everybody," I said. "I admire your taste, Alan, but she says she wouldn't dream of ever doing a Broadway *play* again. Now you tell me musical."

"I've got to have her," he said. "It's her part. A great part of a great woman. She can do it. No one else can. Don't you see that if . . ."

I interrupted. "Don't sell *me*. Sell *her*."

"How?"

"What're you asking *me* for?"

"Because this is delicate," he argued. "It's an odd time and this is a strange offer and I don't want her to turn me down. I need an unorthodox approach because this is an unorthodox situation. You're her friend."

"She has lots of friends," I said, "and, by the way, I doubt that any one of us has any influence on her when it comes to professional matters. Listen, I once spent a year writing a play for her, then she read it and said, 'It doesn't interest me. What would you and Ruth like for dinner tomorrow night?' "

"That's just it!" cried Alan. "This *will* interest her. It must!"

"Coach me," I said to Alan.

"Well," he coached, "mention it to her. She may never have heard of it. And try to arrange for me to see her and talk to her. I have to discuss it with her before she reads it or hears the score."

"Alan," I warned, "she's not snowable."

"I know that," he said. "All I want is a fair shot at her."

"She's lining up pictures," I cautioned. "You may have to wait."

"Gladly," he said, "and I don't care how long. I've *got* to have her!"

I began to get the idea that Alan Jay Lerner had to have Katharine Hepburn for *Coco.*

"You're in luck," I told him. "Kate and Phyllis and George Cukor are coming here to dinner the day after tomorrow. Just us. Family style. George is probably closer to her than anyone. There's sure to be a lot of plan talk. I'll slip yours in."

"Wait," said Alan. "That's good, but what about Cukor? Are you sure he's on our side?"

"Our side?" I asked. "I'm not sure *I'm* on our side."

"Of course you are," said Alan. "Wait. Here it is. Get a hold of Cukor beforehand and brief *him.* Tell him this'll be the crowning glory of her career."

"How about telling him yourself? You know him. He only did *My Fair Lady* for you, for Christ's sake."

"Right," said Alan. *"I'll* tell him." He paused, then added, "And *you* tell him, *too."*

Two nights later, after too much dinner, we lolled about talking of other dinners.

Kate had taken her customary after-dinner position: flat on her back on the floor.

She reported on a number of projects, mostly amorphous. Yes, many scripts were being submitted, but she had not yet got round to beginning to read them.

"And there's something else, Katinka," I said. "Pretty tantalizing."

"Oh? What?" she asked, rolling over and looking at me suspiciously.

That "Katinka" had given me away. She recognized it at once as the variant I use whenever I try to con her about something, great or small. I went on.

"Alan Jay Lerner wants you to play Coco Chanel in a musical he's written with André Previn. Freddie Brisson is going to produce it. Do I sound as though I'm reading? Anyway, he wants to know if you'd be at all interested. It's a great part. Probably be a whale of a show." There was a pause, after which I heard myself say, "He's *got* to have you!"

Kate said, "My—y—y Go—o—o—d—dd!" turning the two syllables into eight.

She laughed. At first I thought it was because she considered the idea ridiculous, but presently I saw that she was truly delighted to have been asked. She was on her feet.

"A musical?" she asked the wall. She turned to us. "Good God! My feet. I couldn't do it. And singing. Eight times a week. Probably dancing, too. I'd go *mad. How fascinating!"* she said, making the last two words equally important.

George spoke. "Anything Alan wants you to do, you should do. He's a great man."

"But George!" Kate pleaded. "Be reasonable." (She seemed to be playing Portia again.) "At my time of life—singing and cavorting."

"Yes," said Ruth, "but as *Coco Chanel*, remember."

"Yah," said Kate. "Yah," the sound escaping her, but her mind elsewhere than on her speech. Then, again: "My—y-y-y Go-o-o-o-dd-dd!!" stretching it this time to *ten* syllables.

I reminded her of the spring of 1941, when I was in Washington, D.C., serving in the Army.

An important documentary called *Women in Defense* was being made, and I was asked if I could get her to do the narration. I hesitated because I did not like to ask a favor, especially one that would be difficult for her to refuse. There was a good deal of pressure on me, so eventually I got her on the phone and outlined the project. To my surprise, she said, "Of course I'll do it. Where do I have to come, and when?"

Later I asked, "How come you agreed so swiftly and easily?"

She replied, "Because it's the first time in my life anyone wanted me for my voice."

Now, I tell her—here is a second time.

The five-part discussion began, and went on for two hours. Kate is as thorough as she is talented, and no aspect of the musical theater, in theory or in practice, was left uncovered. She ate candy and talked; smoked and listened; paced and worried.

In the end she said that of course she would meet with Alan and hear what he had to say, and read the book, and hear the score, and all—but *honestly!*

A year was to pass before she actually signed to play *Coco,* and ten months more before rehearsals were to begin, but as we prepared for bed that night, I said to my wife, "Do you think Kate wants to do *anything?* I mean, yet?"

"Kate knows what she's doing," said Ruth. "She always has. She steers her life. She doesn't let it blow her around. In a way, this is hilarious. All of us sitting around trying to advise her. She should be advising *us.*"

Nevertheless, as the hollow days went by, it became increasingly clear that Kate might talk and not do, might easily fall into a new routine, a pattern of existence devoid of professional activity.

"Too bad we couldn't make it to Edgartown this year," said Ruth. "Kate could have come with us. She'd love it. It would have been just the thing."

Our annual stay at our beloved haven had been canceled because my work was ending just as Ruth's was starting. She was to begin rehearsing *Rosemary's Baby* with Roman Polanski for Paramount in less than two weeks.

"I doubt she'd have come, anyway," I said. "She's pretty rooted. It's going to take more than a pleasant jaunt to tear her loose."

A look I have come to know appeared on my wife's face. It is an expression that usually heralds the birth of an idea for a line, a character, a play, an effect, a theme, a matchmaking scheme, whatever. This look is generally followed by a beeline to the nearest pad and pencil where she may scribble a note, or sit for three hours surrounded by the invisible, impenetrable walls of her most private retreat.

This time, neither of these things happened. Instead, she found a calendar, and began a calculation complete with running commentary.

"We could do it!" she exclaimed, in a way that conveyed we were going to. "Next Tuesday, that's one, two, three from now, we go from here to Boston TWA has that dandy 9 A.M. and then the car or would you rather fly no the drive is so pretty this time of year and Kate'll love all that New England on the way and we can make the seven o'clock ferry if we don't dawdle and be at The Harbor View by dinnertime or if we miss it have dinner at The Landfall and make the nine why don't you see about that part and I'll call the hotel they'll do it for us won't they or should I call Stuart Avery or Alfred Hall to help and we'll need two cars because . . ."

She went on.

When the tide comes in, I do not try to make it go out. When night falls, I let it. When my wife pursues a notion with her brand of conviction, I have learned that it is the better part of wisdom to let her do so to the end.

As expected, Kate declined the invitation. Sweet of us, she said, but impossible. Ruth persisted. As I listened to her word picture of the planned adventure I became eager to go myself. She has a way of describing things to come as though they have already occurred; without, incidentally, any hitch, complication, or difficulty. But Kate continued to shake her head.

We enlisted George's aid. Kate weakened, said maybe, seesawed, said yes, said no again, with finality.

By this time, we were so caught up that we decided to go anyway.

The day before we were to leave, we went over to Kate's to say good-by.

As we were talking along, she said, "You don't *really* want us to come with you, do you?"

It was a straight line if I ever heard one.

Ruth looked at her and said, "Yes, Kate. We really do."

Kate looked at me.

"Yes," I said.

"Okay," said Kate. "What time?"

The short ferryboat ride from Woods Hole to the Vineyard Haven dock on Martha's Vineyard was meaningful. The plane part of the journey had been routine. The rent-a-car drive had been fraught with forms and maps and racing against the clock; but here, on the upper deck of the *Islander,* I could literally *see* my old chum beginning to relax. She glanced back at the mainland, where the tragedy of death had so recently touched her. The widening water was beginning to put it all into new perspective. She turned away now to look forward, ahead to the unknown-to-her island and its beauties and its people and its challenges. She had begun to smile her private smile—not that sudden, radiant, dazzling one everyone has seen, but the inner one, strong and confident and merry, which she shares with no one and which made her look, in the fast-falling dusk, as though she were standing in the subtle incandescence of a well-focused baby spotlight.

We left the ferry, Ruth and I leading in our car, Kate and Phyllis following in theirs. I decided to drive the shore route to Edgartown. It was longer, yes, but more attractive, and we wanted the island to make the best possible first impression. We drove slowly, so that Kate might see and savor the atmosphere. Now and then, she blew her horn, gaily, as a signal of appreciation of something special on the way.

Still, as we approached the hotel, I began to have misgivings. It was, after all, nothing grand or even first class. Its equivalent in the *Guide Michelin* might be rated two stars and one fork. The accommodations were strictly New England "Guests Welcome." The structure was antiquated, and neither its guests nor its appointments had been modernized. True, it had long appealed to us but what charms some often dismays others: a matter of viewpoint. What if Kate didn't like it? Oh, hell. What if she hated it? Oh, well. We would make the best of it for a night or two and decide something. (I suddenly remembered, with a sinking feeling, that she had not thought much of Claridge's in London!) Our arrival was handled unceremoniously. In due course, one of those handsome young college men appeared, wearing someone else's bellboy jacket. He considered the amount of our combined luggage with something this side of ecstasy.

"We have a lot of stuff," said Ruth. "Isn't there someone who could help you?"

"No, ma'am," he said, "I don't think so. Everybody's off or else busy."

"I'm not," said Kate, already on her way, completely laden.

We all followed her lead and began to fetch and carry like an ant family. In and out the lobby, up and down the stairs. Kate's room, Phyllis's room, ours. The bellboy was bewildered not only by the assistance, but by the assistants. At one point, Kate (coming) and I (going) collided in the upper hallway. She dropped her burden and flung her arms about me. She does not often do that. I began to feel relieved. Perhaps it would be all right, after all.

A swift conference involving our full party in Kate's bathroom, during which it was decided to take half an hour to whatever, and walk to the Sea Shanty for dinner.

Thirty minutes later, we assembled. Kate had showered and changed and looked precisely as she had before. Shiny face to shiny face, ragged slacks to ragged slacks, white T-shirt to white T-shirt. We started down.

The miniature lobby was filled with regulars, each in the accustomed wicker rocker or chair that had been a staked claim for anywhere from thirty to thirty-five years.

Kate started through, scattering charm. Ruth and Phyllis followed, I brought up the rear. I stopped to leave the keys at the desk, and saw the elderly gentleman in pongee lean forward out of his wicker chair to address a serene old lady who seemed to be woven of wicker herself. She was wearing an umbrella-like summer hat and white gloves. Now *she* leaned forward, as well, in a remarkable display of supple resilience. The elderly gentleman spoke in that ear-splitting whisper often employed by the hard of hearing.

"They tell me," he rasped, pointing at Kate with his cane, "that *that* is a *motion . . . picture . . . star!*"

Kate went through the screen door, doubled up with laughter.

I knew then that we had brought her to the right place.

Kate, who has it within her to love things and places in the same way that she loves people, fell in love with Martha's Vineyard in a matter of hours.

In our ten days there, she traversed more of its terrain than most off-islanders who have been going there for years. She came to know almost every pond, beach, road, passage, locality, and farm. She talked to many people. She picked masses of wildflowers. She bought all sorts of mementos. She found a beach shack belonging to an old college chum and made a daily trip there with Phyllis to swim and think.

The swimming troubled me because the old shack stood on a marsh and I was not sure the waters there were safe.

"Never mind," Kate reassured me. "Phyllis and I have agreed that if either one of us gets caught in the sea grass or an undertow or mud or whatever, there's to be no nonsense about the other one trying any lifesaving. Do you see?"

I did not see, but said, "I see."

One morning, Roger Edens phoned from Hyannis Port. He was visiting the Kennedy compound and wanted to know how about lunch tomorrow? He and Pat Lawford could come across in the *Honey Fitz.* Fine. An hour later, he phoned again. Jean and Eunice had heard about the plan and wished to be included. Delighted. The next morning, we were informed that Ethel Kennedy was coming, too. What could be finer? A table at a dockside restaurant was arranged and at one o'clock—on the dot—the famed *Honey Fitz* hove into view. Much waving of arms and hallooing of directions.

There we sat, Roger and I, surrounded by a bevy of some of the best women in America. They exuded life. Every one of them had been subjected to the agonies of mischance and catastrophe —and the gentle Ethel on my left bore the unknown weight of disaster yet to come. Still, they ate and drank and reveled in one another. They appeared to have been friends always. They were sisters of a sort, made of the identical fine human material, understanding the same rules of the game.

All through the long, three-hour lunch, opinions were voiced, disagreements aired, scarves exchanged, dates made.

Eunice looked at Kate.

"Where'd you get that jacket?" she asked.

"Oh," replied Kate, casually smug, "up in Maine."

"It *looks* it!" said Eunice.

The busy days and the tranquil nights went by. One of Kate's travel-beaten old sacks (resembling a nosebag for an outsize horse) was loaded with submitted scripts, a covering letter clipped to each.

Slowly reading and patiently sifting, she went through the lot, until only two remained. She returned each of the rejects with a handwritten note, and put her full attention on The Two.

She read and read again, studied and reflected. I would see her from time to time—on the beach, on the porch, in the car, or sitting at the window of her sitting room—looking out across the little lighthouse to the sea, toward somewhere-out-there-Spain, into space, and doubtless into Spencer's wise eyes.

"Damn!" she said one afternoon, flinging down one of the scripts. "Damn!"

"What's up?"

"Wouldn't you know? These are the two best by far, and they go at the same time."

"Wouldn't one of them wait for you?"

"What?"

She was honestly surprised.

"Couldn't the schedules be shifted somehow?" I asked.

The notion had not occurred to her.

In time, the schedules *were* shifted about, and in the fourth decade of her movie stardom, she undertook to play two difficult, foreign-location (partly dead-of-winter) starring roles, consecutively, or, as they say in the movie business, back to back.

The two screenplays she had chosen were *The Lion in Winter* and *The Madwoman of Chaillot*. One in England and Ireland, the other in France. Movement, travel, accommodations, costumes, corsets, wigs, concepts, problems, cast adjustments; on the latter, a change of directors—John Huston, her old friend, withdrawing at the last moment, and Bryan Forbes brought in.

She was to remain abroad for over a year, hard at work every single day.

But all this lay ahead, triggered by the decisions made in placid Edgartown.

The day we were to leave was filled not so much with sadness as with tingling apprehension, and I thought, as we boarded the ferry, that it was a sort of D-day. What lay ahead on that to-be-stormed mainland? My wife was on her way back to California to begin *Rosemary's Baby;* I to start on that terrifying page one again; Kate to arrange one or both of the projects that had captured her imagination. Ruth and I were to stop in New York for a few days; Kate was off for a week of visiting—brothers, sisters, in-laws, nieces, nephews and assorted progeny, stepmother—in various parts of Connecticut; and in Maine, an old friend with a problem.

We all pulled off the road, as prearranged, in front of a grand old antique shop-barn that had caught Kate's eye when we had passed it a week or so earlier. We stepped out onto the gravel driveway, and stood about for a time among the dying flowers of late August. We were all sorry to let the good good time slip from our grasp. Unspoken feelings were running deep there beside the highway and no one seemed to want to be the first to say good-by.

Finally, Kate threw away her cigarette, reached out and took Ruth's hand. At the same time, she took mine in her other hand.

"Well, friends," she said. "Thanks. Y'got me out of my rut."

That was all. There were hugs and kisses, admonitions to drive carefully, and we parted—but not before she had turned back to us and added, "Wouldn't it be great if people could get to live suddenly as often as they die suddenly?"

Our swift, important, fruitful holiday had come to an end. Ruth and I were silent that morning until we stopped at a Howard Johnson's for lunch.

We learned later that what Kate was doing at the barn that morning was buying an opening-day present for Ruth.

It was a rare old papier-mâché lobster that Kate filled with a potpourri of Martha's Vineyard wildflowers she had carefully collected day by day. There were (my wife tells me) chickweed, beach pea, buttercup, daisy, wild rose, devil's-paintbrush, wild aster, bouncing Bet, Queen Anne's lace, pennyroyal, and robin runaway. Gratefully received.

Kate returned to Los Angeles fifteen days later, thoroughly refreshed. She had been home to Hartford, and to Fenwick. She had seen her sisters and brothers, their husbands and wives. She was full of news about the kids. She had been up to Maine to help her beloved Emily Perkins deal with complex medical problems involving Em's son. She had been to New York, had met with Alan Lerner, was mad about *Coco,* and had acquired yet *another* interest.

Her old friend Irene Selznick had sent her two novels by Margery Sharp. Mrs. Selznick had acquired the film rights and was planning a production. Irene has great faith in Kate's literary taste and judgment.

When Kate had finished reading the material, she met with Irene.

"Great," she said. "Absolutely great. It's going to be a *sensational* picture. *But . . .*"

She took a long time finding a cigarette, tamping it down, searching out a match, lighting the cigarette, extinguishing the match, taking a first long puff and exhaling it.

And all the while, Irene hung on that *"But . . ."*

"But? . . ." Irene prompted.

". . . you realize," continued Kate, "there's only one person in the whole world who can direct this particular property."

"Who?" asked Irene, all ears.

"Me!" answered Kate, all eyes.

When Irene recovered from her exploding astonishment, she

was delighted, and by the time Kate had finished expounding her concept, was excited.

Within an hour, the two friends had formed a producer-director partnership.

When the plan became known, there were some who thought it mad. I was not among them. I have long considered Kate a director *manqué*. She has never been, never *could* be a hired hand. Anyone who has ever engaged her knows that in addition to the actress, you get—Free! Bonus! At No Extra Cost!—a play doctor, associate director, co-producer, assistant designer, partner, cheerleader, superintendent, collaborator, speech teacher, expert, guiding spirit, mother hen, moving force, coach, resident psychiatrist, foreman, house detective, district nurse, and welcome buttinski.

Henry Ephron tells me that when Tracy and Hepburn were making *Desk Set* at Twentieth, he was the producer as well as the co-author of the screenplay with his wife, Phoebe. He relates that one of the gags in the script had to do with an enormous philodendron that is supposed to be growing in an office.

Kate came onto the set, looked at it, and asked, "What's *that* supposed to be?"

The prop man replied, "That's the philodendron."

"Ridiculous," she said. "That's not a philodendron."

"Well, the next thing," says Henry, "I was down on the set. I had other things to worry about but she was raising hell, and the set decorator said, 'I don't know what she's talking about. That's a philodendron.' Kate was absolutely furious and kept saying, 'It is *not*. Don't tell *me!*' So they sent for the studio gardener and he looked at it and they asked him what it was and *he* said it was a philodendron. Well, at this, she just gave him a flame-thrower look and stalked off the set. Fortunately, they had something else to shoot. In a couple of hours she came back with a truck, and in the truck was a plant that was too big to get into the elevator, even. She got it onto the set and, sweating, pointed at it and said, 'Now, *that's* a philodendron.' I guess the point of the story is that it was and the thing we had wasn't; so, of course, we used hers."

In addition to her burgeoning duties and responsibilities, Kate found time to immerse herself in the preparation of the Irene Selznick film project. Writers, conferences, first drafts, revisions. She was not satisfied; she flew to England and worked on the script for a time with her friend Bill Rose. When still it failed to materialize to her satisfaction, she returned home, holed up, and wrote a script herself. Those who have read it are enthusiastic but Kate is not persuaded that the best version has yet been achieved.

The idea of her as a director is not new. In 1959, when she was announced for the Stratford, Connecticut, season, it was mentioned that in addition to acting, she would direct a production. It turned out that her acting duties precluded it, but it has long been on her mind, probably from the time of her second RKO picture, *Christopher Strong,* which was directed by Hollywood's first female movie director, Dorothy Arzner.

Since she has always made it a point to become deeply involved in each production, her technical abilities are complete. In addition, she has taste and judgment and an understanding of the problems of the players. Most important, she has a firm notion of total concept.

Long ago, when I was George Abbott's assistant, I asked him what he considered the director's principal problem. Mr. Abbott replied, "The thing you have to learn is how to keep the whole story in your head the whole time. Everything in a show has to hang together, has to be on the main line of what it's about. It's too easy to get carried away by a scene or a piece of business or, say, in a musical, by a single number, but it's only good, it's only important, as it relates to the whole. Have you ever watched a great painter paint? Do you notice how many times he steps away from the canvas and looks at the whole thing? It's because in his head somewhere he's envisaging the entire canvas, and trying to fit every detail into that whole work."

And I remember Ernst Lubitsch criticizing one of our preeminent and successful colleagues.

"Yes, yes," said Ernst, impatiently, "he directs scenes fine and sometimes lines and shots very well but his *pictures* are no good."

Kate understands this instinctively. In my long experience with her, I have never known her to become involved with a detail or a single scene. She understands the totality of a film or a play. She senses that every work of art must have a unity of tone and a unity of intention.

Perhaps it is because in this sense her very life has been a matter of creating a work of art with a unity of tone and most certainly with a unity of intention.

In the days of decision, before Kate had definitely committed herself to *Coco,* we discussed its problems often, pro and con. One evening, she frowned apprehensively and, for a moment, looked unlike herself.

"But what is it that troubles you?" I asked. "The singing?"

She became herself again as she replied, "Good God, no! I've been singing all my life—All over the place—not on the stage—not yet, but I can learn that—I can sing—it's not that—it's the *shoes* I'm worried about."

"The shoes," I echoed, nowhere.

"The goddam ladies' shoes," she explained. "With heels—I haven't had a pair of shoes on my feet in four and a half years, except for a few minutes in a couple of long shots with Stanley Kramer—What if I fall down? Oh, well—I suppose I can learn again—I'll rehearse in them—five weeks." Her shrug combined terror and bravado. "What the hell."

Could it be true? Four and a half years. Yes, it was. Because it was during this time that Spencer's health was failing. Kate continued to work intermittently, but had not appeared on the stage, and only once on the screen. Her social life had been confined to meetings in private places with close friends who could not care less what she had on her feet: sandals, thongs, huaraches, sneakers, or nothing.

Some twenty years ago, the war over and work for both going well, my wife and I decided to buy a house in New York. After the customary exhaustive and exhausting search, we found one that, although not ideal, was at least suitable. While negotiations for it were still in progress, we had dinner with Katharine. In the course of the preliminary small talk, we told her that we were about to buy a house.

"Where is it?" she asked.

"West Eleventh Street."

"Nonsense," she said. "You can't afford to buy a house down there."

"Why not?"

"Because," she said, "a house has to represent an investment for you—you have to own something where the property values are sure to increase—Like here—in Turtle Bay Gardens."

"Thanks loads," I said. "We've only been asking for about two years. In all that time, not more than one came up and we were outbid fast on that."

"Yah," she said, looking through the floor. "Yah. Let me see what I can do."

"All right."

"But *don't* buy the Eleventh Street one."

Although we indicated agreement, it was our intention to go forward with our plans. As it happened, there were legal complications involving title clearance that delayed the deal.

Kate on the phone. "Okay," she said. "You can have the house next to mine—pretty good—needs a little work—not much. They want sixty-five—worth it—but I think you can buy it for about fifty-eight-five."

We went immediately to see it, loved it, and bought it for fifty-eight-five. We love it still.

Later, when we asked her how she had managed it, she explained. "They're terribly nice people—terribly—but they're old—Judge Rublee and his wife—he's sweet—a distinguished lawyer. Dean Acheson used to work for him. He's lived here in the Gardens just about forever—before me—even when Max Perkins and E. B. White did, but they're *old,* and he's rather infirm, so I went in to see them and convinced them they'd be much happier in an apartment. What's more, I offered to help them find one—I will, too—and told them about you and I'm sure it's better for everyone. Yah. Yah. Except—*I* should take that one and give you mine. You're two and I'm one—so I need a bigger house."

I never have figured out the dialectics of that last, but this is how it happens that Kate has been our neighbor for more than twenty years.

Her house is a dream of long accumulation. She began by renting it for one hundred dollars a month, and in 1931, bought it. Since that time, she and her matchlessly tasteful friend, Laura Harding, have lavished four decades of skillful love on it. She is often away from it for months, sometimes years at a time, yet it remains ever alive.

For one thing, the abode of so powerful a presence retains the radioactive properties of its mistress's personality over long periods of time. For another, her faithful man, Charles Newhill, who has been with her for over forty years, provides a surrogate heartbeat for the establishment. He is known as "The Mayor of Forty-ninth Street." Indeed, the life of our block is centered in the kitchen of Kate's house. Lastly, Kate being Kate, the house is frequently occupied by various members of the vast populace that inhabits her world. Brothers, sisters, nephews, nieces, and friends of the above; painters (met abroad) and their wives; old friends; new friends; old beaux and their new girls (or wives); friends of friends.

Kate told us once that a young female relative was in residence.

Thinking of the aspects of safety, I asked, "Is she living there alone?"

Kate looked at me coolly, and replied, "Presumably."

On another occasion, we told her that Tyrone Guthrie was coming to New York to stage *Carmen* for the Metropolitan Opera Company.

"Tell him to stay in my house," she said. "He can't afford rent on what the Met'll pay him."

"Do you know him?"

"No—what's the difference?—tell Charles to give him a key—he can have his meals with you—it'll work—yah."

So ordered, so executed.

The teeming life in and around Kate's house next door once struck me as a possible subject for a play. I spent a few enjoyable months developing it, but although the pieces turned out to be entertaining enough, I was not able to find a workable vessel to hold them.

It was my intention to write a play in which the leading character—based on Kate—never appears. She owns a house, is usually away in Hollywood or London or Africa or Australia (like Kate) and turns it over whimsically to whomever circumstance dictates. Now. Suppose she invites this one or that one to use the house and maybe gets dates mixed—or is it better if *they* do? In any case, the result is that several different parties turn up simultaneously in the course of a single weekend. Act One—Friday. Act Two—Saturday. Act Three—Sunday. I even had a pretty good title for it, *The Cat's Away*. Who turns up? Her ex-husband and his new girl. Her present amour: a brilliant, hard-drinking film director who had planned to hole up here for a few weeks with a husband-wife writing team. The husband, turns out, remembers the aforementioned new girl. From where? When it comes to him—wham! An eccentric brother and a group of his hippie friends (save him for Three?); two girls whom she has asked to redecorate the principal room. They arrive (Act Two) with furniture and paper hangers. Also, a Roman sculptor who brings his wife and his mistress. Her doctor from California, here to attend a medical convention. A niece who is a splendid forthright girl (unconsciously emulating Kate) and becomes the catalyst of the whole adventure. And, of course, Charles, who attempts to cope with growing difficulty and—No, I had better stop. This thing is beginning to seem good again.

It would have been interesting to attempt to create a character by showing the audience no more than her reflection in the eyes of a number of people around her. She would have to be someone to whom others react strongly, which is why it might have worked out at that.

I console myself with the reminder that the best ideas usually make the worst plays. It could have been done, though, about

Kate, because she is vivid and vital and has a galvanizing effect on all who encounter her. I know of no one who has ever remained indifferent to Katharine Hepburn as woman, actress, political activist, dinner partner, friend, or enemy.

Kate's splendid New York house is much admired. It is comfortable and welcoming, and, aside from its enchanting atmosphere, is a carefully wrought living machine.

I was surprised to find that it does not contain a television set.

"How come?" I asked.

Kate shrugged. "Don't need it," she explained.

This is a measure of her practicality. In her California abode, there are several television sets and she uses them often with pleasure. In her New York life, she finds there is neither the time nor the inclination to watch television. So, no set.

"Damn," she said to us one morning. "I wish I had a color-television set."

"Why?" asked Ruth.

"That marvelous ninety-minute documentary on the Queen's trip."

"Oh, yes."

"I'd love to see it," she said. "So would Phyllis. I suppose I could rent a set," she said, "just for the evening."

"What?"

"Certainly. They just put it in and when you're finished—they take it out—nothing to it."

"You must be mad," I said.

Later that day, we phoned and invited her and Phyllis to come over, have dinner with us at our small, temporary apartment, and watch the program.

We were unequipped for entertaining of any sort but arranged to have steak dinners sent in, in the growing fashion of Manhattan apartment dwellers.

"This is a dinner for Katharine Hepburn," my wife said on the telephone. "So get it here right on time. Tell the delivery boy if he's punctual, she'll give him her autograph."

Kate arrived two minutes before the appointed hour and looked about apprehensively.

"You did say 'dinner' didn't you?" she asked.

"On its way," I said.

"It's coming from Stampler's," Ruth explained, "and you're going to give one of your rare autographs. That's the price of getting it here on the dot."

The door buzzer. Dinner. Kate provides the autograph.

"This whole autograph thing is absolutely idiotic," she says, "isn't it?—I remember once, my father—on his way to the hospital to perform an autopsy and—some reason, I don't know —I suppose he thought it would be good for me—he asked me to come along—And there he stood, finally, with another doctor working over this cadaver—and would you believe it?—I don't—and it *happened* to *me*—some idiot, a young doctor or an orderly or something, came over, thrust a prescription pad and a pen at me and asked me for my *autograph*. Think of it!—It's a madness."

We rush through dinner in time to see the program.

During the first break, Kate, who had been watching from the floor, of course, looked up at me and said, "What a marvelous set. Have you had it long?"

"Since this afternoon," I tell her.

"What?"

"I rented it—just for the evening."

"You must be mad," she said, and returned her attention to the program.

Later, she examines the apartment. We have taken it because we are to be away from New York for an extended time, and have rented our house.

She ends her tour of our new home, and says, "You better not stay in this box too long. It'll ruin your personalities."

Kate had never in her life so much as boiled an egg, but when it appeared that it would be convenient if she could cook, she set to and became an expert; mastering one dish at a time, until her menu was impressive. As a carnivorous American, I am something of a steak expert. In New York, the places to get it have narrowed down to Gallagher's, Frankie and Johnnie's, Christ Cella's, and Peter Luger's; in Paris, to the Cochon d'Or. But I have never had a steak anywhere to equal the one she has learned to do out in the driveway. It is the perfect steak, and the reason she learned to do it was that Spence liked steak.

In the long period when she felt she could not undertake to act, she began to paint again. It was during this period that Spencer took to referring to her as "Grandma Moses." Each canvas gained in skill and freedom and life, until she was expressing herself truly. She never shows the pictures, unless urged to do so, will not sell, and has given away only one—to George Cukor. It is a portrait of a chair that looks exactly like Katharine Hepburn.

A few hours after she had finally agreed to do *Coco,* she was on her way to the home of Roger Edens for the first singing lesson of her life. Here was a perfect example of the complete professional in action. Amateurs hope; professionals work. Rehearsals were not scheduled to begin until mid-October, but here she was in early January, beginning to submit to the harsh new disciplines of rhythm, placement, power, range, tone, and tune.

Roger Edens was no coddler. From his early days as pit pianist for Ethel Merman; through countless Metro musicals in their happiest days (teaching Judy Garland to sing); to his final professional involvement with Barbra Streisand as associate producer of the film *Hello, Dolly*—he dedicated himself to the highest standards of musical performance. Working with him daily, Kate began to perceive a good deal of what she was in for.

"I always feel sort of guilty," she said one evening, "when I take a Sunday off and just loll about because Dad worked every Sunday of his life and every holiday—he never stopped—Well, of course, his work was his life, and I don't suppose I can say that about mine."

"How's it going?" I asked her after her first few days with Roger.

"I don't know," she replied. "All I know is that I sweat more up there in the afternoons than I do on the tennis court in the mornings."

After she had been working with Roger for three weeks, she decided that the time had come to perform for an audience.

"I've sung to myself all my life," she explained. "So of course I'm used to it—and up there at Roger's I perform to the furniture which seems absolutely devastated by me but I think I ought to begin to make contact with people, don't you?"

It is arranged. There is to be a small dinner at Roger Edens's house. After dinner, Kate is going to sing.

They have worked up a number of songs. The opening one came about fortuitously. Roger and I had worked together producing a tribute to Cole Porter for The Friends of the Libraries at U.S.C. In the course of our work we had come upon a recording of Cole Porter playing and singing his song "Thank You So Much Missus Lowsborough-Goodby." In later discussion we agreed that the powerful, acidulous, witty lyrics would fit Kate's delivery perfectly. The music and its range would be no strain and the fact that it was a Cole Porter song would give her a great good feeling of confidence. They had also worked up "Miss Otis Regrets" and "Just One of Those Things."

We assembled at Roger's, a group of twelve.

Fifteen minutes later, Kate stood up and said, "Listen, it's hopeless. It's just no use." We were all stunned. She continued. "I mean I simply can't wait until *after* dinner to do it—too damned nervous—putting food down on this tight stomach is going to make me so sick I'll have to go home. Sit down, everybody, and let's get it over with."

We sat down and became an audience. Kate picked up a scarf to use as a prop. Roger sat down at the piano. I saw her face go shiny and moist as she took a deep breath and nodded her readiness to Roger. As he played the long introduction, I could only reflect again on the courage of the acting profession. Kate was singing:

> Thank you so much Missus Lowsborough-Goodby
> Thank you so much
> Thank you so much for that infinite weekend
> with you. . . .*

She was home free. It did not matter that her voice was untrained for singing, that the pitch was often uncertain or the beat a touch early or late. The point was that she was singing as *herself*. She was wisely, confidently, producing her own sound and not pretending to be Merman or Streisand or Callas. As she went on, you felt that at this moment, at this time and place, you would prefer to hear Kate than any of the other three.

The wildly enthusiastic reception of her first number gave her added steam and she whipped through the rest of the program with charm and ease.

We went into dinner. She ate like a horse.

Her new life was beginning. Lessons and learning, wearing shoes, off to the woods with faithful Lobo and her script. Thinking, thinking, looking for a Coco Chanel into whose skin she could fit herself.

One day, I noticed that she talked differently (Consciously? Un-?); she began to move in a new way; unaccustomed expressions were finding their way to her visage.

Rehearsals were still a long way off but the subject already possessed her.

The trip to Paris. Off. On again. When?

On her return, she described the highlight: her meeting with Coco Chanel.

"She said to us, 'Lunch. Come to lunch,' and we turned up. Michael, Alan, Michael Bennett—the choreographer—an absolute *wonder*. Michael Bennett. I don't know what his real name is. I'd *love* to know. It's not Bennett or Michael. Brrrilliant! And there we were in her apartment, the one over her *atelier* in the Rue Cambon—been there since 1922, imagine it." (She worked her newly acquired perfect French accent on the French words.) "Sleeps at the Ritz, of course—eats in her apartment—*exquisite,* perfect—beige and gold—sculpture and some fascinating Dali paintings—a great collection—extremely personal. And s*uch* flowers—silver, linen, china—*devastating*—she was almost an hour late. Alan fidgeted, but I didn't care—goddam scared, I was—used the time to pull myself together. All at once, there she stood—in all her tiny perfection—came toward me, blinking sort of, I think—and I went toward her and we neither of us stopped, so in half a minute we were embracing and then—we both burst into tears!"

I told Kate it sounded like the most momentous encounter of a French and an American citizen since the widely reported meeting between Voltaire and Dr. Benjamin Franklin. They, too, as an assembly watched, had moved into each other's arms and wept.

"Yes," said Kate aimlessly. "But they were older."

Kate hates dressing up and says so. Even when she went to meet Chanel she wore that same old uniform: sandals, baggy pants, white T-shirt, suède jacket, and funny cap.

She went on. "Chanel never sat down the whole time we were there except to eat lunch—and that, she simply bolted. . . . It's important that I went—important to me, because now that I've met her, I think I can play her—We're not so different—she's had terrific ups and downs, like me, and she's always gotten up off the floor and started flailing again—she represents—gloriously—the fight for life—it's what she's about—what I'm about—well, hell—it's what the *show's* about—or should be—will be—and she never listened too much to what the press or the chic people were saying—always stayed in touch with the real world and the stream of life—That's why even the kids now love to wear her clothes or copies of her clothes—I like to think I'm like that, too—Not intimidated—we're really very much alike except I think she's much prettier."

Alan has a report on what followed the meeting: "I went around to see Chanel that evening and she said to me, 'Yes, she's very nice, very impressive, but she's too old. She looks to me like a woman of almost sixty.' What could I say? I sort of double talked about stage lighting and make-up but what I couldn't get through my head was that Chanel was objecting to a woman who looked almost sixty playing Chanel at seventy-one. Of course, she's eighty-six now. I got to thinking about it and now I understand what it is. To someone like Chanel, the numbers game has no meaning at all. She figures her age according to her state of mind and health and maybe even career. Certainly not by the calendar. I think Kate must be like that too. She has that sense of timeless time. People get older, they change their activities and their habits but there doesn't seem to be any change in Kate. She still plays singles and does everything she did at twenty. It doesn't occur to her to change her life style in any way, does it?"

Kate's creative juices flowed wildly on this project, mainly because it was all new to her. Beyond professional necessity, she has never been greatly interested in clothes, and even less in fashion.

All at once she was asked to become—and to perform eight times a week—a woman whose life has been nothing *but* fashion. And clothes. For Kate, this was another language, a new palette, a world she had scarcely known. Thus, each thing in it—personnel, métier, custom, method, aim—became an exciting never-before experience.

While hanging about the Chanel establishment, soaking up atmosphere, Kate bought, for the first time in her life, half a dozen Chanels. She had never owned so much as a copy.

Strange. Here is a girl of whom I am deeply fond; to whom I am greatly indebted, on many accounts; with whom I have spent some of the best and most memorable hours of my life; with whom I have done work of which I am proud, and yet—I have never given her a birthday present. No, not so much as one busted flower, nor sent a cable or wire or card or acknowledged the day in any way. There is a reason for this omission. I do not know when her birthday is. Neither do you and neither does anyone. Kate considers it a private matter. Now that her mother and father are gone, she claims that no one knows the date of her birth. I am told it cannot be found in the Hartford, Connecticut, City Hall; and it has been darkly hinted that since her father, Dr. Thomas Hepburn, was for many years one of the city's leading physicians . . .

She laughs as this is reported to her, her eyes crinkling and her face taking on a look of the Kath who swallowed the birth certificate.

In the sitting room of a suite in a Paris hotel, I once found myself sitting beside a desk on which lay her passport. She sat far across the room, talking to my wife.

I picked up the passport and said, "The jig is up, Missy. I am about to peek and grab your birthday. The code is broken, Mr. President. Knowledge is power."

She regarded me calmly.

"Go ahead," she said. "Look."

"No," I said. "I was kidding."

I put it down.

"Look at it," she commanded.

"My God!" I said. "I knew it."

"Knew what?"

"Taurus!" I said.

"That's my *father's* birthday in there, you ass! You don't think I'd tell them *mine,* do you?"

Foiled again.

Kate thinks nothing of using her father's birthday, her mother's opinion, her brother's toothbrush, or sister's daughter, Katharine, as her own.

Kate has always had an aversion to publicity. In 1933, after *A Bill of Divorcement,* she returned from Europe to find herself a star. The studio insisted she give an interview. She hated the idea. She could not bear the invasion of privacy, and worse, the asinine questions asked by the reporters. They wanted to know about her husband.

"Husband?" she said. "What husband? I certainly don't remember ever getting married. Maybe I did and forgot."

Another reporter wanted to know if it was true, as rumored, that she had children.

"Yes," Kate responded. "I have five. Two white and three colored."

The studio soon gave up on the subject of interviews.

In 1967, in connection with *Guess Who's Coming to Dinner,* Kate began to break her rules regarding public relations. A number of factors were involved. For one thing, she had not made a movie in five years, not since *Long Day's Journey into Night* in 1962. For another, Spencer had not worked since *Inherit the Wind* in 1960. Further, there was the matter of the controversial subject matter. Finally, and perhaps most important, the film was to mark Kathy Houghton's screen debut.

Kate moved into the publicity aspects of *Guess Who's Coming to Dinner.* She astonished the professionals with her bold ideas, her imaginative concepts, and indefatigable execution.

Kate, in order to learn the techniques of avoiding publicity, had become an expert on the subject and in order to *get* publicity, it was necessary only to turn over the coin.

With Kathy Houghton at her side, she held press conferences, submitted to candid photography, gave interviews, tape-recorded radio spots, did countless telephonic interviews with motion picture editors in every part of the country, and succeeded in launching, in great style, not only the film, but Kathy.

When I expressed my own surprise, not so much at her willingness to do all this, but at her ability, she said, "Oh, hell, it's nothing—You know as well as I do that any of us can do anything we really want to do—that's the thing that gets a little harder as the years pile up—We don't seem to *want* to do as much—I remember how I hated Bryn Mawr when I went there —I hadn't picked it—it was just one of those things—all the girls in our family went there, and so I had to go—I loathed it—I'd been tutored, mostly—Dad believed in that, and so I wasn't used to the discipline of regular hours and classes, and also having so many people around—I still haven't gotten used to it—Anyway, I was such a bust that after about two years, they practically asked me to leave. Then one night, I decided to show 'em—and in my junior year, I was an absolute knockout; so what the hell, it's just a question of what you want to do, isn't it?"

As *Coco* rehearsals began, the matter of a Hepburn interview for the Sunday *New York Times* was swiftly broached, and almost as swiftly rejected. After a good deal of urging, she relented on condition that this would be the single pre-opening interview.

"And only," she added, "if you get Ruth Gordon to do it, or the fellow who did the one about *her*."

The "fellow" was Rex Reed, who agreed with alacrity. There was, however, a complication. He was, oddly, involved as an actor in the film *Myra Breckenridge*.

Reed arranged a reshuffling of the film's shooting schedule and, after several postponements at either end, a time was fixed. He flew to New York. When he arrived, preview performances were already under way. The work load was heavier than Kate had anticipated. Numbers were going in, coming out. There were cast replacements and production changes. Daily and nightly cuts, emendations, adjustments. Kate was totally involved, fully concentrated.

"The *Times* interview? *What Times* interview?—Oh, yes—Well—Can't do it," said Kate. "Too busy."

"But Reed. He's here from California. Especially."

"What a shame—I'm terribly sorry—tell him how sorry I am."

"But . . ."

"Some other time?"

"They're *counting* on it!"

"Yes—well—can't do it—sorry."

There was no interview. As it happened, Rex Reed understood perfectly.

"She was right," he says. "What the hell. When you're doing a show, it's a question of what's most important. Hepburn, she's one of the few who understands that getting the number right is going to do more for the show than getting the interview right. I hated to blow it. I'd have loved doing it because I love her. Always have. The loss was mine, not hers. Too bad."

Saint Patrick's Day 1968 approached melancholically. Kate was away, working in the South of France; Spence was dead; there would be no celebration.

We had always made a thing of it when we happened to be in the same city on March 17, which, by design, was almost always.

The year before (with his death less than three months in the future) there had been green derbies, pots of shamrock, a green ribbon for Lobo, Irish music on records sent from the old country, pistachio ice cream, and—the inevitable necktie. For years, I cannot think how many, I had given Spencer a green necktie to be worn on The Day and he wore it. I would look for them everywhere. Spencer was fond of his collection. From France, Italy, Ireland, England, and Lenore's in Beverly Hills, there were ties: from olive-green suède to silk polka dots to Irish linen Kelly green.

This year there would be no party, no necktie, no nothing.

A few days before March 17, I chanced to be shopping at Lenore's and saw a surpassing green tie. I bought it, had it tagged "Made especially for Spencer Tracy," and sent it off via air to Kate.

It reached her on the morning of the seventeenth and she wore it all day and wrote me quite a letter.

Kate arrived in New York to prepare for the commencement of *Coco* rehearsals. She took part, almost immediately, in every department of the production: casting, scenery, costumes, choreography, lighting, make-up, wigs, sound, and, of course, the theater itself.

Experienced professionals know how important the latter element can be, and insist that plays have failed because they were in the wrong theater; too large or too small, or simply not right.

In her long experience, Kate has played virtually every size and shape of theater, but was anxious to become acquainted with the one that had been booked for *Coco:* the Mark Hellinger on West Fifty-first Street.

Alan Lerner's attachment to it was understandable. His *My Fair Lady* had occupied it for the longest run in the history of the American musical theater up to that time.

He and Freddie Brisson, Michael Benthall, and Michael Bennett took Kate over to see it a few days after she reached New York.

After walking about on the stage studying the auditorium and walking about the auditorium studying the stage, Kate announced, "It's a fine theater. Perfectly fine, but we can't use it. What else is available?"

The management was speechless. Theaters, especially sizeable ones suitable for musicals, are not easy to come by in the shrinking world of Broadway. Moreover, the deal for the theater, with its complex terms, had taken months to arrange. The idea of changing theaters was out of the question, but, clearly, the matter would have to be talked out.

Finally Brisson said, "What are you talking about?"

"What's the matter with you people?" Kate responded. "Can't you see anything?"

"Like what?" asked Alan.

"Across the street," said Kate, patiently. "They're beginning the construction of a skyscraper."

"You mean where the Capitol Theatre used to be?" asked Alan.

"I don't know," she said. "Right there, across the road—they're excavating now. It means two things—that this theater is going to be very hard to get to, and what's more, it's going to be impossible to play the Wednesday matinee—I don't care how good we are, we can't compete with riveting."

Michael Benthall tried a joke. "Well, we'll just have to be pretty riveting ourselves, won't we?"

Kate said, "Do you mean to tell me there's no other theater in New York? One that isn't right next door to a construction site?"

The discussion continued. Everyone (probably including Kate) knew that they were committed to the Mark Hellinger Theatre, but Kate wanted to make her point.

As it happened, she was correct on both counts, and had, indeed, been the only one to foresee the difficulties ahead.

The Mark Hellinger turned out to be extremely difficult to get to, and the Wednesday matinees were nightmares, or perhaps it is more correct to say daymares.

The company did its best to work against the noise of the neighboring enterprise, but large sections of the audience, particularly those on the left side of the house and toward the rear, had a tough time.

Kate, as Coco, had several numbers in the first act: "The World Belongs to the Young," "Mademoiselle Cliché de Paris," "On the Corner of the Rue Cambon," and "The Money Rings Out Like Freedom," that she was able to belt out successfully, even against the racket. But toward the end of Act One, came a delicate scene with the memory of Coco's father (projected on a screen behind her) during which she sang the moving title song, "Coco."

At the first matinee, Kate found it impossible to perform the number properly in the overwhelming presence of the noise from across the street.

The following Wednesday, she rearranged her schedule, and left for the theater an hour early. She went directly to the

Uris construction site, found the supervisor's trailer, and asked to see him. He was out on the structure somewhere, but Kate made the matter seem so urgent that an assistant led her out onto the job.

Wearing the mandatory hard hat, she found herself facing the supervisor.

"Look here," she shouted. "My name is Katharine Hepburn and I work across the street."

The astonished supervisor gaped at her. "Holy Smoke!" he said. "What the hell are you doing up here?"

"I have to talk to you," said Kate.

"What?"

"I have to talk to you," she shouted.

"Okay. Come on down. Watch your step. How the hell did you get up here, anyway?"

In the supervisor's trailer, he smoothed his hair and asked, "Can I give you a cup of coffee, Miss Hepburn?"

"Sure," she said, "but I want more than that out of you."

"Go ahead."

"Well, look," she said. "I know you've got to build this building but—on the other hand—we've got to give a show over there—I know we can't ask you to stop—but at least you can help us out—if you want to."

"How?"

"There's one main spot," Kate explained carefully. "It's my 'Coco' number. You know. With *papa*."

"Oh, sure," he said, mesmerized. (Hepburnized?)

"Well, on Wednesdays," Kate continued, "that number starts at three-oh-five and goes on until about three fourteen—so just for that little piece of time—couldn't you possibly hold the hammers?"

"Well, Jeez, I don't know, Miss Hepburn," said the supervisor.

"Sure you could," urged Kate. "Give them a coffee break or something. I'll pay for the coffee."

"Yeah," he said, "but who'll pay for the time? You know what these guys get, don't you?"

Kate gave him The Hepburn Look, and said softly, "You can do it if you want to."

He took a deep breath, and said, "I don't know, but lemme see what I can figure out here."

"You're sweet," said Kate, and went across the street to make up.

At 3:05 that afternoon, as the introduction to her soft number began, the world outside fell suddenly silent. The audience may not have been aware of the abrupt change, but everyone connected with the *Coco* company was. The dancers, the singers, the orchestra, and the crew. Some of those who were momentarily free stepped out into the street to see what had happened.

Up and down the structure they saw the workers signaling for silence and looking at their watches. At 3:14 P.M. the applause for the number was all at once augmented by all hell breaking loose across the street.

In the darkness of the scene change, Kate was able to allow the radiant smile, which she had kept hidden in her rib cage, to burst forth on her face.

She went over to thank the men after the matinee, but their day's work had ended, so she made a special trip over the following day to clamber all over the job, thanking her new friends. So it went for week after week. Every Wednesday afternoon at the specified time, the construction gang gave Kate a gift of silence.

Then came the afternoon when a Consolidated Edison crew, not connected with the Uris construction, turned up on the corner to make a cable repair. At 3:05, when the building work stopped, the uninformed Con Edison crew continued.

Whereupon, from every part of the structure, the shouts came raining down.

"Hey, hold the noise, you guys!"

"Shut up down there. Katie's on!"

"Hey, what's a matter with you bastards? Don't you know Katie's doing her number?"

"Quiet!"

In addition to the hollering and yelling, an *ad hoc* committee went dashing over to enforce the admonition.

At the end of the matinee, Kate was handed a note from the supervisor, explaining that the short burst of noise at the beginning of her number was ". . . not us, but that crazy Con Edison which we have now straightened out."

The first act of *Coco* ends as Chanel's comeback collection is about to be shown for the first time. The room is ready, the mannequins are standing by, Coco goes to the top of her famous staircase, raps wood for luck, and sits—confident and excited. The curtain falls.

Intermission.

The curtain rises on Act Two. The room is a shambles, the atmosphere uncertain. Coco (Kate) rises, moves slowly down the steps, picks up a dropped accessory, and starts out. Front and center she stops for the merest moment and says, with deep feeling, "Shit!"

The opening-night audience was, by turns—startled, unbelieving, and shocked. A moment later, it exploded into laughter and applause.

After I had first heard it, I asked Alan, "How on earth did you get her to do it?"

"Easy," he replied. "She wrote it."

I found this difficult to believe, but she later confirmed Alan's report.

"When we began, there was a lot of stuff before my entrance—explaining the failure and so on—it seemed wrong to me—dissipated the effect of Coco—I thought it would be better form for it to pick up where it left off, sort of—me on the steps at the end of One—there I am at the opening of Two—and, in between, the disaster—but how to convey that?—We all thought about it and one day, this idea struck me—I must say it made *me* laugh—so I told Alan—he was shocked—liked it, but shocked—then he said, 'Okay, but how about *"merde,"* instead?'—but I said not enough would know what I'd said—so we tried it straight—went great from the start—did it bother you?"

"Hell, no," I said. "Nothing that gets a response like that

could ever bother me. I was just surprised. Not that you said it, but that you knew the word."

It leads us into talk of language and fashions in words.

Ruth remembers Fanny Brice saying, in all seriousness, "I have found out that anybody who doesn't say 'shit' is deceitful!"

"I don't know about that," said Kate. "I just know I needed it to start Act Two with a bang."

Some time later, Robert Emmett Dolan, the musical director of *Coco,* tells us of seeing Kate to her car one night. Among the waiting stage-door fans, there is a young girl with a large camera. She photographs Kate.

Kate walks up to her and asks, "Are you the one who sat in the first row taking pictures all through the performance tonight?"

"Yes, I am," says the girl.

"Well, you know what you are?" asks Kate, and replies, "You're just a little p-i-g!"

Bobby tries to explain to Kate that the word has a current new meaning.

"She knew what I meant," Kate insists.

It strikes him as odd that Kate would say "shit" in front of 1,581 people and then feel compelled to spell out p-i-g in front of *one*.

I explain that all actresses practice schizophrenia. It is Coco, not Kate, who says it up there. And Kate, not Coco, at the stage door.

As friends, Ruth and I attended an early preview performance of *Coco*. A musical of this sort would normally have gone out of town for a six-to-eight-week tryout, but, because the production was extremely heavy and since Kate's contract was for a limited time, it was decided to play five preview weeks in New York instead.

The second performance was uneven, although Kate appeared to have been playing her part for a year. In a way, she had been.

She was surprisingly at home in the musical form, or was successfully pretending to be, which amounts to the same thing.

It was clear that at this point she was carrying the evening. She stopped the show twice and took a standing ovation at the end. Yet, when we went back to see her afterward, she lay sprawled out disconsolately on the couch in her dressing room, surrounded by Alan Lerner, André Previn, Michael Benthall, Freddie Brisson, the inevitable Phyllis, and a few others.

We told her what we thought of her.

She punctuated our praise with "Yah. . . . Yah. . . . Yah," but seemed disinclined to believe us, and looked more morose by the minute.

"Well," she said at length, "I'll tell you what *I* think. I think the boys put together a great show, but they picked a lemon to play it. Me."

We protested.

"No, no," she insisted. "I know what I'm talking about. Well, maybe I'll improve. Let's go get some food."

Stars are not inclined to blame themselves if something is not going as it should. They are more apt to find fault with the text, the director, the sets, the lighting, their fellow players, the size of the theater, the weather, the costumes, the sound system, the musical conductor, or the audience.

Kate's concern was with herself.

We saw subsequent preview performances. The show was improving and she was finding more and more confidence.

Opening. It was one of *those* opening nights. The hottest ticket in town. People flew in from every part of the country, from many parts of the world.

As the glamour audience poured in, spectacularly dressed and celebrity-filled, one wondered what on earth could take place on the stage to compete with the performance in progress in the auditorium. It is at times such as these that the theater, which after all is meant to be a forum, becomes instead an arena, a bull ring. The spectators have come to see whether the matador or the bull will triumph.

On this particular night, Kate, the matador, conquered the

bull in a series of brilliant thrusts. Even the scoffers were won over, and the show, as a whole, seemed better than it was.

Afterward, there was unanimous agreement that the show was "in."

The post-performance assemblage at Kate's house was, in a sense, the story of her life. Family, old friends and new, a cross section of the variously shaped parts of her jigsaw history.

Her brother Bob: Dr. Robert Hepburn, a rugged New Englander, a distinguished urologist, the staid son who followed in his father's footsteps. He embraces his sister and says, "Proud of you, Kath." It means much to her, because she knows he means it.

Her sister, Marion: A comfortable, rather buxom small-town lady, full of big-town excitement. Talking with her, I searched carefully for a vision of another time. A photograph by Munkasci which appeared on a full page in *Life* magazine. I had clipped it and pinned it up on a wall. Three surpassingly beautiful girls and of the three, Marion the most beautiful. The years pass and a metamorphosis takes place. Kate's life adds character and enthrallment to her looks, and tonight, up there, she was certainly more beautiful than she has ever been. Marion, as a result of another sort of life, is now settled and sedate. The beguiling beauty has become a nice lady. It is difficult to believe that a younger edition of this proper matron worked at Hull House in the Chicago slums; in the offices of John L. Lewis of the United Mine Workers; as a secretary for the United Federal Workers, with whom she once picketed the Hotel Harrington in Washington, D.C.

Dick: Ever the individualist, he is wearing bright red trousers with a matching turtleneck, and a dinner jacket over this. On closer inspection, the outfit turns out to be simply red pajamas.

"Well, Richard," I say to him. "You're pretty resplendent tonight."

He winks at me, and says, "Well, I was pretty sure nobody else would be wearing anything like it."

He is a wildly talented writer, but has never been able to make working contact with the world as it is. His plays are written for audiences that do not yet exist. In his own way, he is as original as Kate. Looks like her, in fact. Loves her and she him.

"I suppose I should have married Dick," she mused one day. "As it is, I guess maybe I ruined his life."

There are college friends, and Irene Selznick, and Kate's best friend, Laura Harding.

Laura, a lady of considerable private means, accompanied Kate when she first went to Hollywood in 1932.

I believe it is from Laura that Kate has acquired her ability to transform a hotel room, almost instantly, into a charming abode.

They met when they were both studying with Frances Robinson-Duff and took a shine to each other. Laura was at that time an aspiring actress and had already had a summer of stock in Stockbridge, Massachusetts, at the Berkshire Playhouse. Miss Robinson-Duff thought Kate needed practical experience and asked Laura to try to get her into the Berkshire Playhouse company the following summer. Laura did so and they went off together. Laura remembers they both had bits in *The Admirable Crichton,* and that Kate bitched all through rehearsals because she thought they should be playing the leads.

A few weeks later, Laura relates, to her great surprise, Kate got a good part and made a sensational success. It was so impressive that Laura decided to give up.

"I could see right there in front of me what it took and I knew she had it and I didn't, so why bother? I suppose the thing I admire most about Kate is that she's so damn practical."

"How do you mean?"

"Well, here's an example. She was having dinner one night right here in this room with me and a beau of mine, a rather pompous one, I'm afraid, and he was badgering Kate about her religious beliefs or lack of them. We were having fried chicken and corn on the cob, and as we ate and argued and talked, a great glob of melted butter ran down his chin. He was so passionately involved in the discussion that he was unaware of it, and it went on for some time. I tried to signal to him. I was about to have hysterics. I could see that she was on the verge of breaking up as well, and all at once I heard her say, 'Just a moment. Do you not agree that if God created the earth—you've got butter on your chin—that He is responsible for it in all its manifestations?' The poor fellow dove for his napkin, wiped his chin, and wasn't able to utter again for the rest of the evening. That's what I mean by practical."

Another guest at Kate's opening-night party is the illustrious Dr. Seymour Gray, down from Boston. He was Spencer's friend and doctor, and represents another continuing link with the great days.

The atmosphere at the party is charged with confidence and enthusiasm. *Coco,* after a long and stormy journey, has, at last, made it safely into port.

There is a great deal to eat and drink. The evening is a celebration.

Kate has a cold, is physically and emotionally exhausted, and promises us all she will not go to the chorus party later on.

She waits only long enough to dispose of the last of her own guests, and at 1 A.M. makes her way uptown to the chorus party.

It does not help her cold.

Nor does the press reception for the show, the following morning. To almost everyone's surprise, the notices for *Coco* are uniformly poor. To no one's surprise, those for Kate are excellent.

I can only explain that reviewers review the show, not the event. As professionals, they are seldom affected one way or another by laughter, applause, or apathy.

Apparently, those of us who had been caught up in the intoxication of the occasion had seen something other than had actually existed.

For myself, I may have fallen into a common theater trap, as a result of having seen the production several times. The snare is that as we see a thing getting better and better, we begin to think it is getting good. The fact is that it is not getting good. It is simply getting better. This illusion explains why so many of us fail in the theater so many times.

But *Coco* was not a failure, even with its weaknesses. Kate's drawing power transcended the unfavorable press. Long queues continued to form at the box office, and what is most important, the hard core of the audience continued to respond enthusiastically. Kate's standing ovation at the end became a standard part of the evening, almost as though the audience had been rehearsed.

She had cautiously signed for a limited engagement and her contract would expire in April.

The problems of the show now behind her, Kate put her attention on the business aspects and began a series of conferences with Lerner and Brisson. When it was pointed out to her that, because of the costliness of the production and the high weekly operating cost, the show would not quite pay off by the time she left, she immediately agreed to extend her engagement.

"What the hell?" she said. "People have a right to get their money back."

In addition to this, she swiftly renegotiated her terms and cut her salary in half, to the dismay of the William Morris Agency. At the same time, she traded the bird in hand of her salary for the two in the bush of increased participation. She had been around long enough to know that in the theater, anything is likely to happen, and usually does.

She later extended her contract once again, agreeing to play through July, although this new schedule would involve her with an old enemy, summer heat.

Kate likes almost everything in nature with the exception of humid heat. She seldom spends a summer in the city, considering it a hell on earth. She is not happy unless she is physically active, and physical activity is hardly stimulated by July or August in New York City.

Air conditioning, which solves the problem for many, is not the answer for her. She cannot bear air conditioning. It seems to her tampered-with air. She has a religious respect for fresh air.

"Dries up your nose," she says of air conditioning. "Ruins

your throat—and if you care a damn about your lungs—you won't feed 'em with air-conditioned muck."

Another time, she revealed that instructions in her will call for her to be buried in Hartford, Connecticut. "I considered Southern California," she says, "but I decided against it—too damned *dry!*"

She recently had her house in New York entirely air-conditioned at great expense. When I questioned her about this contradiction, she explained that she had done it for the staff, for friends, and for the other people who use the house.

The outlet in her own bedroom on the third floor is shut off when she is there, and the windows opened wide.

Coco went into rehearsal in the course of a raw October in New York, but she found the theater stifling and insisted on keeping the exit doors open most of the time. The rest of the cast complained to the management. They were freezing, they said.

The management went to Kate, discreetly, and reported their problem.

The next day she appeared at rehearsal with several boxes of sweaters, shawls, gloves, and knitted wool caps.

"All right," she said to the astonished company. "Help yourselves—any of you who think you need it—but for God's sake, let's not seal ourselves hermetically in here—we'll strangulate."

The play opened on the night of December 18. It was an unusually cold night, but Kate had arranged with the front of the house to have many of the doors at least partially open.

"If I don't get some air," she said, "I'll never get through it."

She got through it all right, but a number of people in the audience caught bad colds. I know this to be true because I was one of them.

Katharine is a dramatic human being. As such, dramatic things happen to her and to her life each day.

Late one afternoon in March 1970, I was walking down

Seventh Avenue, in the vicinity of the Fifties. I was on my way to pick up my wife, who had been taking a singing lesson. On the corner of Fifty-fifth Street, I stopped as I saw a street altercation in progress. Cars were parked oddly. A woman, her back to me, was having a screamer with a burly truck driver.

A sparse semicircle of onlookers stood watching, bored, hoping, no doubt, that the argument would develop into something more entertaining, such as a zestful fist fight.

They did not have long to wait because suddenly, without warning, the man hauled off and punched the woman in the head. As she reeled away, I saw that it was Kate.

I ran to her, hoping all the way that someone else would restrain that truck driver before my arrival, but he had already returned to his wheel. Two policemen were on their way to the scene and Kate's driver was writing down information.

As I approached, Kate seemed not at all surprised to see me. What could be more natural? When you're in trouble, a friend turns up. Doesn't she always turn up when *her* friends are in trouble?

"Are you all right?" I asked.

"Oh, sure," she said. "He socked me."

"I know. I saw him."

"Not very hard," she said. "Was it?"

"*I* should ask *you.*"

"I'm all right," she said, vaguely.

"What's it all about?" I asked.

"Well, he was so wrong," explained Kate. "That's why he got so mad—people always get mad when they're wrong—he's had us blocked in here for twenty minutes—illegal as hell—and even when he finally came down, he wouldn't move."

I moved over to the delivery truck where one of the policemen and Kate's driver were attempting to make contact with the stolid truck driver.

"He punched her," I reported. "I saw him. Right in the head."

"*No*body kicks *me,*" said the driver, looking straight ahead. "I don't care who. Movie star or *what.*"

"What's he talking about?" one of the cops asked. "Do you know?"

"Sure," I said, and pointed to where his partner was talking to Kate.

"Holy Christ!" he said. "It's Katie." He looked up at the truck driver, incredulously. "You belted Katie in the head?"

*"No*body kicks *me,"* said the driver.

Kate came over with the other cop.

"She wants to drop it," he said.

"Oh, sure," said Kate. "What's the use?" She stepped up to the truck driver, looked at him gently, and said, "Will you admit you were wrong?"

*"No*body kicks *me,"* he said, his needle apparently stuck.

"You think about it—You'll be sorry before the day is out—That's no way to behave—I could make a fuss—you know that—you'd be in a lot of trouble—but it wouldn't be all that fair because you're you and I'm me—but you *think* about it—Just think about it."

*"No*body kicks *me,"* he said, as Kate walked away.

The cops were dispersing the small crowd.

"Okay. Break it up. Let's go, friends. It's all over."

As the people drifted off, they said variously, "Nice going, Katie."

"Get him in the next round, Katie."

"You okay?"

"Lock 'im up, Katie!"

As I put Kate into her car, I inquired quietly, "Did you kick him?"

"Of course not," she said, indignantly.

"He kept insisting," I said.

"Of course I didn't kick him." She shrugged. "I may have given him a little push with my foot, but that's all."

Whatever actually did happen, it was thus that the incident would be permanently locked in her mind.

We have gone home with Kate after a performance of *Coco,* and are warmly ensconced in her arms-around-you sitting room. The unglamorous supper tray is at her elbow, the piece of cold chicken (her favorite second joint), a slice of buttered bread, a glass of milk. She is still, at this hour, more Chanel than herself: bobbed hair, free mouth, flashing eyes. In an hour or so she will have thrown off the character and returned herself to herself.

"I love doing this show—mistake to be leaving it, I suppose—can't be helped, though—it's tiring, yes, but exhilarating, too. Getting into the evening was a probb-lemm. Solved now—I go on early—sit up at the top of the stairs by myself and get myself to cry—cry until the opening scene begins—then I pull myself together—so when I come on—perfectly composed and smiling, there's all that pent-up, unreleased emotion underneath—pretty soon I need it and it's there—don't have to start from scratch to build it. You know that moment when I tell them I've decided *not* to reopen the salon—then I hold up my hands and look at them—and the tears come? That's Dad."

"How do you mean?"

"When Dad was ill—dying, actually—he would sit and look at his hands, studying them—remembering, I suppose, all they had done—He had the most beautiful hands I have ever seen on any human being in all my life. But to him, they meant something else—useful—they'd done so much good and now they were going to be useless and do good no more."

She reaches out, picks up the glass of milk and gulps some down, before continuing.

"What I love about Chanel is the way she embodies the theme that interests me most: the fight for life. We all have to do it—as individuals, or families, or theatrical troupes, or nations. Life doesn't come automatically—and it isn't easy to come by—it's a daily struggle—every day. Fight for life—what it's all about, really, isn't it? Think of Spence—how gallantly he fought for *his* life."

"And won," I say.

"Yes, I suppose so."

"Lloyd Lewis," says Ruth, "once wrote that you could always measure an actor by the size of the hole he left when he left the stage. Well, that Spencer certainly left a void on our stage."

"It's another life," says Kate. "Isn't it?"

"I miss him," I say, "more than I can say. And need him."

"I think I'm much changed since his departure," says Kate. "Have you noticed?"

"In what way?"

"Lots of ways. I don't seem to plan as much as I used to—I've always been a great one for planning." She laughs. "I think sometimes I enjoyed the planning even more than the doing."

"Hell, yes," I say. "One of the indelible decals on my memory is of you sitting around—usually on the floor somewhere, surrounded by calendars and maps and timetables—scribbling away, writing and rewriting, planning."

Kate nods. "I'm less and less like that, though—getting to be much more of a *now* person—I loathe having appointments or dates—much prefer to do things on the spur of the moment—I've never been terribly interested in the past—but the future always fascinated me. That's fading—it's *now* that matters to me now—this moment—this hunk of chicken."

The Broadway season of 1969–1970 produced few musicals of quality. As the quasi-official end of the season (April 1) approached, it began to appear that The Antoinette Perry Awards would be something less than suspenseful. *Coco* would obviously win the Tony for Best Musical and Katharine Hepburn was a shoo-in for Best Actress in a Musical. No competition.

Alexander H. Cohen, the producer of the Awards show, went to Frederick Brisson and outlined the dilemma.

"Is there a way out?" asked Freddie.

"Well, yes," said Alex. "We could ask the League of New York Theatres to extend the date. That would give *Applause* and maybe even *Company* a chance to open—then we'd at least have the look of a contest."

"Well," said Freddie, reluctantly, "I don't know. . . ."

"Coco is sure to win it, anyway," said Alex. "And Kate. But in the other categories it would make it more interesting."

Freddie demurred. Alex sold a bit harder.

"What kind of a victory will it be," he argued, "if it's a one-horse race?"

Freddie asked for time to think it over. He discussed it with Alan Lerner and they both took it up with Kate.

"Of course you should let the other shows in," she said. "Silly to stick to an arbitrary date—Let them all in—What's the difference?—It doesn't matter all that much."

A compromise was reached. The date would be extended to allow *Applause* to qualify.

Applause came in, swept the town and the bulk of the Tony Awards, among them Best Musical and Best Actress in a Musical for its star, Lauren Bacall.

Kate was truly delighted. Betty Bacall is a close friend. They came to know each other when Kate was making *The African Queen* with Humphrey Bogart, to whom Betty was then married. Kate and Spence were of inestimable help to Betty during the awful months when Bogart was dying. They were, in fact, the last visitors to see him alive and the first to turn up when his death was announced.

"Isn't it simply *great* about Betty!" Kate exulted on the phone. "She tells me she's never won a prize for anything—think of it—so you can imagine how much this one means to her—and after all she's been through lately—it's a sort of balm. Freddie and Alan are furious—I can't imagine what's got into them."

Kate on the phone in the early part of 1970.

"I've been going up to Fenwick every weekend," she says. "All winter. And I've been swimming in the sea."

"Good God!" I say. "Why do you do that?"

"I *have* to," she replies. "I have this terrible cold, and I can't seem to get rid of it."

To Kate, this makes perfect sense.

She is riding her bicycle in the park every day, or walking, or running. On her way home one morning, she passes the Wildenstein Galleries on East Sixty-fourth Street. There is an exhibition of French impressionist paintings being shown. She parks her bike and strides in. A voice stops her.

"Just a moment, please."

She turns. There at the entry desk sits an Edna May Oliver, looking put upon.

"It's two dollars," she announces.

"Two dollars," says Kate, blankly.

"The admission."

"Oh."

For a moment, she had thought these were reproductions for sale at bargain prices. Now it comes to her. She reaches into the pockets of her torn slacks. Empty. She is carrying no handbag.

"I don't have any money," she says.

The woman at the desk looks her over, studying her chagrin.

Looking for a way out of the awkward patch, the woman asks, "Are you a nurse?"

Kate laughs and says, "Well, I have been. Right now, I'm an actress."

"Oh?" says the woman. "Which one?"

"I'm Katharine Hepburn."

The woman squints, attempting to find the person she remembers within the figure before her. She succeeds. "Oh, yes," she says flatly. "I saw you in *The Warrior's Husband*. I don't know *why* I haven't seen you since."

Kate shrugs. The woman returns the shrug.

"Will you take a check?" asks Kate. "Do you have a blank one?"

"Oh, hell," says the woman. "Go on in."

On Saturday, August 1, 1970, we attend the performance of *Coco*. Kate's last, on Broadway. It is an event filled with emotion. A standing ovation on her first entrance. Dr. Seymour Gray, Laura Harding, Phyllis, Ruth, and I sit together. Strangers come to us. They know, somehow, that we are her friends. They grab us by the arm and say, "Can't you make her stay?"

We explain that her commitment to make *The Trojan Women* with Michael Cacoyannis in Spain can no longer be postponed.

The performance is slightly marred by show girls weeping their mascara down their faces.

Kate goes up completely in "The Money Rings Out Like Freedom," and is too rattled to take the prompt from Gale Dixon onstage or Bobby Dolan in the pit.

When she speaks those lines that can have a second meaning, such as "The Maison Chanel is closing," she chokes on them.

The curtain call. A second standing ovation. Kate is visibly moved and in tears. All at once there is a parade of the show girls and chorus girls and singers. Each one carries a single red rose which is handed to her with a kiss. By the time the whole group has done so, Kate's arms are filled with roses. The last girl has a basket of rose petals that she strews at Kate's feet.

The audience cheers. Kate makes a speech in which she says, "This is all very moving and very confusing—to stop something in the middle." She goes on to say how much she owes to Alan Jay Lerner for having faith in her and about what it means to have people believe in you. She thanks "Roger Edens, who is dead," and Sue Seton, "who worked with me every day." She says, "And all these people standing here behind me have given me the support and faith and even the love that I needed." There are shouts from the audience. Finally she shrugs and says, "Well—I love you and you love me and let's leave it at that."

On Friday night she had distributed presents to everyone in the company. Tonight the presents come to her. They are not the kind one goes out and buys. There is a huge, circular tablecloth, in its center the *Coco* logo in needlework, Kate's name, the date, and the hand-embroidered signature of every member of the cast and crew. It must have taken the wardrobe mistress months to work it out.

Later, George Rose, who played Coco's manager, says to Ruth, "Curious. There was something the whole company felt, not only I. Once she was in the theater and in her dressing room, we all felt safe."

Before she goes to the party downstairs she says, "I'd better go out and see the fans, otherwise they'll have to wait too long."

She goes to the door, signs autographs, does the expected waving, goes down to the party. When we leave, hours later, there are several hundred fans still waiting.

She had done matinee and night on Wednesday, matinee and night on Thursday, a Friday performance, a matinee on Saturday, yet her energy seemed to be at peak level. I had never seen her giving out more energy.

The next day, Sunday, she went downtown to see Zoe Caldwell in *Colette*.

In a profession where an inconstant public is ever interested in novelty, and quickly tires of favorites, she remains a permanent standard.

Kate says, "And the curious thing is—when I started out, I didn't have any great desire to be an actress or to learn how to act. I just wanted to be famous."

Movie stardom is, by and large, short lived. Where are the stars of yesteryear? Strangely enough, many of them are still around. Able, highly experienced, some extremely attractive. They seem to have lost nothing except sufficient thrust and ambition and energy. How else can one explain the fact that they are no longer in the game?

The difference between them and Kate is that she will not be put down. She will not be silenced or denied. She is tenacious. She is strong when she needs to be.

In a theater-film career where the normal life span may be likened to that of the common housefly, she continues unflaggingly, as up-there as she has ever been.

In a time of fear, she is fearless.

"I don't regret anything I've ever done," she told me recently, "so long as I enjoyed it at the time."

That is quite a statement if you think about it.

We were talking about a play of mine that failed some years ago. It was called *The Smile of the World*. Kate asked me what the title meant, and I quoted the source.

It was from John Morley who once wrote: "And what is this smile of the world, to win which we are bidden to sacrifice our moral manhood; this frown of the world, whose terrors are more awful than the withering up of truth, and the slow going out of light within the souls of us?"

As I spoke the words, tears came into Kate's eyes, her chin quivered, her throat caught.

She cries often on the stage and on the screen (too often, some think) but, in all our years, I had never before seen her cry in private life. . . .

. . . Don't cry, old friend. You've got it all now (and what you haven't got, you can remember) and what matters most is that you got it on your own terms. You have the applause and the devotion and the admiration and the respect and the love and the smile of the world—and you have never sought it. You have sought only excellence in all things, including yourself.

Needless to add, Kate, that I love you, and for the sake of what is left of the human race, I hope you live forever. What the hell. You already have. Love to Spence. Sincerely yours.